Humanizing Research

Decolonizing Qualitative Inquiry With Youth and Communities

Django Paris
Michigan State University

Maisha T. Winn
The University of Wisconsin-Madison

Editors

Los Angeles | London | New Delhi
Singapore | Washington DC

Los Angeles | London | New Delhi
Singapore | Washington DC

FOR INFORMATION:

SAGE Publications, Inc.
2455 Teller Road
Thousand Oaks, California 91320
E-mail: order@sagepub.com

SAGE Publications Ltd.
1 Oliver's Yard
55 City Road
London EC1Y 1SP
United Kingdom

SAGE Publications India Pvt. Ltd.
B 1/I 1 Mohan Cooperative Industrial Area
Mathura Road, New Delhi 110 044
India

SAGE Publications Asia-Pacific Pte. Ltd.
3 Church Street
#10-04 Samsung Hub
Singapore 049483

Acquisitions Editor: Vicki Knight
Editorial Assistant: Jessica Young
Production Editor: Brittany Bauhaus
Copy Editor: Rachel Keith
Typesetter: C&M Digitals (P) Ltd.
Proofreader: Rae-Ann Goodwin
Indexer: Rick Hurd
Cover Designer: Candice Harman
Marketing Manager: Nicole Elliott
Permissions Editor: Adele Hutchinson

Printed in the United States of America

Library of Congress Cataloging-in-Publication Data

Humanizing research : decolonizing qualitative inquiry with youth and communities / editors, Django Paris, Maisha T. Winn.

p. cm.
Includes bibliographical references and index.

ISBN 978-1-4522-2539-5 (pbk.)

1. Action research. 2. Social justice. 3. Qualitative research. I. Paris, Django. II. Winn, Maisha T.

H62.H742 2014
001.42—dc23   2012037727

This book is printed on acid-free paper.

13 14 15 16 17 10 9 8 7 6 5 4 3 2 1

Humanizing
Research

With our youth, for our futures

BRIEF CONTENTS

DETAILED CONTENTS

To Humanize Research

Django Paris and Maisha T. Winn

I feel valued and I feel like you witnessed things and you were a legitimate witness. You are a worthy witness.

—Joseph Ubiles (Winn & Ubiles, 2011)

HE IS A FRIEND WHO UNDERSTAND FULLY

HE KNOWS WAT WE GO THROUGH

CAUSE HE'S BEEN THROUH IT

HE'S INSPIRED ME THE WAY AND TOLD ME TO DO IT, TO IT

—"Rahul" (Paris, 2011a)

What does it mean to be a "worthy witness" in qualitative inquiry with communities, and how can researchers become "a friend who understand fully"? In the opening quotes, participants in our work expressed how they viewed our presence in their work and worlds. Joseph Ubiles, also known as "Poppa Joe" in Maisha's earlier work, and "Rahul" (a pseudonym for the youth quoted by Django) capture a particular methodology that seeks to decolonize and thus humanize the research process. We use the verb *seek* because we, like the contributing authors in the chapters that follow, are still in the process of "becoming" as we grapple with the tensions that arise from being primarily concerned about equity and social justice while simultaneously engaging in research with youth and communities. In the first quote, borrowed from Maisha's research with her teacher/comrade/friend Joseph Ubiles, Joseph was reflecting on the many months of fieldwork Maisha had done with him and the African American, Dominican, Puerto Rican, and West Indian youth poets in his Bronx, New York, classroom (see Fisher, 2007). For Joseph, Maisha's presence and participation—through her ethnographic inquiry using video, field notes, and interviews to document and analyze the dialogue between his teaching and the work of the youth poets—made him "feel valued." And while Joseph did not ask for or even need Maisha's approval, he, like many teachers, was in his classroom with his students wanting a partner to join him in forging literate identities with youth marginalized by systems of inequality. Through a collaborative effort, Maisha became a co-teacher with Joseph and reflected on her practice as a researcher as much as Joseph reflected on his practice as a teacher. It was through this collaboration that Joseph deemed Maisha a "legitimate" partner in his work, one who was "worthy witnessing" as opposed to solely gathering data for a study.

In the second quote, a youth rapper, friend, and research participant in Django's ethnography and social language study in the California city of South Vista provides a critical youth voice in naming the role of a researcher. Rahul, a Fijian American emcee, emailed this impromptu rap to Django in the latter months of his yearlong study of youth language, literacy, and ethnicity in this changing multilingual urban community (Paris, 2011b). In his rap, Rahul was communicating that Django's many months of participating and observing, of interviewing, and of reading and recording his rapping and formal schooling had forged a "friend who understand fully," someone who had, through the activity of research, "inspired" Rahul to find a path "to do it, to it"—to continue forward with his life and work.

We do not lead this introduction with these two quotes to claim that, as ethnographers and qualitative researchers, we have arrived at some complete understanding of how our relationships with Joseph and Rahul were formed and what they meant to the processes of fieldwork or to the knowledge we built with participants in these studies. As researchers, we have many miles to travel in our collaborations with youth in communities and schools. Rather, we call on the contributors to this volume (and many others in the research community) to provide a roadmap to foreground the worth of such processes of humanization for inquiry and for society.

In the fall of 2010, the two of us exchanged our most recent writings: Maisha shared the chapter she had co-authored with Joseph, *Worthy Witnessing* (Winn & Ubiles, 2011), and Django shared his article, *Humanizing Research* (Paris, 2011a). This sharing inspired the dialogue that led to the conception of this book. As we read each piece and reflected on what was at stake in such qualitative inquiry with youth and communities, we decided to invite other researchers to join us in further exploring the interconnected terrain of worthiness, witnessing, friendship, vulnerability, shortcomings, and positive social change as it occurs across the research process in our professional lives. Contributors to this volume embody the commitment and work we were after as we began our collaboration, and we invited them to write essays on the humanizing elements of what we view as their revolutionary research approaches and outcomes. As we developed this volume and shared our ideas with contributors, we found that they were grappling with similar issues in their research and writing and were passionate to work on such a book. Our goal in this book is to provide methodological insights about what makes social justice research possible. We believe these insights are necessary for all of us committed to the intersection of equity and qualitative inquiry in education and across disciplines in the social sciences and the humanities.

In this edited volume we address researcher positionality as well as the many roles researchers play in the communities where they do their work. The contributors in this volume work with youth or in youth-centered communities and have a range of research interests. Contributors also have a range of disciplinary groundings and commitments, for example, in Indigenous and American Indian, Asian American, African American, Chicana/o, feminist, or queer studies; cultural anthropology; cultural and social psychology; sociology; literary studies; rhetoric; sociolinguistics; and linguistic anthropology. While many of these scholars locate themselves significantly in educational research, they approach their work as transdisciplinary explorations of teaching and learning both inside and beyond classroom walls. From understanding LGBTQ youth exploring identity in Philadelphia to understanding the assault on undocumented youth in the Midwest to understanding the linguistic and cultural identities of Indigenous youth in the Southwest, scholars raise difficult questions about whom research is for and if it is possible to decolonize methodologies. We invited contributors to offer reflective questions to start and sustain dialogue about the tensions researchers who consider themselves "a friend who understand fully" and youth advocates grapple with as they straddle working in the academy and working with communities facing historical and continuing inequalities. We do not offer step-by-step recipes for research in this volume; however, we do demystify the research process in hopes that a new generation of researchers and scholars will continue to trouble, complicate, and extend the conversations spurred by these chapters. We imagine this book in the hands (note "in the hands" as opposed to on the shelves) of scholars both seasoned and emerging as they sift through their research notebooks, analyzing field notes and ethnographic videos, wondering when and where to enter. This volume supports a multidisciplinary approach to thinking about the ways one conducts research with youth and communities in that it positions researchers as evolving and situated, always being mindful of how critically important it is to respect the humanity of the people who invite us into their worlds and help us answer questions about educational, social, and cultural justice.

DECOLONIZING WHAT AND HOW WE KNOW THROUGH WORK WITH YOUTH AND COMMUNITIES

We focus this book on research done with youth and communities who are marginalized by systems of inequality based on race, ethnicity, language, class, gender, sexuality, citizenship status, and other categories of difference and (in) equality. We and the authors in this volume have made marginalized and oppressed young people the focus of our work because we all are committed to working to end a long history of colonizing approaches to research, policy, and practice in communities of color and other marginalized communities. The history of qualitative and ethnographic work seeking, at worst, to pathologize, exoticize, objectify, and name as deficient communities of color and other marginalized populations in the U.S. and beyond, and at best, to take and gain through research but not to give back, stretches back across the 19th century and forward to the current day (see Ladson-Billings, 2012; Paris, 2012; and Wilson, 2008, for further critiques of this history). It is our express goal in this book to join with others in cultural anthropology, sociology, psychology, linguistics, ethnic studies, feminist studies, queer studies, education, and related areas who have pushed against this history. Our work here, then, joins what we view as a trajectory toward a stance and methodology of research that acts against the histories and continuing practices, ideologies, and accompanying dehumanizing policies of discrimination and unequal treatment based on the race, ethnicity, and belief systems of Indigenous peoples, other U.S.-born people of color, and people of color who immigrate to the U.S.; of class stratification and economically impoverished communities; of patriarchal norms and the unequal access to opportunities for girls and women; of the unequal, heteronormative, and discriminatory treatment of LGBTQ people; of the mistreatment of immigrant people due to citizenship status; and, broadly, of the discriminatory treatment of those who speak languages other than Dominant American English (commonly referred to as "standard English").

Building on our previous work with youth of color and their communities, we conceptualize humanizing approaches as those that involve the building of relationships of care and dignity and dialogic consciousness raising for both researchers and participants. Furthermore, we view such a research stance and its processes as involving reciprocity and respect. By relationships of dignity, care, and respect we are naming what Joseph in Maisha's research experienced as "feeling valued" by a "worthy witness." Reciprocity and dialogic consciousness raising, for us, speak to what Rahul called being "inspired" to action on the problems of interest in the study.

A series of questions and pressing issues emerge from our conception of humanizing research. We offer chapters that take up these interrelated methodological issues from researchers across an array of disciplinary perspectives within education and related applied social sciences. And, true to our commitments and focus in this volume, the chapters are written by scholars who not only represent a rich, necessary range of identities and positionalities within and across differences, but also enact their scholarship with youth and communities who represent the same necessary range within and across races, ethnicities, classes, genders, sexual orientations, languages, and citizenship statuses.

We introduce each section in the book by offering seasoned and emerging researchers a series of questions and considerations to guide their engagement with each chapter. At the end of each chapter, we offer a set of reflective questions to bring to your own research and teaching. We begin the book with a section centered on the interlocking themes of "Trust, Feeling, and Change: What We Learn, What We Share, What We Do." In Chapter 1, "Too Close to the Work/ There Is Nothing Right Now," Strong, Duarte, Gomez, and Meiners take a critical stance as researchers working with undocumented youth in order to humanize their experiences against the backdrop of dehumanizing practices and policies on immigration in the United States. This team of collaborators not only offers a window into the lives of the youth they work with but also the ways in which these stories have impacted them as scholars, in some cases previously undocumented students themselves, and citizens of the world. Chapter 2, "The Space Between Listening and Storying: Foundations for Projects in Humanization," offers a framework for scholars who are interested in understanding space and place through listening. In the chapter, Kinloch and San Pedro creatively synthesize their dialogue as social justice educators and researchers with the notion of "storying," or listening for the stories in their work with youth and communities—and acting on those stories. In Chapter 3, "Conducting Humanizing Research with LGBTQ Youth Through Dialogic Communication, Consciousness Raising, and Action," Blackburn explores how lesbian, gay, bisexual, transgender, and questioning (LGBTQ) youth helped her understand her responsibilities and positionalities as a White, lesbian woman doing research with LGBTQ youth of color. Reflecting on two long-term literacy and literature studies with LGBTQ young people, Blackburn offers her learnings about what it means to do compassionate, humble research that works to combat homophobia and heterosexism.

The second section of the book is titled "Navigating Institutions and Communities as a Participatory Activist Researchers: Tensions, Possibilities, and Transformations." Within this set of issues, Irizarry and Brown offer Chapter 4, "Humanizing Research in Dehumanizing Spaces: The Challenges and Opportunities of Conducting Participatory Action Research With Youth in Schools." Drawing on their own experiences of conducting school-based Participatory Action Research projects (PAR), the authors give examples of the ways schools, teachers, and administrators in their PAR projects were often at odds with the explicitly transformative goals of their research and often felt threatened by the knowledge the youth of color in their work gained about education and inequality. In Chapter 5, "Activist Ethnography With Indigenous Youth: Lessons From Humanizing Research on Language and Education," McCarty, Wyman, and Nicholas share how they have humanized their work with Indigenous youth around practices involving and commitments to heritage language. The authors provide vignettes of the interrelationship of researcher positionalities and activist stances grounded in participatory ethnographic work with Hopi, Navajo, O'odham, and Yup'ik youth. In Chapter 6, "Critical Media Ethnography: Youth Media Research," Jocson describes her work with youth poets, digital media, and critical ethnography in Northern California. Jocson works through tensions and ethical concerns when digital narratives written and produced by youth reveal complicated issues such as immigration and citizenship.

In the third section of the book, contributors take up "The Complex Nature of Power, Relationships, and Responsibilities" by focusing on researcher-participant relationships and the ways they map onto our responsibilities to the youth and communities in our work. Mangual Figueroa offers Chapter 7, "La Carta de Responsabilidad: The Problem of Departure." In the chapter, Mangual Figueroa investigates the often unexplored challenges of exiting the field as she recounts the difficulties she faced when the undocumented migrant parents in a family she worked with asked her to sign a letter to become a legal surrogate for their children in the event of their deportation. In Chapter 8, "Doing Double Dutch Methodology: Playing With the Practice of Participant Observer," Green examines her positionality in her work with youth radio participants as she juggles her roles as adult ally, teacher, community organizer, and scholar. Using an autoethnographic framework, Green's work speaks to the ways in which many of the scholars in this volume mediate tensions in their multiple roles. Romero-Little, Sims, and Romero take up the transformative possibilities of long-term learning and action in Chapter 9, "Revisiting the Keres Study to Envision the Future: Engaging Indigenous Pueblo Youth, Elders, and Teachers in Intergenerational Collaborative Research and Praxis." The authors describe how a 1990s study of giftedness with New Mexico Pueblo youth who had been placed in special education has influenced the design of a current study in the same community. Through reflections on the earlier study and an account of the current state of Pueblo education, Romero-Little and colleagues illustrate how learning with youth and elders over many years in collaborative research has the potential to help sustain a way of life and traditional languages for future generations of Pueblo people.

The fourth and final section of the book, "Revisiting Old Conversations Toward New Approaches in Humanizing Research," offers chapters that push existing tools and theories of qualitative inquiry into new methodological ground. In Chapter 10, "Why I Study Culture, and Why It Matters: Humanizing Ethnographies in Social Science Research," Kirkland explores how the complex literate cultures of the African American young men in his work became visible through his years of conversation about books, tattoos, raps, and magazines with a small group of boys called "the guys." His chapter offers a vision of why many of us do humanizing social and cultural inquiry. In Chapter 11, "Critical for Whom? Theoretical and Methodological Dilemmas in Critical Approaches to Language Research," Souto-Manning distills the complex methodological and theoretical underpinnings of discourse analysis and narrative analysis to argue for a more culturally grounded, humanizing, action-oriented approach to studying language with youth and communities. Providing dialogues from her research in Brazil, Souto-Manning crafts a novel set of critical interpretive moves with liberatory goals for her research participants. In Chapter 12, "R-words: Refusing Research," Yang and Tuck imagine what research methods that refuse "damage-centered" approaches could and should look like with Native youth and communities and the responsibility scholars have to protect some of the sacred stories that are shared in the research process. Their chapter explores the necessary question of whether research is the answer to pressing social issues and, if and when it is, how research must be decolonized before it can attempt equity work with communities.

Each chapter in the book concludes with "Reflective Questions" meant to foster critical engagement with some of the pressing methodological issues at stake. Winn ends the book with the epilogue, "Reflecting Forward on Humanizing Approaches." In her reflections on her recent work with formerly incarcerated girls, Winn reflects as well on what we have learned from the chapters in this book. She asks us to cast our gaze to the future, imagining what humanizing research must look like in the continuing project of social and cultural justice through disciplined inquiry.

REVELATIONS FROM THE CUTTING ROOM FLOOR: BEYOND KNOWLEDGE AND TOWARD SOLUTIONS

Together, the essays in this volume show how research for equity with young people happens in processes of human relationship, respect, and care. As editors, scholars, educators, teacher educators, and people of multiple ethnic and racial heritages who are committed to cultural and educational justice, we are concerned that continued and longstanding efforts to make the process and product of qualitative inquiry fit into positivist notions of what research is and how it should look often silence and minimize what it is we actually do in coming to know and know about the youth we spend months and years with. We are especially concerned that what we don't report—what doesn't make it into the article and ends up on the cutting room floor— may sometimes be what has allowed our learning and that of our participants to happen. In short, we are concerned that the culture of power in research is minimizing our learning and doing and reporting of research with youth and communities who are marginalized and oppressed by systems of inequality based on race, ethnicity, language, class, gender, sexuality, documentation status, and other categories of difference. Our concern is deep and heartfelt. We are driven to understand how our research can be further dedicated to understanding not only how inequality happens across multiple communities and from multiple perspectives, but also how we can be part of solutions that support equality within our research practices and in the lives of the young people and communities we learn from.

REFERENCES

Fisher, M. T. (2007). *Writing in rhythm: Spoken word poetry in urban classrooms.* New York, NY: Teachers College Press.

Ladson-Billings, G. (2012). Through a glass darkly: The persistence of race in education research and scholarship. *Educational Researcher, 41*(4), 115–120.

Paris, D. (2011a). "A friend who understand fully": Notes on humanizing research in a multiethnic youth community. *International Journal of Qualitative Studies in Education, 24*(2), 137–149.

Paris, D. (2011b). *Language across difference: Ethnicity, communication, and youth identities in changing urban schools.* Cambridge, MA: Cambridge University Press.

Paris, D. (2012). Culturally sustaining pedagogy: A needed change in stance, terminology, and practice. *Educational Researcher, 41*(3), 93–97.

Wilson, S. (2008). *Research is ceremony: Indigenous research methods.* Halifax, Nova Scotia, Canada: Fernwood.

Winn, M. T., & Ubiles, J. R. (2011). Worthy witnessing: Collaborative research in urban classrooms. In A. Ball & C. Tyson (Eds.), *Studying diversity in teacher education.* New York, NY: Rowman & Littlefield.

ACKNOWLEDGMENTS

Our deepest appreciation goes to the youth and communities in our work and to the youth and communities in the work of the extraordinary group of scholar activists who contributed to this volume. And to those scholar-activists: What a privilege it has been to learn from your work—our thanks for humanizing us as editors through your necessary research and writing. We are indebted to the Community Rejuvenation Project (CRP), and more specifically the incredibly talented muralists Lavie Raven, Mike 360, Release, Beats 737, Desi, Rate, Abacus, Pancho, Yesenia, and Dora for their visionary "Decolonize" mural as part of the Decolonize Oakland Mural Reactionary Art to the Occupy Movement. We are especially grateful to photojournalist Eric Arnold for the use of his photograph of this mural and movement. Many thanks are in order to Emory University and specifically Emory College and the Laney Graduate School for their generous support in securing permissions for our cover photo. Our sincere thanks as well to our editor at SAGE, Vicki Knight, who called us during the summer of 2011 to tell us she thought this would be a very important book. Her encouragement and guidance, and that of the entire SAGE team, has been essential to this project. And our gratitude to the scholars who reviewed the prospectus and manuscript for SAGE: Kristen Campbell Wilcox, The University at Albany; Francine Morin, University of Manitoba; Patricio R. Ortiz, Utah State University; Kara Smith, University of Windsor; Cristóbal Rodriguez, New Mexico State University; Simone Schweber, University of Wisconsin; Susan Letvak, University of North Carolina at Greensboro; Donna Martinez, University of Colorado; Steve Howard, Ohio University; Travis Wright, University of Wisconsin; Janette Habashi, University of Oklahoma; Doris Boutain, University of Washington; Shailesh Shukla, University of Winnipeg; William "Ted" Donlan, Portland State University. Your feedback and suggestions were of great value to this project.

Django: I would like to thank Rahul, Ela, Miles, Rochelle, Julio, Pedro and the many other youth I learned from in California and Arizona. You taught me what humanizing research was. I continue to try to live up to the model you have provided. Thanks as well to the Spencer and Ford Foundations and the NCTE Cultivating New Voices Among Scholars of Color (CNV) program for their generous support of my research. My many mentors and colleagues at Stanford University, Arizona State University, and Michigan State University have helped make the thinking in all my work possible. And finally, to Rae Paris, for being my best friend and my partner in this work and life.

Maisha: I would like to thank Joseph Ubiles and the Power Writers for teaching me what it means to be a "worthy witness." I am also grateful for the support of my students and colleagues at Emory University and the University of Wisconsin–Madison. I wish to thank Rae Paris for her warmth and support. Last, but certainly not least, I wish to thank my partner, Torry, and our son, Obasi, for believing in this work and believing in me.

ABOUT THE EDITORS

 **Django Paris** is Assistant Professor of Language and Literacy in the Department of Teacher Education in the College of Education at Michigan State University. He received his PhD in Education from Stanford University. His teaching and research focus on languages, literacies, and literatures among youth of color in changing urban schools and communities. He is particularly concerned with educational and cultural justice as outcomes of inquiry and pedagogy. He is author of *Language Across Difference: Ethnicity, Communication, and Youth Identities in Changing Urban Schools* (2011) and has published in many academic journals, including the *Harvard Educational Review* and *Educational Researcher*. Paris is also the Associate Director of the Bread Loaf School of English, a summer graduate program of Middlebury College.

 **Maisha T. Winn** is the Susan J. Cellmer Chair of English Education in the Department of Curriculum and Instruction in the School of Education at the University of Wisconsin, Madison. She received her PhD in Education from the University of California, Berkeley. Her work examines the ways in which youth build and sustain literate identities as well as how educators teach freedom in confined spaces. She is the author of *Writing Instruction in the Culturally Relevant Classroom* (with Latrise Johnson, 2012), *Girl Time: Literacy, Justice, and the School-to-Prison Pipeline* (2011), *Black Literate Lives: Historical and Contemporary Perspectives* (2007), and *Writing in Rhythm: Spoken Word Poetry in Urban Classrooms* (2008), as well as articles in journals such as *Harvard Educational Review*; *Race, Ethnicity, and Education*; and *Research in the Teaching of English*.

Photo of Django Paris: By Anthony Cepak/Michigan State University College of Education.
Photo of Maisha T. Winn: By Anne Almasy.

PART I

Trust, Feeling, and Change: What We Learn, What We Share, What We Do

Maisha T. Winn

Although Blackburn closes this first section, I begin with her invitation for readers to reconsider Freire's argument that all of us are in the process of "becoming more fully human" (see p. 43). To understand what it means to "humanize" research, it is important to consider the ways in which people, and more specifically youth, are often "dehumanized" or—to borrow Blackburn's words—"made less human by having their individuality, creativity, and humanity taken away, as when one is treated like a number or an object" (p. 43). Something that often gets omitted from both qualitative and quantitative research methods courses is how we as researchers can and will get close to the work, as Strong, Duarte, Gomez, and Meiners remind us in Chapter 1. Methods courses also often ignore the obvious; some of the dehumanizing processes, conditions, and experiences that our participants/students/friends have encountered will remind us of our own lived experiences. No one tells emerging scholars that, yes, sometimes "we cry." Strong, Duarte, Gomez, and Meiners recount the emotions that are inextricably linked to being and becoming human, and that I argue are also part of being and becoming a researcher. How can one not feel "upset, depressed, and sad while trying to think and to write" (p. 5), especially when memories of their own (im)migration experiences taunt them in the course of

1

this work? Similarly, Blackburn, in her efforts to reflect on whether or not she is "living up to the expectations set forth in these articulations of humanizing research" (p. 44), juxtaposes her own coming out as a lesbian to her work with girls who are coming of age.

Something I carry with me from my work with teacher/scholar/youth ally Joseph Ubiles and his Power Writing class is the ritual of "catching words" (Fisher, 2005, 2007). As students and teachers exchanged original poetry and prose, attended public lectures and cultural events, and journeyed throughout the five New York City boroughs, Joseph gave them one job—to collect words while out in the world. These words, phrases, concepts, or ideas could be new to students, or they might be words they hoped to use one day. Throughout Part I, contributors offer words, ideas, and concepts to further efforts to open the research space to relationships where respect in central. If I were to engage in the ritual of "catching words," I would look to Strong, Duarte, Gomez, and Meiners's use of "leveraging resources," "collectivizing," "self-educating," "justice mobilizers," "immigration justices," and "researching feelings" in Chapter 1. In Chapter 2, Kinloch and San Pedro inspire us in the ways we can build "projects in humanization" while thinking about both "self/selfed identities" and "other/othered identities." Ultimately, Kinloch and San Pedro offer a roadmap for researchers to engage each other about their work through the process of "storying." And while contributors do not claim all of these words to be their own, they employ them in new contexts for us to consider. Blackburn's (re)introduction of words like *derailed*, *unraveled*, and *dehumanized* help us think about what it means to become "more fully human" and conduct research that is, indeed, "mutually beneficial."

And finally, the work in Part I leaves us with important questions. In what ways does our work shape, sort, and decide who counts? How does revisiting field notes or our questioning practices during interviews help us prepare to be better researchers? Can we, in fact, create new sets of rules at sites where we are not researchers only but wear multiple hats?

REFERENCES

Fisher, M. T. (2005). From the coffee house to the school house: The promise of spoken word poetry in school contexts. *English Education, 37*(2), 115–131.

Fisher, M. T. (2007). *Writing in rhythm: Spoken word poetry in urban classrooms*. New York, NY: Teachers College Press.

Too Close to the Work/
There Is Nothing Right Now

1

Daysi Diaz-Strong, Maria Luna-Duarte, Christina Gómez, and Erica R. Meiners

E ach one of us gets phone calls looking for hope. Sometimes these phone calls are from allies to undocumented students, other times from young people wanting assistance related to higher education. Every time we do a public talk someone hangs around after, by the door, ducking in and out, waiting for one of us to be alone. On the phone, at a talk, in a school, the questions are always the same. *Is there anything you can do for me?* We recycle the same responses: our time and care, lists of advocacy organizations and groups, and sometimes rhetoric about "revolution," "organizing," and "justice," but the end result for the many young undocumented men and women who ask us if we can do anything for them is the same. *There is nothing right now.*

In 2012, there are still no pathways for legalization for those undocumented in the United States, a population of approximately 11 million by current conservative estimates (Passel & Cohn, 2009). Routes that might have been opened in the past, such as marrying an American citizen or being sponsored by a family member, are now more complicated or simply unavailable. This leaves most people, including students, without hope.

In 2007 we collectivized and began to educate ourselves about higher education and immigration policies that affect undocumented students, as we are invested in progressive and just immigration reform that unifies families, offers clear legalization pathways, and eradicates punishing immigration policies. We—Maria, Erica, Daysi, and Christina—joined together in part because of our overlapping research areas of interest, but also because we wanted to work together on a project that at the start appeared overwhelming, unwieldy, political, and complex. We also recognized that as a collaborative, we could do more with our resources and skills. While this project started as a politically motivated scholarly project, we quickly found that we ended up at many scholarly conferences responding (to the best of our ability) to "basic" and "practical" questions from the audience. Since few researchers besides us were doing this work, the folks in the room often had little knowledge about the complexities of immigration policies and had few structural ideas about what their educational institution could (or should) do. These experiences pushed us into offering workshops for high school, community college, and university staff to educate our colleagues and ourselves.

We also wanted to gather better data about what was happening to undocumented students and their families. Therefore, over a four-year period (2007–2011), we interviewed 40 currently and formerly undocumented students—27 females and 13 males—about their educational pathways and other issues, including family, border crossing, relationship to U.S. identity, and future plans. Our participants self-identified as Latinos and students who were at least 18 years of age, enrolled in high school or college, and working to be academically successful. Clearly, this is a select sample and not representative of the total population of undocumented youth in the Chicago region or the nation.

After years of working very closely on these issues, we also interviewed ourselves about our methodology and how we had been impacted by our participation in this (ongoing) four-year project, and over the 2011 summer we wrote short reflective essays to each other about our processes. This chapter draws from all these sources: our interviews with participants, our organizing, our self-interviews on methodology, and our own essays.

We formed this team because we were angered by ongoing media coverage that routinely depicted immigrants as "illegal aliens" and offered little historical context for immigration policies and trends in the United States (Newton, 2008). Immigration continues to shape the lives of each of us. Two of our core team members were formerly undocumented immigrants, one of us is not a U.S. citizen, three of us have undocumented family members living in the United States, and all of us have relationships with nonfamily undocumented individuals. As students, faculty, and staff, we work at different federally designated "Hispanic Serving institutions" (HSIs) with over 25% Latino enrollment, where students often disclose to us that they are undocumented. We have published editorials in local papers; participated in strategy meetings, rallies, and marches; circulated information on access to resources for the undocumented; advocated policy changes in higher education and immigration; and helped youth to informally network and gain access to support and resources. Our goals, as this chapter outlines, continue to shift. We understand ourselves as allies to those most impacted, and we are also invested in making more visible the experiences of a criminalized population. We work at the local level to leverage resources and educational access for those in need, and to use our research and power to support systemic and structural changes in immigration and educational policies. We struggle to juggle these goals with our other full-time demands as caregivers, students, workers, and justice mobilizers in other movements.

Throughout our process, we found ourselves, many times, overwhelmed by the feelings associated with this project. As Maria states below, being personally connected to the research continuously changed the process:

> For me, this research project was so intimate. I cannot detach it from who I am. While I was listening to the stories, it was also very depressing, and I would cry when I would leave them because many of their stories were my story, but fortunately

I've been able to adjust my status, but they haven't. As they ask what could we do for them, in many ways they pushed me and I think pushed some of us to continue doing things around our community. Like putting on workshops for undocumented parents or going to conferences to educate people.

Driving away from a meeting on immigration mobilization or a conversation with a young person, we would cry. We found ourselves angry during our planning and writing meetings; upset, depressed, and sad while trying to think and to write. Our anger was associated with legislative and institutional failures, our anxiety and fear linked to the political realities of people whose presents and futures we cared about deeply. We were depressed thinking about how little we could offer. Sometimes our engagements triggered memories of our own immigration experiences of separation, anxiety, fear, and loss. Occasionally, we were exhilarated and motivated by our collaborations and the work of many in the immigrant justice movement. We were also inspired by the ability and tenacity of many women and men to overcome tremendous obstacles and to be politically active and to retain hope. We were, we told ourselves, *too close to the work*.

Throughout our four years of work we have not paid significant attention to these feelings, yet they persist and continue to shape our work. They still cause pain and invite us to pay attention. Through engagement with work on political feelings, including affect theory, this chapter focuses on our "feelings," particularly our *bad* feelings, and names these as public and pervasive rather than simply individual or private. Affect is the body's response to the world—amorphous, outside of conscious awareness, undefined, full of possibility—and we use the term "feelings" or "emotion" to refer to how *affect* is marshaled into personal expressions and shaped by social conventions (Massumi, 2003). Our feelings demonstrate how affect not only is used to regulate political practices such as immigration policies, but also shapes our investments and labors as scholars, including our resistance to retaining the veneer of objectivity in scholarship and our desire to move beyond research to support and participate in justice movements. The twin titles of this piece point to the focus of this chapter: to share narratives from our participatory action research surrounding what it means for us to be "too close to the work," and also to share how we negotiate internal and external demands on this project to actually make desperately needed material differences in the lives of many.

Highlighting how emotion is threaded throughout this project and changes shape according to whom and how we are accountable, this paper starts with a short description of the political contexts for our work and includes some basic findings from our participatory action research project. The second part looks at feelings, focusing particularly on our process and how emotion emerged and continues to reshape this project. In particular, this second section looks at how the increase in undocumented students "coming out" shifted our feelings about our roles within the work.

THE POLITICAL LANDSCAPE

Access for undocumented students has always been controlled in part by federal and state policies. In the 1982 U.S. Supreme Court case *Plyler v. Doe*, the court held that states could not discriminate against students enrolling in K–12 public schools in the United States on the basis of their citizenship or legal permanent residency status. The decision, however, did not address public education beyond high school. In the absence of federal guidelines for higher education, states have created their own rules. Although undocumented students can apply to most colleges, they are not eligible for federal or state financial aid. Consequently, most undocumented students can attend only community colleges or affordable state universities. As of August 2011, 12 states had tuition equity laws on the books: California, Connecticut, Illinois, Kansas, Maryland, Nebraska, New Mexico, New York, Oklahoma, Texas, Utah, and Washington. In addition, Minnesota has a "flat tuition rate" available in some of its college systems. At least two of these states, Texas and New Mexico, also offer state financial aid to eligible students, regardless of their status (National Immigration Law Center, 2011). Other states have laws that ban undocumented students from receiving in-state tuition (Arizona, Colorado, Georgia, and North Carolina), or from attending community colleges (Alabama and South Carolina) altogether.

While it is difficult to assess the total and direct impact immigration status has on the lives of these young people, our work clearly indicates that undocumented youth are under particularly severe psychological stress. As children, they may not have fully experienced the impact of their immigration status, but during high school they become all too aware of the grim futures awaiting them in the United States: physically demanding work earning less than minimum wage, no mobility, constrained options for economic advancement, and possibly deportation. As one of our participants, a 23-year-old student named Mario who attended a community college and successfully transferred to a four-year university, stated, "There are so many things you can't do and so many limitations that make you feel out of place and make you feel like your arms and legs are tied up and you can't move."

While undocumented students confront difficulties similar to those encountered by many low-income and first-generation college students across the United States, they also face unique challenges. For example, in most states, undocumented students cannot legally drive and have to depend on public transportation and rides from family and friends or put themselves at risk by driving without a license. Unable to work legally, their ability to access postsecondary education is predicated on their ability to pay for tuition through non–living wage work, familial support, or a small number of private scholarships. Their lives and those of their families are at the center of often vicious public debates regarding employment, health care, and social services; recently, even the right to U.S. citizenship of children born in the United States to undocumented parents—known derogatively as "anchor babies"—has come under attack. Chavez

(2008) suggests that the public discourse on Latinos has been "plagued by the mark of illegality, in which in much public discourse means that they are criminals and thus illegitimate members of society undeserving of social benefits, including citizenship" (p. 3). Furthermore, with the 2001 folding of Immigration and Naturalization Services into the Department of Homeland Security, the undocumented have become an integral and expanding component of a criminalized class subject to raids, detention in a network of private and public prisons, and deportation.

While the 1980s were characterized by prison construction, fueled by the war on drugs, the post-9/11 decade is about detention center expansion, scaffolded by the war on terror. In 2010, Immigration and Customs Enforcement (ICE) removed 392,862 undocumented immigrants—a 35% percent increase over 2007. With a workforce of more than 17,000 and a 2009 budget that topped $5.5 billion, ICE is the largest enforcement agency in the United States, deporting an average of 977 noncitizens daily (U.S. Department of Homeland Security, 2009; U.S. Immigration and Customs Enforcement, 2008).

> [ICE] is responsible for one of the largest, most transient and most diverse detainee populations in U.S. custody. On any given day, at more than 300 ICE-managed detention facilities and contract facilities nationwide, the agency is responsible for overseeing the well-being of thousands of detainees hailing from countries around the world. ICE detainees include men, women and juveniles of all ages, including families. . . . ICE detention bed space has grown from 18,500 beds in FY03 to approximately 32,000 beds in FY08. (U.S. Immigration and Customs Enforcement, 2008, p. 19)

The *Washington Post* calculated that

> with roughly 1.6 million immigrants in some stage of immigration proceedings, the government holds more detainees a night than Clarion Hotels have guests, operates nearly as many vehicles as Greyhound has buses and flies more people each day than do many small U.S. airlines. (Hsu & Moreno, 2007, p. 8)

Given this context, many undocumented students have extreme difficulty knowing whom to trust with their status and how to negotiate the most basic registration pathways for college. This tension is exacerbated by the hesitation of most institutions to formalize resources or widely communicate possible strategies to students—or even to faculty and staff. Those ostensibly closest to the students—their teachers or counselors—often lack basic knowledge of the barriers and are sometimes unaware of state and institutional policies. This lack of awareness and transparency means that it is up to the student to navigate the system and locate the one or two knowledgeable and trustworthy advocates at the high school or college campus. Most students rely on informal networks among students or on the one great high school teacher or counselor who knows their status and can assist them in accessing pathways to college.

Our research and organizing project transpires during a particularly oppressive context for immigration "reform." Comprehensive immigration reform has achieved no success. For almost a decade, proposed federal legislation has floundered. The only legislation that has received any mobility has specifically targeted undocumented students. The Development Relief and Education for Alien Minors (DREAM) Act, first introduced in 2001 by Senator Orrin Hatch of Utah, attempted to provide a legal path to citizenship for undocumented students. As of December 2011, the most current iteration of this legislation would provide undocumented students who had arrived in the United States before the age of 16, had lived in this country for at least five years, and were of "good moral character" temporary residency for six years, during which time they would be required to obtain at least an associate's degree or complete two years of military service. After satisfying these requirements, a young person *could* be eligible to receive permanent residency. Those who did not meet the requirements would be subject to deportation. While the DREAM Act, if it passes, will help undocumented students enrolled in postsecondary education, it will not help their families. Additionally, within a few years undocumented students graduating from high school will once again have no pathway for legalization. The military service provision must also be questioned, as Latinos have some of the lowest rates of college entry and college completion.

In 2007, Hispanics represented about 15% of the American population and about 12% of full-time college students. However, Hispanics received only 7.5% of the bachelor's degrees awarded that year. Even more discouraging are the low attainment rates among Hispanics. According to a 2003 report by the National Center for Education Statistics (NCES), about a decade after graduating from high school, only 23% of Hispanic students in the National Education Longitudinal Study of 1988 had earned a postsecondary credential—half the percentage of white students in the same cohort (Kelly, Schneider, & Carey, 2010).

Given this gap in postsecondary educational attainment, undocumented students who do not enroll in college may view military service as their only option. A comprehensive immigration reform that would allow students to select among the workforce, college, or the military would be a more viable option for these students. Ten years later, the DREAM Act has been the only the viable immigration legislation on the table, and still it has not passed.

While there is limited hope for other legalization options in the future, the landscape for immigration justice work has changed remarkably in just two years. Starting in 2009, young undocumented students, often participating in DREAM Act campaigns, began to "out" themselves as undocumented (Preston, 2011) while organizing nationally and locally. The 2011 campaign of the Chicago-based Immigrant Youth Justice League is "Undocumented and Unafraid," and many members of this group (and others across the U.S.) have not only publically outed themselves at rallies and in interviews with mainstream media sources but have also continued to be arrested at high-profile and public mobilizations in Georgia; Washington, DC; Arizona; Alabama; and Illinois. These tactics are the result of trainings and collaborative consultation processes within the immigrant justice movement. These outing tactics have politically educated the nation about the impact of our punishing immigration policies and engendered limited public sympathy for select young people. Amid a bleak political landscape for legalization, youth and immigrant justice organizing has reframed the context of our work and also made us feel hopeful, worried, and galvanized.

RESEARCHING FEELINGS

Feelings are not simply byproducts of organizing or research; they are a central component of contemporary political life. From George Bush's "compassionate conservativism" that masked the further privatization of the state to Barack Obama's campaign evocation of hope, politics is, as Feel Tank Chicago points out, a "world of orchestrated feeling" (2008, para. 3). Immigration policies and other punitive policies are built on affect, and the (attempted) production of feelings to regulate and to secure state-sanctioned goals is not new; panic, terror, and shame are central to the stories of dismantling welfare and public education and maintaining a permanent warfare economy. The fear of terrorist violence, of "illegal aliens" taking U.S. jobs, of prisoners using tax dollars—the feelings of disgust, fear, and anger produced through the public repetition of these tropes—all help to justify expanding the punitive arm of the state. The circulations of these feelings become "affective economies" that "seduce us all into the folds of the state" (Agathangelou, Bassichis, & Spira, 2008, p. 122). Fears are also often framed as threats—to marriage, safety, traditions—requiring *defense*: Department of Defense public schools, a Defense of Marriage Act, the U.S. Patriot Act, and on and on. Feelings matter.

As feminist theorists from Audre Lorde (1984) to Dorothy Smith (1990) have realized, affect is also used by the state to disqualify and to control those targeted for violence. While anger is a legitimate response to institutions that systemically propagate hate or deny the rights of full humanizing participation to many, it can be dangerous for some to be angry. Lorde (1984) warned that displays of "outlaw emotions" will be used against those who are marginalized. Outlaw emotions can be defined as feelings like anger and resentment that are considered wrong and denied to marginalized groups precisely because these emotions challenge cultural hegemony and open avenues for social change (Jaggar, as cited in Steinberg, 2011). Outlaw emotions can be tools to mobilize communities and individuals for change, yet simultaneously these affects can be used to devalue or erase the responses or analysis of those who are marginalized.

In this analysis of political feelings, we are careful to note how affect is also used by justice movements with problematic consequences. As exemplified in the earlier discussion, the DREAM Act trades on tropes of "innocence" and "merit" directly linked to the identity of the student. The DREAM Act (the 2010 version is also a de facto racial and economic draft) separates a population that typically accrues the most sympathy—youth and students—and provides this limited group access to pathways for legalization, thus possibly making it difficult to pass wider legalization initiatives for other undocumented groups that are less able to engender sympathy or are potentially the "real" criminals and undeserving or guilty immigrants (day laborers, domestic workers, or those over the age of 30).

The DREAM Act and associated organizing is not unique, as other justice movements have historically struggled with negotiating difference. Images of enslaved and beaten women (and children) were used by abolitionists as a strategy to challenge slavery, as the assumption was that an image of brutally beaten pregnant women would trigger more sympathy or pity than one of a man being attacked. Yet, this often functioned to produce pity that would work in the long term to weaken demands for abolition. As Angela Davis writes, we should not permit "emotions such as pity to foreclose possibilities of solidarity" (2010, p. 36). Even when deployed by "progressives," emotions can be problematic and leave audiences "touched" but not moved (Morrison, 1994, p. 211). The mobilizations surrounding the DREAM Act created sympathy for young undocumented college students, who therefore might merit legalization pathways, but not for day laborers, domestics, or queers.[1] Feelings are political and central to shaping common sense about who counts in our communities.

Aiming at "emotional epistemology" (Feel Tank Chicago, 2008, para. 2), or evaluating feelings as political and methodologically strategic, is a central component of our research. This section explores some of the "bad" feelings that continue to emerge—depression, fear, and shame—and chart our own engagements with these feelings throughout our research and organizing. These feelings are rarely discrete; they intersect and overlap in our work and in our engagements with students and shape us.

This chapter is primarily focused on *our* negotiations; that is, we examine our "bad feelings" and less those of our participants. The focus of this chapter is not intended to encourage sympathetic responses from readers to the plight of the emotionally overburdened scholars who sacrifice all, or to center ourselves. Instead, we contend that focusing on feelings can help us see and challenge norms, including those of professions and institutions that often value only objectivity and rationality. We offer snapshots to these discussions to encourage opportunities to think through how feelings circulate and shape our work.

Depression

Sadness and depression are laced throughout this project. Most concretely, in our interviews, participants routinely named themselves as depressed, or identified the experiences of others undocumented as depressed.

Carlos (age 20):   I guess; I was basically raised up here. This is what I know. To me this is my country. What makes me not believe I am American, I guess, is all the hate, all the prejudice. I guess you can only take so much before it breaks you down.

Angela (age 19):   So it was just kind of like those [high school years] were the worst years of my life, because I just felt, like, so useless, almost in a sense . . . You know, like, it just . . . it wasn't . . . it was really, like, depressing and I just . . . where I just felt, like, useless, like what's the point.

Elena (age 21):   It's not easy being like this you know, especially as you grow up every day, some people give up. I think it was before I started college, someone who had straight A's through grammar school and high school because of the same reasons as me and he just killed himself, he committed suicide.

Frequently students would apologize for their public expressions of depression and sadness during interviews, as Daysi describes:

I had one student that I interviewed and he cried, and that wasn't abnormal; a lot of the students cried during their interview. But what was weird was that later that day he emailed me and apologized for crying. . . . I'm so sorry. I could sense that he was very embarrassed that he had cried, and I was trying to reassure him: "It is okay; it's very personal, of course," and he said, "Yeah, I've never talked to anybody about this except my family."

The persistent expressions of sadness, anxiety, isolation, and depression by the young people we spoke with had a ricocheting impact on our ability to negotiate what we initially identified as professional boundaries between this work and ourselves, and this wore us down.

Christina: Yeah, I cried in the car afterwards. I saw a lot of sadness in the students that in the beginning, when you start the interview, they usually . . . they know how to do the interview; they say all the right things, but somewhere, usually in the middle, something happens, often, and you ask a question and then you can see it almost in their eyes that they understand how hard this is, and the stress . . . and they get emotional and they start crying, and often this came up because so many of them drove without licenses, and the stories about being stopped by the police and the fear that brought them about being deported. For me that was hard because I knew I couldn't do anything; there was nothing I could do for them and I think they knew it too. I'm always surprised when we give talks; students always linger behind at the end and want to talk. All the rules that you learn when you're in graduate school have disappeared for me. I don't care if I cry anymore.

The inability to hold this sadness refracted back into the work, and pushed us to question exactly why we were doing research and the expectations these young people possessed. As faculty and staff members at postsecondary institutions, much as we tried not to represent ourselves as lawyers or in possession of any magic pathways or useful resources, we struggled with our absolute lack of ability to offer material options.

Erica: I got super depressed after I first did a few interviews, and while sometimes, yes, people wanted [their story] to be heard, . . . they also, almost all the time they asked me, what can you do? What is there? Even though I never made any promises, there was always the assumption that there must be something that I could do, right? I still feel that today; I feel like I still have those kinds of interactions with people.

Fear (or Lack of Fear)

Participants offered divergent statements about their own levels of "fear." In one breath, a participant would state both that she was not afraid of the police or deportation and also that she did not drive on any freeways or expressways or ever go to the airport or the train station. These deep contradictions, however, made sense. The young people we spoke with self-identified as students, were in educational programs, and were "successful." We argue that a certain amount of disidentification is required to function in a world where your life is erased.

While we argue that some participants worked hard to keep their fears at a distance, we had not practiced these skills. Fear mobilized us in complex ways and shaped our organizing and research. Recognizing that this is possibly very patronizing, as the young people and the families we spoke with were extremely competent and skilled, we still are often afraid for the students and for their families. Our fear increased as the political context shifted between 2009 and 2011 and increasing numbers of young people publicly identified as undocumented.

Erica outlined her anxieties when she first heard young people identify publically as undocumented:

I remember a panel a couple of years ago, which was one of the first times I heard somebody come out [as undocumented], and it was a packed room. There was one young White guy with a baseball cap and one young African American guy that looked like they were not our students; they totally looked like they did not belong in the room, and I remember all the little hairs on the back of my neck went up and we were thinking, like, "Oh my god, they're, like, cops or ICE agents. What are they doing here?" I remember taking photos of them with my cell phone thinking, "Oh my god, we have to track them down and find out who they are," because I felt like they were there infiltrating and watching and taking notes. I talked to some of the other professor types in the room, like, "Don't they look weird? Who are they?" One actually stood up and tried to, like, agitate, which I think is a total textbook 101 tool, and I was, like, we're so screwed! I think they're brave [those that come out], but I still think they're very vulnerable; I don't trust the government, the police.

For Daysi, formerly undocumented herself, her *loss of fear* reshaped how she thought of engaging with the "research" components of our project:

The interviews were harder, or they got harder the more that I was distanced from being undocumented. When I did this the first time as a graduate student, I was still in the process of adjusting my status; I had a work permit, but I was still in fear of what my status meant and possibly getting deported and what if things didn't work out. I could approach the students a little bit more easily. I had some contacts and I had some people who I thought would help these students because I still felt like I could relate. It was easier. I felt like I was trustworthy and now I notice a little bit of a shift now I'm a citizen. I don't have that fear, and somehow you begin to forget what that felt like.

Often our fears for the students triggered our own memories of fear and anxiety in relation to border crossing. Maria remembers how the fear does not leave with the possession of legal status:

Three years ago, after I became a resident, I actually forgot my Green Card, and my husband and I drove down to Texas and it was so horrible. We were in El Paso and a few miles from the border, and I could see the border and I could see the border patrol, and the whole night I couldn't sleep, like, thinking because I forgot my Green Card here [in Chicago]. I had to call my mom and she FedExed it the next day, because every 10 miles [there was] a border stop, so that brought back a whole bunch of memories. The first night that I was there I could not sleep because I thought, "Oh, somebody is going to come for me and they're going to pick me up and deport me. What am I going to do, going back to, I guess, a country that is no longer mine?" My husband said, "You're crazy; you're a U.S. citizen already." I'm like, "I'm not, I'm just a permanent legal resident," and I remember having a big argument with him about it. I'm like, "You don't know what it means to be undocumented. You don't know what it's like driving, being afraid the police are going to catch you if you're driving."

As members of our team held varying positions in postsecondary education (faculty, students, staff) and thus very different levels of academic freedom and employment protections, the political nature of the work translated into very different abilities to participate in the various levels of advocacy and organizing. Given the immigration policy context in Illinois, some of us were afraid of retaliation.

Daysi: I work at a public community college, and we have a group of students that are coming together to advocate for the DREAM Act on campus. I backed away from that because I'm an administrator. I'm at will. If what I do is not in line with what administration wants, then they can say bye-bye tomorrow? I wish I could really afford to go to meetings. If they need help with something I'll help them. It's moments like that where I feel like I'm failing or somehow giving in to pressure. I have to keep my job at the same time.

Shame and Shifting Contexts

Our situations and memories of either being undocumented or having family members who were undocumented have continued to emerge throughout this work. In particular, interviewing respondents has triggered memories of our own shame about immigration and the tensions involved in pursuing a research agenda when movement building is also required. Below, Christina discusses her understanding of who was undocumented and what it meant to be undocumented when she was a young girl. As she grew up in the 1970s in the Mexican South Side neighborhood of Chicago, there was little discussion of immigration or the undocumented. Silence about being undocumented signaled the "wrongness" or "shame" of the situation—being undocumented or "illegal" was understood as "bad"—it would undermine your character.

When my father first came to the U.S., he was undocumented, and it was only ever brought up when my mother was really angry at him and it would come out as something negative, but otherwise it was never talked about. One time I asked my dad and he said, "Oh, we don't talk about that," and the idea was because it was shameful, and the people that we knew who were undocumented, it was always like they were shady characters, like "Roberto." The joke was he would let himself get caught so he could get a free trip to Mexico for the holidays. It was very funny. . . . The big thing was always, especially for the women, "Don't hang around with the wetbacks, because they only want to marry you for the papers." Everyone bought that: "Yeah, yeah, yeah, if someone is from Mexico and he's kind of after you, it's because you're an American. He wants the citizenship." It was very negative, rarely talked about, but if it was talked about it was to criticize. It was a bad thing, but clearly people were around and clearly there must have been [undocumented] kids, but who knew?

In response to a discussion about the changes in context for undocumented people, particularly students, in the last 10 years, and the small but highly visible numbers of young people who have chosen to "come out," Maria reflects on how this change has impacted her:

Back in 1996, when the law changed, I would have never . . . I mean, I never told anybody that I was undocumented. I did not tell anyone until I was going to get married, and my college mentor was wondering why I was getting married so quickly since I had these other plans. I remember I went to her office and asked her to close the door because I didn't want . . . it was like a shameful thing. Even the people that were my friends [made] it very difficult because they never knew that I was undocumented. Simple things like going out to a nightclub: I remember one time I tried to go to a nightclub with a Mexican ID card, and they actually didn't let me in and it was embarrassing because my friends couldn't get in because they didn't want to leave me alone, but I couldn't tell them I was undocumented. Now students are very vocal about that; it's definitely a different time. I tell my students that are undocumented that they need to be careful. There are students that have those political connections to be very vocal and unafraid and apologetic, and there are those students that are not as vocal, in the background just trying to stay above the ground, and trying to be involved in school but also not open about their status. I don't know why that is, if it's because of shame? Is it because they're afraid? Some students feel really open and able to share their status . . . because they know they have rights and have advocates that could fight alongside them to be able to stay, and not being deported, but there are other students that I'm not sure would be willing to disclose their status.

Both Maria's and Christina's comments remind us that shame, circulating within families and institutions, also works to maintain social and institutional silences. As researchers, we negotiate shame when working to advocate for, or even to make visible, those targeted by the state for destruction and surveillance. Maria's and Christina's comments highlight the shifting landscape of immigration policies and how young people publically identifying as undocumented, along with years of immigration justice organizing, has reduced the shame surrounding being undocumented, although the dangers of being deported are still very much alive.

Maria and Daysi outline the shifts between their experiences in the 1990s and the lives and work of undocumented young people today, and specifically how shame has shifted:

Maria: I mean, I think that they're really brave, because I would have never done that [come out]. I would have never done that because of shame more than anything, because being undocumented was kind of, like, shameful.

Daysi: Yeah.

Maria: Well, it was shameful and also it was like . . . I was scared to be undocumented, you know? I was not scared, but afraid because my mom always told me, you never tell anybody.

Daysi: When we were undocumented, I think we operated much more secretly, because there was just a lot less knowledge; they didn't have student ID numbers instead of Social Security numbers, so you had to come up with what you had to come with. If you did tell someone they probably knew very little about it, but now people know what it means to be an undocumented student; it's kind of out there in the mainstream. It wasn't like that for us. There were no scholarships. On the other hand, it was easier because it was easier to get a driver's license. I had a driver's license. I've never had that fear in me, of "I'm going to get pulled over," you know. It was fine. I could travel because I had a driver's license. I could get on an airplane. You never heard about people like you, positive or negative. Now it's like there are so many messages out there and it could probably get a little overwhelming, I can imagine.

It is important to note that the contexts for undocumented youth today are uneven, as Maria and Daysi pointed out. Many young people we spoke with were not organizing and did not identify themselves as undocumented to anyone, and a lot of them, particularly those living outside Chicago, had experienced unsafe encounters with police. One of them had been arrested after running a stop sign in a county adjacent to Chicago that is notorious for racial profiling by the police:

> Matilda (age 22): He [the police officer] told me, "I'm going to have to arrest you; I'm not going to tow your car; you can leave it here," and of course I started crying. I'm like, "Do I have to sit in the back of the car?" "Yeah, you do," and so I did. I was embarrassed more than scared. I didn't want anyone to see me because I'm always afraid someone is going to know that I'm undocumented. (Matilda, Age 22)

Conclusions: Reshaping Our Work

The constellation of these "bad feelings"—depression, fear, and shame—in ourselves, laced throughout our wider political moment, and from the people that participate in this project and related organizing work, have reshaped our work and often left us, at our monthly or bimonthly meetings, feeling frozen. Participating in this process has moved us to continually think about the relationships between research and organizing. Below, Daysi charts her own shifts, from undocumented individual to researcher to someone who also engages in advocacy and political support:

> When you're doing the interview, you know the questions, you almost kind of know the answer a little bit, or at least you have a sense of their responses. You forget that for them this is very real and this is very emotional and they haven't talked about it. I realized, wow, I sort of have forgotten a little bit and I sort of have gotten away from it, and that made me feel bad. Now I'm a little more cautious about asking people to interview, because now somehow I feel like I am taking advantage of them. I meet somebody; they tell me they're undocumented and then the first thing I do is go, "Would you like to get interviewed?" I've backed away from that. I feel like I don't want to take advantage of them. I don't want them to feel like my interest in them is for something outside of just my interest in them, and so unless we can build a little bit more of a relationship I don't want to introduce that. So that's been kind of weird for me, feeling distanced from the experience more now and feeling guilty about that.

The research project and engaging with students also push us to continue to think about our participation in movements. Christina describes how she was moved to do more while driving an undocumented student to her volunteer position in the 2008 Obama campaign:

> She made me really think, we as professors need to come out and support them, we should be doing more, not them. We have nothing to lose; she has everything to lose. We needed to do more. As time has gone on I now worry much more and I think things, in a weird way . . . because they do this [organize] and do it so well, they let us off the hook, right?

Thus far the "more" has often led to guilt and internal conflict, because there is always work to do, and we never feel like we are doing enough. We never started this project to be saviors, and those undocumented students we work with don't need to be saved; yet we feel as though there is more we can do. Writing about it and reporting on our research is not enough. The students we work with live a very different experience that we try to understand and document, but don't fully comprehend.

> Christina: I always feel guilty. There's a march or there's a meeting and I'm like, I can't go. I have to go home or I have to . . . I always feel guilty, like it's moving ahead without me and I want to be a part of it, but then there's also the whole issue with the DREAM Act and some of our criticisms of it, and so even that . . . I just feel a lot of guilt. It's like every week and this week we signed four petitions on email and again it's very small; it doesn't take much for me to do it, right, organizing is so much more than that; it's easy to sign those petitions. I sit down in front of the computer and I can just do it. But the difference is to go out and be at the marches. I'm always really aware of that; there are different levels of commitment to this.

We have no answers for the right way to negotiate the many tensions and "bad feelings" mentioned throughout this paper, and instead see that publicly naming the complications when one is *too close to the work* is vital and potentially transformative. Research and organizing matter, particularly in desperate times. We close this chapter with a pointer for our future thinking and feeling. We recognize that our varied professional trainings did not prepare us to be workers in justice movements, or even to work collaboratively. We have felt isolated, like the only ones who have ever felt so depressed about their work and completely bereft of ideas about how to move. Generally, scholars are professionalized to produce discrete products, to acquire and to keep jobs, to build expertise, to be objective, and to advance the discipline or the field. As we move between research and advocacy and participate in organizing, we recognize the immense resource— time, money, technology, and more—that are located within universities, and we want better linkages between justice movements and scholars. This is our work to do and we must build these networks, train ourselves, and reframe what counts as scholarship. For example, if we are conducting work with human subjects, we must go through an Institutional Review Board (IRB) process (generally to protect the institution from any liability). What if we develop processes that asked the question, how is this work linked to other justice mobilizing scholarship? Or, how will this work redistribute resources or access to life pathways? Changing how and to whom we are accountable can move us away from "research of convenience" to research that responds to express material, political, or historical needs. Our networks can develop pathways among organizations, people, and institutions to focus work and channel resources (e.g., graduate students desiring experience in participatory action research) toward entities that need this labor (i.e., "This is what we know" and "This is what we need assistance with"). Collectivizing moves against so much of what the academy centers on—individual expertise and success (or failure)—but as resources for justice work continue to diminish inside universities, pooling our labors will provide needed strength.

REFLECTIVE QUESTIONS

As you plan and carry out your research, consider the questions that have guided us in the collaborative research we shared in this chapter:

1. Why are you engaging in this research project? Whose lives will it impact? How and why will these lives be impacted?

2. Who will you collaborate with to engage in this research? How will these relationships be established? When and how throughout this process will you talk about race, gender, sexuality, and other relationships between identity and power?

3. What are your political goals for this research project? What contributions can you make toward these political goals in addition to your research?

4. How have your emotions shaped how and what you research? What emotions are produced through your research, in the researchers and in the participants? How are these individual emotions linked to wider circulations of public feeling? How have your emotions shifted throughout the research process?

5. After the research has been completed, what are your ongoing commitments to the political goals you identified as important in this research? What are your ongoing commitments to your participants and collaborators?

NOTE

1. Nancy Fraser's (1997) analysis of how our tactics result in recognition but not redistribution (of resources, state systems, and more) is instructive. For Fraser, justice strategies all too often agitate for recognition (a liberal multicultural model), thus inviting additive responses that are not capable of transforming systems of power, oppression, and privilege. In addition, recognition can often only be on a single axis (race, gender, or sexuality).

REFERENCES

Agathangelou, A., Bassichis, D., & Spira, T. (2008). Intimate investments: Homonormativity, global lockdown, and the seductions of empire. *Radical History Review, 100,* 120–143.
Chavez, L. R. (2008). *The Latino threat: Constructing immigrants, citizens, and the nation.* Stanford, CA: Stanford University Press.
Davis, A. (2010). *Narrative of the life of Frederick Douglas, an American slave, written by himself: A new critical education.* San Francisco, CA: City Lights Books.
Feel Tank Chicago. (2008). *Manifesto.* Retrieved from http://www.feeltankchicago .net/ (accessed November 13, 2008)

Fraser, N. (1997). *Justice interruptus: Critical reflections on the "Postsocialist" condition*. New York, NY: Routledge.

Hsu, S., & Moreno, S. (2007, February 2). Border policy's success strains resources: Tent city in Texas among immigrant holding sites drawing criticism. *The Washington Post*, p. A01. Retrieved from http://www.washingtonpost.com/wpdyn/content/article/2007/02/01/AR2007020102238.html?referr

Kelly, A., Schneider. M., & Carey, K. (2010). Rising to the challenge: Hispanic college graduation rates as a national priority. American Enterprise Institute.

Lorde, A. (1984). *Sister outsider: Essays and speeches*. New York, NY: Crossing Press.

Massumi, B. (2003). Navigating movements: An interview with Brian Massumi. In M. Zournazi, (Ed.), *Hope: New philosophies for change* (pp. 210–243). New York, NY: Routledge.

Morrison, T. (1994). *The bluest eye*. New York, NY: Plume.

National Immigration Law Center. (2011, August). *State campaigns on education for immigrant students gain momentum in 2011*. Retrieved from http://www.nilc.org/immlawpolicy/DREAM/2011-ed-legislative-session-summary-2011-08.pdf

Newton, L. (2008). *Illegal, alien, or immigrant: The politics of immigration reform*. New York, NY: NYU Press.

Passel, J., & Cohn, D. (2009). *A portrait of unauthorized immigrants in the United States*. Pew Hispanic Center. Retrieved from http://www.pew hispanic.org/files/reports/l07.pdf

Preston, J. (2011, February 8). After a false dawn, anxiety for illegal immigrant students. *The New York Times*. Retrieved from http://www.nytimes.com/2011/02/09/us/09 immigration.html

Smith, D. E. (1990). *Texts, facts, and femininity: Exploring the relations of ruling*. London, England, UK: Routledge.

Steinberg, S. (2011). Teaching and (Re)learning the rhetoric of emotion. *Pedagogy: Critical Approaches to Teaching Literature, Language, Composition, and Culture, 11*(2), 349–369.

U.S. Department of Homeland Security. (2009). *Budget-in-brief, fiscal year 2009*. Retrieved from http://www.dhs.gov/xlibrary/assets/budget_bib-fy2009.pdf

U.S. Immigration and Customs Enforcement. (2008). *ICE fiscal year 2008 annual report: Protecting national security and upholding public safety*. Retrieved from http://www.ice.gov/doclib/pi/reports/ice_annual_report/pdf/ice08ar_final.pdf

The Space Between Listening and Storying

Foundations for Projects in Humanization

Valerie Kinloch and Timothy San Pedro

2

But we do language. That may be the measure of our lives.

—Toni Morrison (1993, p. 22)

Writer-scholar Toni Morrison (1993) describes how the power of language

> lies in its ability to limn the actual, imagined and possible lives of its speakers, readers, and writers. Although its power is sometimes in displacing experience, it is not a substitute for it. It arcs toward the place where meaning may lie. (p. 20)

The utility of language provides opportunities for the emergence of multiple, related, and conflicting experiences through use of various channels and spaces of communication. These channels and spaces can include technology, face-to-face speech interactions, linguistic and cultural diversities, geographical distances, and the space between listening and "storying." However, as Morrison reminds us, language—even in its power to displace—"is not a substitute for" experience. Therefore, we (Valerie and Tim) do not limit ourselves to the vitality of oral language to fully communicate our streams of consciousness around listening, storying, and authoring. We rely on (a) written texts, especially the ones we create, exchange, and reflect upon, including passages from the various authors who open the sections in this chapter (e.g., Charmaz, Jordan, Morrison, Okakok, Silko); (b) body language, or nonverbal cues, such as facial gestures and random up-and-down or left-to-right head nods; and (c) untimed verbal interjections such as, "That's deep," "You're right," "Mm-hmm," and "Exactly."

Specifically, we take up Morrison's claims around language to expand understandings of, and experiences with, language as listening by turning our gaze on

21

how we position ourselves (*self/selfed* identities) and get positioned by one another (*other/othered* identities) through the stories we exchange. We do this by recognizing the act of and embodied performances around listening as a literacy-rich practice that can foster what we refer to as Projects in Humanization (PiH). These projects, as we discuss, are grounded in a theoretical consideration of listening (Bakhtin, 1981, 1990; Bartolome, 1994; Schultz, 2009) as a framework for telling, retelling, and re-presenting stories in nonlinear ways—from left to right or right to left, from conversations on the telephone, via email, or over Skype. Such nonlinearity leads us to present stories in ways that appear messy, complicated, complex, and multivoiced, which is why we rely on storying. While the stories presented in this chapter are from our individual research experiences, we argue that these stories are simultaneously interconnected in ways that lead us to raise questions about expansive forms of literacy engagements, ethics, and trust in relationship building. They also help us to critique the shifting roles of researcher as listener, learner, advocate, and participant. Therefore, we frame this chapter within, but do not confine it by, the following questions: What does it mean to listen and engage listening as a framework in literacy research? In what ways do practices in listening converge with acts of storying/storytelling/authoring? How might these acts and actions foster innovative processes for conducting critical research and PiH with young people?

To address these questions, we engage in storying as we co-create, or co-author, narratives about literacy grounded in critical listening. As we have briefly acknowledged, such co-creation occurs in nonlinear ways; therefore, this chapter represents deliberate moves between "traditional" academic writing and "reflexive" vignette writing. It also represents movements, or shifts, among stories—movements that do not come equipped with visible road signs, or the subheadings traditionally found in published academic writings. With these attempts, we hope to make visible our thinking processes (streams of consciousness), ways of listening and responding to one another (in dialogue), and encounters (storying) that occur across the approximately 1,900 miles that separate us. In making these things visible, we begin this conversation by turning to vignettes from our individual research projects to illuminate our growing desire to engage listening and storying as practices in literacy *with* young people that serve as foundations for PiH. We engage in these practices (e.g., listening, storying) *with* and not *on* or *about* youth participants as a way to learn from, collaborate with, and center the narratives of young people in educational projects.

Our vignettes take us to different places: (a) a theoretical place in which we call on Bakhtin (1981, 1990), among others, to question how listening can motivate us to act differently in various context-specific situations; (b) a methodological place that challenges us to employ multiple means by which to listen to ourselves and interact with others as we conduct research in schools and communities; and (c) a place of storying, where the convergence of theory and method, and theory and practice, intersect to push us to listen to the questions we raise and vignettes we offer as we move toward Projects in Humanization. As we explain in this chapter, our theoretical, methodological, and storying selections contribute to the significance of conducting humanizing research in ways that privilege the co-construction of knowledge, human agency and voice, diverse perspectives, moments of vulnerability, and acts of listening. Additionally, PiH can contribute to how researchers, especially methodologists, make explicit connections between selected theoretical frameworks (e.g., New Literacy Studies, Ethnography of Communication, critical race theory) and methodologies (e.g., ethnographic interviews, participant observations) in ways that relate to how researchers interact with, and subsequently "report" on, participants (e.g., children, youth, adults). As these theoretical and methodological connections are made, researchers can meaningfully and openly collaborate with participants to learn about the complexities of human lives, the conditions under which people engage in teaching and learning, and the ways positions (e.g., as researcher vs. participant, or as teacher vs. student) can shift as relationships are fostered. As we argue in this chapter, such factors serve as the foundations for PiH.

We invite you (the reader) into these different places, beginning with our vignettes, as we ask you to consider establishing your own educational efforts as Projects in Humanization.

VIGNETTES IN STORIES AND STORYING

But as long as you remember what you have seen, then nothing is gone.

As long as you remember, it is part of this story we have together.

—Leslie Marmon Silko (1977, p. 215)*

Valerie and I sit across the table from one another sharing stories about ourselves over New York–style pizza during our Cultivating New Voices Among Scholars of Color meeting in St. Louis, Missouri. The conversation that moments ago was light with laughter has suddenly shifted. The napkins that once hid our pepperoni-infused smiles are now being used to jot down notes from a conversation that has become filled with stories about interactions with research participants. It is only then, when I see Valerie taking out a pen and covering her napkin with ideas spawned by my stories, that I do the same with her stories. I tell her about Michael, a participant in my pilot research, who told me that he looked up to me and thought of me as an advocate, as someone who pushed him to do better.

"I wonder what I had done up to that point to become that person to him," I ask Valerie.

"Perhaps you listened," Valerie said.

A silence falls between us, filled by reflections on a simple statement. She does not interrupt this silence as we usually do in academic conversations.

After some time, I say, "I have often thought about the power of listening. Often what we want as human beings is to have someone hear our stories, connect with us, pay attention to us. I wonder if by listening to his stories and asking follow-up questions that further the conversation, I had become something more than just a researcher. Bakhtin discusses how we are continually helping others further their understandings of themselves by answering their stories, listening, and being present in the conversation." Later, Valerie adds into my thinking the idea of researchers moving beyond doing work *for* a purpose or *for* people to researchers doing work *with* and *alongside* others. I tell her that working *with* is the type of work more people should be engaging in.

"Mm-hmm," Valerie says, nodding her head up and down. "That's deep."

"See, like right now . . . simply offering verbal and nonverbal cues like 'Mm-hmm' and saying 'That's deep' and nodding your head give me the confidence to continue my train of thought because you are listening. You are showing me that you are connecting with me. We need others to reflect back onto us who we are. Bakhtin says that our identities are a collection of how others see us, believe in us, and know us. If, however, you do not reflect back onto me in a way I can comprehend, or if you give me nonverbal cues to indicate that you've stopped listening, then I might be more hesitant to engage in meaningful conversations. I think for the many students I've seen, they've been burned either intentionally or unintentionally by teachers, administrators, or other adults who can't or won't . . . really listen."

As I talk, Valerie continues to give affirmations, verbally and nonverbally. My story spurs a story of her own that involves listening to youth inside their communities. As she tells her story, she immediately reflects on ideas articulated by Schultz (2009): "She focuses on listening to learn, which impacts how we listen to teach, work with, and gain deeper understandings of who people are and of who we are in different and complex contexts we find ourselves moving in and out of."

***

Our storying continues as I share ideas with Tim about listening and working with young people by turning our focus to Phillip and Khaleeq, two participants in a long-term research study on place, race, and literacy. Tim sits there, listening to me describe a moment when I was standing alongside Khaleeq and Phillip on a street corner in New York City, just having finished a video walk-through tour of Khaleeq's neighborhood. I explain to Tim, "We were standing their talking about survival, race, and . . . Black people being misunderstood by people in power, or as Phil said, 'especially White people.' Phillip continued, 'We have to recognize those who paved the way for us, like King and X, et cetera.' Khaleeq agreed: 'That's why we gotta hear stories of perseverance, hope, and civil rights.' I stood on that corner listening to these young men, and when they asked me what I was thinking, they, in turn, listened to me. I repeated their points about survival and race, recognizing who came before us, and about civil rights as I tried to make connections to my thoughts on . . . my thoughts on . . . on . . . ”

My hands fly up in a helpless gesture and my head lowers to the table. “Oh, what was I saying? I just lost my point!”

Tim looks at me, smiling. Then he intervenes in my frustrating moment of loss by saying, “You were on an exciting train of thought.”

Later on, Tim shares his reflections with me about this moment. He writes, “You were in the middle of your thought when something happened that happens to me quite often. You admitted that ‘Oh, I lost it.’ You could not proceed with the idea that was forming. However, because this conversation was shared, because it was vocalized in the space between us, and because I was a listener, I was able to provide the ideas you almost lost. It wasn’t the conversation that you had lost, it was your train of thought, and because we shared it, I was able to provide a bridge to help you find your ideas and get to that lost thought. When you got back there, you were able to share your thinking in that moment.”

According to Tim, “Bakhtin would say I completed the dialogic circle. The idea that was emerging for you was not in isolation in just your mind; it was between us, emerging not necessarily by you speaking or me listening, but in this space between us where we were interacting and engaging an idea together. What you ‘lost’ was simply your train of thought; however, the idea was still alive and well between us and I simply helped you to retain it.”

“Exactly,” I say to Tim. I realize that Tim’s active listening helped me to reenter the moment I temporarily lost during our meeting in St. Louis. Doing so allowed me to continue my line of thinking regarding listening to people (and in this case, Phillip and Khaleeq) as we rethink our beliefs and reshape our positions, perspectives, and pedagogies.

Back on that street corner in New York City listening to Phillip and Khaleeq’s ideas, they listen to me as I say, “I’m taking this all in. Making connections between your points and my beliefs about place and race. I just need to listen more.”

Khaleeq chimes in, “I’m learning to do that thing you do, Valerie.”

“What thing?” I ask.

Phillip and Khaleeq laugh, then Phillip explains: “You know, how you listen to us like that. You really be listening.”

Our conversation ends in laughter followed by silence. We stare at each other and at the people passing us by. We stare into the busy space that surrounds us as we reflect on our listening to, for, and because of one another.

And later on, when I recount the story to Tim over pizza, he gives me an exaggerated nod. “That’s deep,” he says.

***

Laughter breaks between us and ends the conversation where it started—with napkins hiding our smiles. Only this time, those napkins are filled with notes (and a touch of tomato sauce), which are the genesis for this chapter and the foundations by which we examine listening and storying within what we refer to as Projects in Humanization. As we later explain, such projects are grounded in acts of listening that situate us as researchers, advocates, and humans who work with, and not for, each other and other people. In this way, our identities become a collection of how others see us, believe in us, and know us, even as our vulnerabilities and feelings of care emerge from "the space between." Even now, as you (the reader) read this, you are entering into this conversation with us, interacting with this story, and thinking of ideas that connect with or that push past our storied experiences. It is through this interaction with readers, participants, co-authors, and people in general that we seek to discover deeper interactions through language and the experiences of listening.

A THEORETICAL CONSIDERATION: LISTENING AND PROJECTS IN HUMANIZATION

> I am a stranger learning to worship the strangers around me whoever you are whoever I may become.
>
> —June Jordan (2005, p. 3)*

The stories we share about our interactions with Michael, Phillip, and Khaleeq frame our conversations on meanings of, and engagements in, Projects in Humanization, or PiH. While we believe literacy research is strengthened by the inclusion of diverse perspectives by and about young people, we also believe that researchers have a responsibility to listen—closely and carefully—to *what* young people are saying, and *how* and *for what reasons* they are saying it. Such listening—careful, critical, and deliberate—can help educational researchers "gain insights that can be used to begin crafting a nuanced understanding of . . . lived experiences" (Ball, 2006, p. 129). In this way, listening requires us to be attentive to people's utterances, voices, vulnerabilities, body language, lived conditions, backgrounds, and ways of being in the world. Our understanding of listening is grounded in Bakhtin's (1981; see also Wertsch, 1991) semiotic mediation in which dialogicality, utterance, and voice play essential roles. For Bakhtin, dialogicality involves "the ways in which one speaker's concrete utterances come into contact with . . . the utterances of another," and utterance refers to the ways meaning exists within the context of how words are used and received, and not simply in the use of words (Wertsch, 1991, p. 54). Voice, for Bakhtin, "is concerned with the broader issues of a speaking subject's perspective, conceptual horizon, intention and world view" (Wertsch, 1991, p. 51), and thus represents language—spoken and written. These three concepts—dialogicality, utterance, and voice—and the role played by them, speak to the value of listening and understanding, which are activities that are dialogic in nature and that are collaboratively constructed.

*By June Jordan from *Directed by Desire: The Collected Poems of June Jordan*. Reprinted with the permission of the June M. Jordan Literary Estate Trust, and Copper Canyon Press, www.Junejordan.com.

Additionally, the idea of listening takes shape from our recognition that there are multiple worldviews that often get negatively positioned in conflict with one another instead of being constructed as different and diverse. According to Okakok (1989), "We need to catch a glimpse of the world through other eyes" (p. 248) as we move toward understanding how our thoughts, actions, world, and words exist in relation to those of other people. Okakok's sentiments on seeing through various lenses connect well with Greene's (2000) call for people to engage in collaborations as a means to "constitute a newly human world, one worthy enough and responsive enough to be both durable and open to continual renewal." Greene explains:

> Of course, this has to begin in local places, in schoolrooms and schoolyards and neighborhood centers; it has to begin where people know each other's names. But it can reach beyond, toward an enlarging public space where more and more common interests are articulated. It can radiate to inform the "conversation" and to empower individuals to open themselves to what they are making in common. Once they are open, once they are informed, once they are engaged in speech and action from their many vantage points, they may be able to identify a better state of things—and go on to transform. (p. 59)

Seeing more deeply, realizing the importance of others' words (and names), utilizing speech and action, and collaborating for transformation are fundamental principles by which to deeply and deliberating listen to and with others. Only through these acts and actions can we honestly question who we are at the backdrop (or forefront) of who others are in relation to us, in relation to how we perceive them and they us, and in relation to sustaining meaningful relationships.

What might this—way of viewing, seeing, and ultimately, listening—mean for educational research concerned with collaboration, problem posing, and social justice? How might this work point to expansive forms of literacy engagements predicated on ethics and trust in relationships, one to another? In turning, again, to Bakhtin (1981) and in recalling the vignettes that locate us (Valerie and Tim) in collaboration with Michael, Phillip, and Khaleeq, the presence of an "ideological struggle" involving discourse, voice, and perspective emerges. Bakhtin warns:

> One's own discourse and one's own voice . . . will sooner or later begin to liberate themselves. . . . This process is made more complex by the fact that a variety of alien voices enter into the struggle for influence within an individual's consciousness. . . . All this creates fertile soil for experimentally objectifying another's discourse. Fertile soil for facilitating an ideological struggle that needs to occur, a struggle that will result in more inclusive attitudes toward diversity. (p. 384)

Ideological struggles result, in part, from listening with others as we consider, question, and debate diverse views that may, in fact, conflict with our own. Hence, "this process is made more complex." Yet our ideological and epistemological stances are heavily shaped by what we hear, do not hear, and understand about our and others' thinking as we engage in listening. These things occur in light of, and not in opposition to, dialogicality, utterances, and voices in ways that make silence (e.g., the speechless moments that often exist between us [Tim and Valerie]) significant, in ways that make words (spoken, unspoken, written, and repeated) accepted, and in ways that make collaborations across researchers and with participants (e.g., Valerie and Tim with Michael, Phillip, Khaleeq, and others; the space between) humanizing. The language we utilize to talk, write, and listen to one another, even in moments of silence, shapes the ideological struggles we are already a part of as we engage in educational projects. Thus, literacy and literacy's engagements become expansive. Moreover, utilization of language encourages us to move beyond traditional educational projects and into human (and humanizing) projects in which relationships become redefined against dichotomous categories of researcher versus participant to researcher-as-participant-as-listener-as-learner-as-advocate.

Within this movement—that of positions and categories—listening as well as talking, storying, and authoring become important acts and actions for (re)defining our human relationships within a discourse of trust, care, and ethics. For example, Tim and I (Valerie) trust one another, hence our decision to co-story this chapter on Projects in Humanization and to share our vulnerabilities with each other through online, telephone, and face-to-face means. Michael trusts Tim, hence his decision to view Tim as an advocate. Phillip and Khaleeq trust me, hence their choice to regularly invite me into their familial communities. Therefore, within such discourses of trust, care, and ethics that become reciprocated across "researchers" and "participants," multiple perspectives, worldviews, and readings of texts and contexts proliferate human interactions. This proliferation occurs in ways that get us to listen to stories and inquire into our own and one another's thinking about experiences. We can do this type of inquiring only if we intently, purposefully, and openly listen to what is said and not said, and if we meaningfully transact with texts and interact with people.

And these here are the exact principles that define PiH, projects that are grounded in the actions, languages, perspectives, and concerns of people generally and young people particularly. We understand such projects as experiences we have *with* people that are directed by the desires for social, political, and educational change that can only happen if relationships are forged in light of, and because of, human differences. PiH are framed within a discourse of care (Greene; 2000; Noddings, 1993) and listening (Bakhtin, 1981, 1990; Schultz, 2009) as relationships with people are created, as conversations among those people are exchanged, and as interactions rooted in difference, conflict, vulnerabilities, and respect are forged. In this way, PiH is an extension of what Kinloch (2012) describes as "Democratic Engagements," or situated practice contextualized within the lived conditions, voices, and histories of, as well as interactions among, people within various defined communities. To say it another way, Democratic Engagements (DE) are grounded in "the ideals of education, the values in literacy acquisition, and the principles of creative pedagogies [that encourage] conversations and relationships people have with one another in multiple spaces of interaction" (Kinloch, 2005, p.109). Connecting DE to PiH, insofar as listening is concerned, requires us to engage education as a social process that calls into question what we know and do not know about other people, about ourselves, and about our relationships. It means allowing room for conflict, complications, silences, and pauses to exist between and among people as they learn to listen to each other in *the space between* language and silence, language and action. It also means encouraging people to collaborate for change, and to work at being and becoming *with* other people in the world.

Additionally, PiH—much like DE—take seriously the following things: listening as a fundamental factor in learning (Bakhtin, 1981, 1990; Schultz, 2009); collaborating for meaningful change and action (Greene, 2000; Tuck, 2009); seeing vulnerabilities as authentic reactions that should be acknowledged (Kinloch & San Pedro); viewing language as something we do and create (Morrison, 1993); and constructing knowledge as shared and relational (Brayboy & Maughan, 2009). Together, these factors encourage us (Valerie and Tim) to recognize how divergent perspectives contribute to the ways we learn, live, and listen as we walk through the world with other people.

METHODOLOGICAL CHALLENGES: LISTENING TO OURSELVES, INTERACTING WITH OTHERS

> *We all know that we can go through life convinced that our view of the world is the only valid one. If we are interested in new perceptions, however, we need to catch a glimpse of the world through other eyes. We need to be aware of our own thoughts as well as the way life is viewed by other people.*
>
> —Leona Okakok (1989, p. 248)

By using the voices of authors like Charmaz, Jordan, Morrison, Okakok, and Silko as well as research participants like Michael and Khaleeq to begin each of the chapter sections, we illuminate how we construct, together, the methods and processes of Projects in Humanization. The root of our work is based on Bakhtin's notion of dialogism or citationality, which we take to mean that whenever we speak, we are citing the words of others who have meaningfully impacted us: "Another's discourse, if productive, gives birth to a new word from us in response" (Bakhtin, 1981, p. 346).

Beginning each section with the words of others does two things: It gives homage to conversations that have happened before us, and it reveals that our voices, words, and understandings are a collection of others' discourses. In this way, we are using others' words and ideas as catalysts for our own construction of thoughts. In addition, we are using listening and storying as methods of constructing this chapter by engaging in the *dialogic spiral* (see Figure 2.1). We have come to understand the dialogic spiral as the construction of a conversation between two or more people whereby the dialogic process of listening and speaking co-creates an area of trust between speakers—the space between. In this between space, the speakers' discourse reveals vulnerabilities and feelings. The conversation moves back and forth when the speaker becomes the listener and the listener becomes the speaker. In order for the conversation to continue, we must see or hear that the other is listening to what we are saying. We can see and hear this in a number of ways: by seeing them nod their head, by hearing verbal callbacks like "Mm-hmm" and "Exactly," and by hearing the other person extend our ideas by adding their own thoughts based on their understandings and experiences. If constructive, this dialogic spiral moves back and forth, while it also advances forward and upward by expanding prior understandings of listening and storying. According to Bakhtin (1981), when we speak, we hope those we are speaking to—our audience—will listen and reciprocate our words by answering them genuinely. Words either grow by way of the dialogic spiral or, if our ideas are neither reciprocated nor validated by another, they may die within the world:

> When discourse is torn from reality, it is fatal for the word itself as well: words grow sickly, lose semantic depth and flexibility, the capacity to expand and renew their meanings in new living contexts—they essentially die as discourse, for the signifying word lives beyond itself, that is, it lives by means of directing its purposiveness outward. (pp. 353–354)

Thus, if a word is spoken and there is no one there to listen to and expand it, to try to make sense of it, does it exist? We argue alongside Bakhtin that it does not, and the effects of this invalidation and ignoring have been felt by both of us personally and seen through our participants' eyes in many of their classrooms.

By using the dialogic spiral as a central method of co-writing this chapter, we have engaged in meaningful dialogue that has spurred ideas from each of us to the other. Every week for a month and a half, we have engaged in conversations via Skype, email, and/or phone. During these one- to two-hour conversations, we recall what was said in prior conversations in order to continue our discussion. By recalling, we are engaging the ideas of who we were a week ago as we move forward with new understandings and new selves in the present moment. As we talk, we both take note of what the other is saying; however, we do this differently. When Valerie speaks, I (Tim) type notes and ideas nearly verbatim on my computer, which Valerie can hear. When I speak, Valerie jots down notes on paper with a pen, which leaves a silence between us. She creates more overarching notes and draws lines and connections between them to see where her ideas are connecting with mine. When I reread her words verbatim, they bring back to mind ideas I had while listening to her words, which I then add to later as we make ideological connections. I have come to relish this silence, because I know that she is connecting my words and thoughts with her own. As we build off of each other's ideas through conversation, we are creating between us a sense of trust and mutual respect.

Figure 2.1 The dialogic spiral

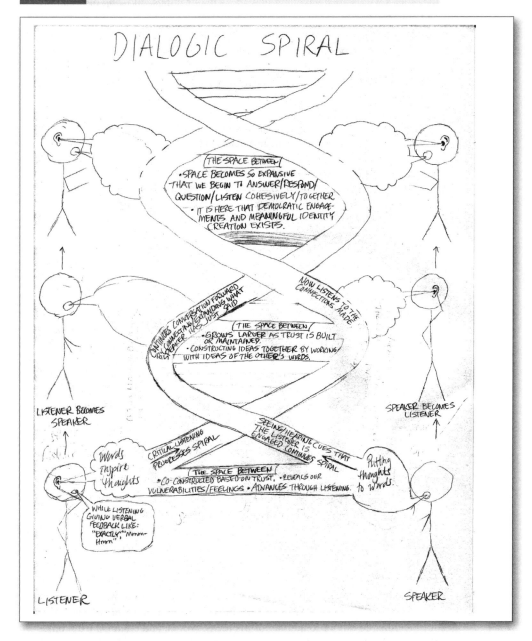

It is these notes created in conversation between us that act as the foundation for the structure of this chapter. As Bazerman (as cited in Ball & Freedman, 2004) states, "As one realizes the importance and variety of the words of others, there is a consequent awakening to the importance of taking those words seriously and attempting to understand them. One comes to see their value more deeply" (p. 101).

Through careful construction of our dialogic spiral, we have shown each other that the other's words are awakening new ideas in our minds, allowing our relationship and conversation to continue, expand, and grow.

While we may be typing the words onto this page separately, we realize that our words are merely citations of each other's. Neither of us "owns" certain words or sections, since they were co-constructed through storying and listening over a range of communicative means. Charmaz (2006) refers to this sort of engagement as "reciprocities":

> Remember that human beings are unlikely to relish being treated as objects from which you extract data. Reciprocities are important, and listening and being there are among them. Some researchers may command access on the basis of their authority and the prestige of their projects. Many other researchers cannot. Instead we gain access through the trust that emerges through establishing on-going relationships and reciprocities. Ignoring such reciprocities not only weakens your chances of obtaining telling data but, moreover, dehumanizes your research participants—and yourself. (p. 110)

This is central to our thinking of what PiH can be. If we see our participants as those who are in the process of constructing knowledge with us rather than as separate from us, we break down the artificial boundaries or binaries of researcher/subject that have been building over time. Rather, we suggest that we are all participating (thus we use the term *participants* as opposed to *subjects*) in the construction of knowledge, which has implications not only for research, but also for teaching. As Battiste (2002) says:

> Knowledge is not what some possess and others do not; it is a resourceful capacity of being that creates the context and texture of life. Thus, knowledge is not a commodity that can be possessed or controlled by educational institutions, but is a living process to be absorbed and understood. (p. 15)

It is in this absorption and understanding in the space between us, between participants and ourselves and between teachers and students, that we focus our attention.

Even using Charmaz's and Battiste's words here points to the idea that words spark ideas from others. When listening to Valerie, I (Tim) have often thought of another author who stated something similar to what we have discussed. Those authors are in conversation with us—perhaps not physically, but mentally over great distances of time, space, and place—as we connect to the conversations that have come before us. Glimpses of those we are citing are seen here and are catalysts to our thinking and the identities that we project at the moment of writing this chapter.

In addition, while writing our words on and in this document, we each allowed for the other co-author to add her or his ideas, words, and citations from others so that this chapter could expand through listening, reading, and connecting. Even when writing our final section, we attempted to co-construct our ideas within a Google document based on our conversations and the notes we co-created in order to give life to our collaborative voice. In this way, we purposefully merged our ideas and moved beyond our own words as knowledge was created in the space between (leading the way to a shared understanding of co-authoring and storying).

We have also used vignettes between various sections to direct our thinking of this work back to the young people with whom we work. How might our methods of constructing this chapter together relate to our construction of relationships with participants through listening and storying? Vignettes also open up avenues for readers to connect with the process and the emotion of the events that have occurred in research with participants. By including stories that evoke emotion, we hope that you (the reader) engage with us in the space between by revealing your own vulnerabilities and stories. This connection reveals that the space between us does not have to be the three-feet area between two people in a face-to-face conversation. Rather, conversations via listening and storying can happen over time, distance, and varying ways of communicating. By co-constructing this chapter based on the dialogic spiral, we acknowledge that the document we have created is alive, moving, and re-creating. Eventually, however, we have to take a snapshot of it, and pause to reflect on it, which you see here. This does not mean that it stops. Perhaps someone reading this 10, 20, or 100 years from now will find meaning in what has been said here and add it to their understanding as they reshape our ideas with others. Perhaps you may be able to catch a glimpse of our process, of our ideas, of our understandings, for as Okakok (1989) says at the beginning of this section, our world is not the only valid one. When we overlap our under-standings, perspectives, and viewpoints, we may begin to engage in a mean-ingful dialogic spiral based on storying, listening, and reciprocating. In so doing, we hear the other and see each other in the space between, and thus achieve Bakhtin's definition of ideological becoming.

"DO YOU HAVE A SECOND TO TALK?" ANSWERING BY CONTINUING THE DIALOGIC SPIRAL

Everything is just starting to come together for me, but at the same time it's falling apart.

—Michael (participant in Tim's research)

It's about 8 o'clock at night and my cell phone is ringing. The caller ID says the incoming call is from Michael, a participant in the research I concluded about four months ago. Answering Michael's call, I hear his voice crack as it makes its way through cell towers and static air into my phone.

"Do you have a second to talk?"

A seemingly simple question between two people who have gotten to know and respect each other has become deeply complicated as I think about the competing ideologies that often limit interactions with participants. Michael's question raises a quandary: Who am I going to be, for and with my participants?

When the spring semester came to an end, I thanked everyone for welcoming me into the classroom, told them I hoped they would do well in the future, said good-bye, and walked out the door. From conversations I have had with others, this is when interactions with participants should end, forever. We have already collected enough data to report our findings to the academic community and, perhaps, to the community we have researched. We should now cease contact with participants. For me, this way of thinking has about half a second to do battle in my mind after I hear Michael's voice on the phone.

A short pause divides us for a split second.

"Of course," I reply. "What's going on?"

He tells me that he is about a month away from graduating from high school and has been making plans for the big day that will honor him for where he comes from and what he has accomplished. In light of this, he asked the assistant principal at Desert View High School to grant him permission to wear traditional Native American clothing during the ceremony. He was quickly denied and given an alternative:

> They told me, you can wear [traditional Native American clothing], you can wear whatever you want; it just has to be underneath [the gown]. That wasn't enough for me. I owe my parents and my grandparents because there was only so much I could learn culturally from them, so to me everything goes in a cycle. For me, this is something leading to the end. Something like this to happen, it just doesn't make sense to me. The more I got into it, the more confusing I got.

By answering Michael's call, I have crossed a line that some researchers have deemed unethical. Yet I cannot ignore Michael's dilemma and how he is trying to make sense of it, for if I did, I would be severing the dialogic spiral between us that started at the beginning of the year. How can I refuse Michael's call? It would seem inhuman, cold.

As we talk, I ask myself, who am I to and *with* him? Bakhtin (1981) says that to make

> real meaning of others' words in everyday life, the following are surely of decisive significance: *who* precisely is speaking, and under *what* concrete circumstances. . . . And the entire speaking situation is very important: who is present during it, with what expression or mimicry is it uttered, with what shades of intonation? (p. 340)

In other words, when two or more people are engaged in a conversation, who are they to and with each other? The answer to this either fuels the conversation or leads to a breakdown in communication. In listening to Michael, I attempt to remain neutral, asking a string of questions. In a sense, I remain a researcher:

Tim:　　　So what was their reasoning for denying you your request?

Michael:　Y'know this is where she went off on a tangent. She said, "Oh, it's just policy, you know." That's how they always handle things. They'll let me walk, but it's still going to be a policy next year and the fact that I know kids that are juniors who want to do this.

Michael wants me to weigh in, to validate his thoughts, to complete the dialogic spiral. Perhaps I do by asking questions that push him to voice emotions and ideas he is grappling with. When I reflect on the conversation later, I am convinced I was not answering, but questioning him. On this point, Bakhtin (1990) says,

> We are constantly and intently on the watch for reflections of our own life on the plane of other people's consciousness, and, moreover, not just reflections of particular moments of our life, but even reflections of the whole of it. (p. 16)

As a young researcher thinking about "the whole," as Bakhtin would have me do, I admit that I fought the urge to answer Michael. I kept asking questions as if we were in an interview. For example, my next three questions were as follows:

1. So where are you at right now with the process?

2. What are your thoughts right now as far as all this is concerned?

3. So what are you doing to correct this wrong?

While these questions seem crafted, they provided Michael an invitation to voice concerns to someone he knew would listen and provided him an avenue to be heard: "Every discourse presupposes a special conception of the listener, of his perceptive background and the degree of his responsiveness" (Bakhtin, 1981, p. 346). By uttering small sounds like "Mm-hmm" and "Yes," I was giving Michael cues that I was listening, which may have given him confidence to make sense of a confusing situation.

However, we had become different people. According to Bakhtin (1990), we react to situations, people, and feelings that surround us as we decide who we are in these situations. Although we are one person, we carry different identities that we either reveal to or hide from others. Thus, I realized I needed to reveal more of who I was to answer Michael's call. Near the end of our conversation, I had a profound realization: Who we were to and with each other had changed; the researcher-participant relationship that existed in the classroom had become something more. He saw me as an advocate, and I needed to answer him genuinely in order to allow this change to take place.

I provide the last part of our conversation in its entirety to illustrate this transition:

Tim: Yeah, I appreciate the call. This is important work that you're doing.

Michael: I respect that you understand that, and it's like the minute I say this to my mom, she just immediately just goes to what God says. That in and of itself is another conflict. I'm not going to get through to her and that's the way the world is, so these are just smaller incidents of the bigger thing, and this to me is just how I'm going to go about it, how I will do it. I'd like to see where it could go. To have people believe in me—I feel honored and privileged and, like, at the same time, I always just joked in class and said, "Hey, remember my name man?" and I don't know, it's just a lot of little things like that, and it just makes . . . everything is just starting to come together for me, but at the same time it's falling apart. I guess when you do confront something like this, I'm already going to have problems with my own identity because who's to say that to some extent I'm already assimilated myself and that's something that I accept.

Tim: That's something that we all have to try to question is, what are the colonial aspects that are within our mind frame already and how can we combat that and how can we move beyond that, and it's not an easy thing to do because we've been living in this system for a long, long time and the things that we are doing may be hidden and it's a process of awakening, of realization, of what you're going through right now, and I share the path you're on right now, Michael. I'm going through it right now myself, so you're not alone and knowing that you're not alone helps.

Michael: That's the thing that I told my other friends—it's like, what the hell am I? I'm not Jesus. I'm just some other kid and people are like amazed by what I'm doing and I'm like, "No, everybody has this. You just have to bring it out." I don't want to have people go through what I have to go through; there's an easier way.

Tim: What you're gonna be doing will help someone behind you do what they want to do in this sense, and then you can move beyond that. There's no limit to what you can do.

[Five-second pause]

Tim: It's good, though, Michael.

Michael: [Audible sniffles heard.] Yeah, I know, man; it's just so . . . ugh . . . whew.

Tim: What you're feeling right now is a good thing. You're waking up, man.

Michael: Yeah, and that confusion is just me, like my other part of my mind just wanting to stick to what's already . . . what's the norm, besides every other problem that's outside of my head; it's just that's what it is and something that I have to work out myself.

Michael and I had transitioned into something new for and with each other. At the time, I did not know what to call this transition, but in co-creating this chapter with Valerie, I now know that this exchange speaks to Projects in Humanization. Michael and I engaged in a conversation that allowed us to reveal vulnerabilities because we engaged these things with trust. In a way, I was giving back by sharing in his emotion and answering his call. According to Bakhtin (1990),

He must become another in relation to himself, must look at himself through the eyes of another. . . . We evaluate ourselves from the standpoint of others, and through others we try to understand and take into account what is transgredient to our own consciousness. (p. 15)

By continuing the dialogic spiral, we see ourselves in the faces, voices, and reactions of others, and in so doing, we engage Projects in Humanization.

BECOMING AND BELONGING IN THE SPACE BETWEEN

We belong, our identities wrapped up in our place.

—Khaleeq (participant in Valerie's research)

As I reflect on Tim's encounters with Michael—receiving a surprise phone call, debating whether to offer answers or a series of questions—I cannot help but recall exchanges I shared with Phillip, Khaleeq, and many of their high school peers. Various exchanges suddenly rush to the front of my mind in vivid detail, and as they do, I reach for my blue notebook. I jot them down, one after another, and instantly I am taken back to those spaces where we interacted, one with the other: the high school classroom, the teachers' lounge, the sidewalk in front of Phillip's family's apartment unit, on the side of a school in close proximity to where Khaleeq lived with his family, the platform to one of the local-bound Manhattan subways, my university classroom and office, and, among other spaces, the streets and corners that converge to make New York City's Harlem community.

A quick glance at my notes reveals specific situations that Phillip, Khaleeq, and I shared. In my notebook, I have scribbled the following moments: "Khaleeq & Phillip helping me think about community by thinking about civil rights and struggle"; "Phil talking about doing something great with his life for himself and family"; "Khaleeq sitting in a chair as we—his peers, teachers, and I—look on, and when Phil asks him if he's on grade level, Khaleeq saying he's a senior by standing, but a sophomore by knowledge." I also write, "Was it Sam or Kim who talked about living in Harlem and needing to improve the community and schools without building more high-rise condos Black people can't afford?" I end my reminiscing by writing, "We grew together, and I had my moments, like when Phil asked me what I thought about gentrification in Harlem. This came a year or so into our project. I stared at him wondering, 'You don't know what I think?' Maybe he read my mind because the next thing he said was, 'I know what you think about it, but I'd like to hear you say it. Put words to it.'"

Those words continue to impact me: "Say it" and "Put words to it." Here was a teenager on the brink of graduation—a teenager who voluntarily participated in this project on gentrification, race, and literacy—encouraging me to attach words to my internal thoughts and to say what was already known, but not yet heard. Phillip was asking me to make visible (and public) reciprocity. That is, if I can ask questions, then I can make space available to be asked and to answer questions. Phillip probably did not realize it at the time, but his request humanized the way I conduct research and interact with people. For what Phillip was asking of me was what I regularly asked of him and his peers: to name actions and thoughts and to use words or signs to communicate ideas, even if the results of our communication opened spaces of discomfort and vulnerability, criticism, and question.

For Phillip to ask me to do what I was already asking him to do signified his level of engagement in *our* work, one marked by care and grounded in acts of critical listening. For example, when he inquired into my stance on gentrification, he posed questions similar to the ones I had long been asking him (and others) to consider: How do you define gentrification? What signs indicate gentrification in the area, and what might those signs imply? How do you put into words your feelings on community change? How do you see gentrification: as creating a new and different community, as a race and/or class issue, or as something else, more, different?

In essence, what Phillip was asking me to do was to become and belong in the space between thought and action, researcher and participant, interview and conversation, asking and being asked questions. I had an obligation to become and belong in ways that aligned and/or conflicted with how Phillip, Khaleeq, Kim, Sam, and so many others were becoming and belonging. It was not that Phillip wanted to know my thoughts on gentrification, for he knew them. He sought to include my *other* voices (e.g., my personal/vulnerable/emotional/less-than-academic voices) into the conversation because, as he explained, "You know me, and I'm coming to know you."

What does this knowing mean, entail? How might I take up Phillip's challenge to "put it into words" and make openings for him to come to know me in ways that lead to humanization? In the following excerpt (see Kinloch, 2010, pp. 94–95), I revisit a conversation on gentrification and White-ification in Harlem between Phillip and me. I do so to rethink how my engagements with Phillip led me to take up Projects in Humanization or, as Bakhtin would have me say, to realize that "true understanding is dialogic in nature" (Wertsch, 1991, p. 54).

Phillip: You know me by now. You know I'mah speak my mind and tell my truth, Valerie, and the way I see things around here is quite simple: They coming in and taking over by using privilege to get what they want [. . .]

Valerie: Again, who you talking 'bout when you say "they?" Seems like you ain' comfortable giving a description for this "they." And what are they taking over?

Phillip: My Harlem, your Harlem, you know, Black people's Harlem. I'm talking about White people, but you already know that. And I'm not just talking about White people, but like I said, White privilege. So, I've been fortunate to live in Harlem all my life and I've had to make do with what is here, but now that they want to gentrify this, gentrify that, I'm suppose to just sit back and smile. This my home. I might be a teenager, but I got a right to this place, and my right runs deeper than theirs.

Valerie: Why's that the case? This thing about your rights running deeper?

Phillip: From when I can remember from living here, I ain' never seen so many White people in Harlem walking the streets, moving into the 'hood, you know. And when I'm talking with folks in the 'hood, like residents who been living there forever, it's like we don't know what's going on. Nobody talks to us; they [White people] just walk by. Then before you know it, with new folks come new businesses. [. . .] That's not my Harlem. [. . .] It's complicated.

Revisiting the above excerpt helped me to see my relationship with Phillip through a different lens. Clearly, Phillip became more than a research participant in a study I was conducting. As Tim says of his relationship with Michael, Phillip and I became "something new for and with each other." He knew, without my ever suggesting it, that I had come to know him and his habits (e.g., speaking his mind, telling his truth, pointing out what I "already know"). In my knowing him, he had come to know *of* and *with* me, and was not hesitant to vocalize opinions on race, privilege, and rights—hence his assertion, "My Harlem, your Harlem, you know, Black people's Harlem," an assertion that created our shared sense of place and belonging. Phillip invoked Bakhtin in this discussion by asking me to "look at [myself] through the eyes of another" and engage in ideological struggle (Bakhtin, 1990, p. 15).

As Tim and I describe throughout this chapter, we seek to enhance collaborations *with* people, and as we do, we are continuing the dialogic spiral. We should answer our participants' calls—whether it's Michael's call for Tim to "stand with him" or Phillip's plea for me to "say it." When we engage answering as inquiring by listening to and working *with* others, we become better positioned to respond to questions of becoming and belonging. Within such situations, we can better contemplate who we will be for ourselves and with other people in the multiple spaces in which we interact. As Khaleeq says, "we belong, our identities wrapped up in our place."

IMPLICATIONS FOR PROJECTS IN HUMANIZATION

Strong bonds build trust and foster open conversations with research participants about areas ordinarily left unspoken.

—Kathy Charmaz (2006, p. 113)

Throughout this chapter, we have pushed ourselves beyond our individual comfort zones while refusing to retreat behind the phrases "I don't know" and "That doesn't make any sense." Our use of those phrases led to moments of vulnerability that revealed the complexities of our interactions with one another and with participants. Discussing our vulnerabilities allowed us to engage in a dialogic spiral conversation in which we co-constructed knowledge. The process of co-constructing was a scary experience. That is, we exposed ourselves to each other in the hopes that the other would understand who we were and who we sought to be/become, which are critical factors in storying, listening, and, thus, in Projects in Humanization. Because we openly recognized the spaces between us (e.g., distance, time, utterances, silences, speechlessness, ideological struggles) within actions of safety, support, and trust, we were able to construct that which we might not have had the confidence to build alone.

For example, when trying out a new thought, Tim said, "I don't know, " to which Valerie responded, "You do know, because that's exactly what it is." In this moment, Tim pulled back for fear of not being understood, and Valerie pushed ahead by providing the confidence Tim needed to move forward. At other times, the roles were reversed. The point is that we engaged in PiH by listening, co-constructing ideas, and displaying vulnerabilities and human emotions. The inclusion of vignettes pushed us to consider the implications of our arguments for the people with whom we interact. Specifically, the vignettes helped us to tell stories about the space between listening and reading, and between storying and authoring, as we shared emotions that contribute to Projects in Humanization. Such projects are grounded in interactions that allow people to ask, answer, and receive questions that transcend space-time limitations. Thus, we are careful to name such work "projects" as opposed to "research." This distinction is important, because we view PiH as occasions that make space for people to engage in personal, reflexive conversations that might initially occur because of research, but not for the sake of research. Such conversations do not have a set expiration date or a definitive ending point, because the interactions, teachings, and knowledge do not end after a set time frame. Hence, the research and ensuing publications (which we realize are important by-products) do not take precedence over interactions we have and relationships we build with (and not for) people.

While we are fully aware that research studies have ending points, we also understand that connections, conversations, and teaching and learning encounters we construct with others will always impact our work and our human interactions. The measure of this impact is evident in how we come to see, hear, and learn things beyond what we know through collaborations that foster role reversals (e.g., as researchers, participants, advocates, etc.) and expanded understandings of constructed knowledge. For instance, Phillip and Valerie reconnected via Facebook when Valerie sent him a "friend" request, and he sent her an email about a videotaped experience they had shared years before. Talking about that experience encouraged Phillip and Valerie to revisit prior arguments on urban gentrification. As well, Tim received a message from another participant, Edgar, who asked if they could meet during the writing of this chapter. Tim met Edgar at a coffee shop and entered into a dialogic spiral. The result was the co-creation of a Native American discussion group with past and current students in the Native American literature class Tim is currently researching. These interactions can lead to Projects in Humanization.

We see implications for PiH and the dialogic spiral for teaching, researching, and co-authoring. However, what is most valuable to us is engaging in authentic human interactions that can mold, shape, and teach us how to be ourselves in various spatial-temporal contexts. How do these humanizing interactions take shape in ways that look different? How can our interactions with others support a range of engagements? As we pose these questions, we admit we are always in a process of becoming as we consider who we are and might become alongside other people in the space between.

REFLECTIVE QUESTIONS

1. What is the dialogic spiral, and how has it or could it operate in your research?

2. How can the creation of reciprocal trust through conversation and relationship building aid in the development of research, teaching, and becoming human, both in academia and in our communities (which should not be separated)?

3. What does it mean when our participants feel we are critically listening as they engage in stories with us? How is such a feeling dialogically constructed in this chapter? How might you construct it in your current or future research?

4. Whereas power relations often place researchers at an advantage and participants at a disadvantage, how can power be better shared in Projects in Humanization, thus breaking down or breaking through the dangerous binaries that have guided research methods in the past?

REFERENCES

Bakhtin, M. M. (1981). Discourse in the novel. In *The dialogic imagination: Four essays.* Austin: University of Texas Press.

Bakhtin, M. M. (1990). Author and hero in aesthetic activity. In *Art and answerability: Early philosophical essays.* Austin: University of Texas Press.

Ball, A. (2006). *Multicultural strategies for education and social change: Carriers of the torch in the United States and South Africa.* New York, NY: Teachers College Press.

Ball, A., & Freedman, S. (2004). *Bakhtinian perspectives on language, literacy, and learning.* New York, NY: Cambridge University Press.

Bartolome, L. (1994). Beyond the methods fetish: Toward a humanizing pedagogy. *Harvard Educational Review, 62*(2), 173–194.

Battiste, M. (2002). *Indigenous knowledge and pedagogy in First Nations education: A literature review with recommendations.* Ottawa, Ontario, Canada: Indian and Northern Affairs Canada.

Brayboy, B., & Maughan, E. (2009). Indigenous knowledge and the story of the bean. *Harvard Educational Review, 79*(1).

Charmaz, K. (2006). *Constructing grounded theory: A practical guide through qualitative analysis.* Los Angeles, CA: SAGE.

Greene, M. (2000). *Releasing the imagination: Essays on education, the arts, and social change.* San Francisco, CA: Jossey-Bass.

Jordan, J. (2005). These poems. In J. H. Levi & S. Miles (Eds.), *Directed by desire: The collected poems of June Jordan* (p. 3). Port Townsend, WA: Cooper Canyon Press.

Kinloch, V. (2005). Poetry, literacy, and creativity: Fostering effective learning strategies in an urban classroom. *English Education, 37*(2), 96–114.

Kinloch, V. (2010). *Harlem on our minds: Place, race, and the literacies of urban youth.* New York, NY: Teachers College Press.

Morrison, T. (1993). *Lecture and speech of acceptance, upon the award of the Nobel Prize for literature.* New York, NY: A.A. Knopf.

Noddings, N. (1993). *Educating for intelligent belief or unbelief: The John Dewey lecture.* New York, NY: Teachers College Press.

Okakok, L. (1989). Serving the purpose of education. *Harvard Educational Review, 59*(4), 248.

Schultz, K. (2009). *Rethinking classroom participation: Listening to silent voices.* New York, NY: Teachers College Press.

Silko, L. M. (1977). *Ceremony.* New York, NY: Viking Press.

Tuck, E. (2009). Suspending damage: A letter to communities. *Harvard Educational Review, 79*(3).

Wertsch, J. (1991). *Voices of the mind: A sociocultural approach to mediated action.* Cambridge, MA: Harvard University Press.

Humanizing Research With LGBTQ Youth Through Dialogic Communication, Consciousness Raising, and Action

3

Mollie V. Blackburn

As humans, we are always "imperfect, unfinished, incomplete beings, who exist in and with an ever-changing world" (Freire, as cited by Roberts, 2000, p. 41). Or, also in Freire's (1998) words, "No one is born already made. Little by little we become, through the social practice in which we participate" (p. 79). We are, he argues, always "becoming more fully human" (Freire, as cited by Roberts, 2000, p. 51). This is what humanization is—the infinite process of becoming more fully human. But the process does not necessarily keep moving along unhindered or uninterrupted. It can get stalled out or stuck; it can even get derailed or unraveled. This happens when a person is dehumanized, that is, made less human by having their individuality, creativity, and humanity taken away, as when one is treated like a number or an object. This is especially true for those marginalized by systems of inequality based on race, class, gender, sexuality, religion, or language, among other identity markers. Consider, for example, lesbian, gay, bisexual, transgender, and questioning (LGBTQ) youth. These young people are often forced, sometimes implicitly, other times explicitly, to hide who they are and to conform to their straight peers. Sometimes, when they fail to hide and conform, they are treated as less than human; sometimes this means being physically assaulted, at other times it means being verbally abused, and at still other times it means being ostracized and isolated. But such a state of dehumanization need not be a permanent one. One has agency to resist and rebut dehumanizing forces, to reassert one's humanity, and to play a part in work that humanizes others. Certainly, these things are integrally intertwined.

Paris (2011) asserts that researchers "can humanize through the act of research" (p. 11). Moreover, Bartolome (2010) states that humanizing work with youth is imperative to "get on with the business of sharing and creating knowledge" (p. 177). Although Bartolome is talking about teaching, her claim applies to research in the humanizing tradition as well. Such humanization is not only "ethically necessary," it also often "increases the validity" of research (Paris, 2011, p.1). Such assertions, indeed, are the driving force behind this book.

And the driving force behind reading it, at least for me and I imagine for many readers, is to figure out how: how I, as a researcher, can engage in humanizing research with young people in the project of educational and social justice. Winn and Ubiles (2011) advocate demonstrating "responsibility in the research community," establishing opportunities to "exercise reciprocity," "ritualiz[ing] respect" (p. 305), and collaborating (p. 306). For his part, Paris (2011) talks about being friends with participants, understanding them, and, even if in small ways, inspiring them and being inspired by them. He talks about "building relationships of dignity and care" and engaging in "dialogic consciousness-raising" (p.1). These ideas resonate with me deeply, and I find myself reflecting on my past and current projects to see whether I am living up to the expectations set forth in these articulations of humanizing research. I find myself imagining future projects and ways I can strive and struggle to become more fully human and humanizing.

Here I describe a study with LGBTQ youth in Philadelphia, which is the focus of this chapter, and then tell three stories that challenged me in my struggle to conduct humanizing research. The first and second stories focus on humanizing fieldwork, the first attending to the role of dialogic communication and the second attending to the role of consciousness raising. Like the second, the third also attends to consciousness raising, but focuses on humanizing through data analysis rather than during fieldwork. The final section of this chapter focuses on the importance of action—that is, getting up and doing something about the injustices you've come to know and understand—in the work of humanizing research.

WORKING WITH LGBTQ YOUTH AT THE ATTIC

For the purposes of this chapter, I draw primarily on the qualitative and ethnographic inquiry I conducted at the Attic (Blackburn, 2002–2003, 2003a, 2003b, 2005a, 2005b). The study was, primarily, an exploration of the ways LGBTQ youth used literacy to advocate for themselves and others. The Attic was and is a youth-run center in Philadelphia that serves LGBTQ youth ages 12 to 23. I came to know of it via an instructor's recommendation of a place where I might start developing and practicing research skills. Her recommendation came at a pivotal time in my life. I had recently left teaching in middle and high schools, and I desperately missed being around adolescents. I had also only recently come out as lesbian. In fact, these two events, leaving teaching and coming out, were almost simultaneous, and not just coincidentally. In retrospect, I think I did not come out before I taught because I was financially dependent on my rather conservative parents, but once I started teaching, coming out seemed even more impossible. I did not even consider the possibility for most of the time I taught. It was not until my final year of teaching that I developed a crush on a co-worker and began imagining what it might be like to come out as lesbian. Right around that time, two women teachers were seen by a parent and a student during a school day kissing in a car in the parking lot of a nearby shopping area. They were fired from their jobs. The articulated rationale for the firing was about their having taken sick days when they were not really sick, but everyone I knew believed these women were fired because they were kissing each other. It was hard to imagine coming out as a teacher at this particular time and place. Once I decided to leave teaching, though, I started the seemingly endless process of coming out. At least in one way, I started becoming more fully human. It was at this time that I came to know of the Attic.

I worked so hard to connect to the Attic. I called and left messages, which were never returned. I stopped by, but, appropriately, adults who were not hosted by youth members were not permitted to be on the premises. I tried to make an appointment. Eventually, I was contacted by a youth representing the Youth Planning Committee (YPC), who scheduled me for an interview by the committee. Although I didn't know it then, the YPC was facilitated by the Attic's executive director, Carrie, and the assistant director, but it comprised mostly youth who came to the Attic and were invested in making decisions that impacted the center. They volunteered to serve on the YPC, and in doing so, they made program and policy decisions in collaboration with Carrie and the assistant director. They also, as it turns out, decided who was (and was not) allowed to volunteer in the center. I eagerly accepted the YPC's invitation for an interview. When I showed up for the interview, Theo, a young biracial gay man, gave me a tour of the center and asked me to wait in the lobby until the YPC was ready to interview me.

The interview wasn't easy. I proudly referenced my experience working with adolescents in schools and was quickly put in my place by a young person who asked me what I was going to do to *not* be a teacher in the Attic. I confidently talked about wanting to conduct research that would be mutually beneficial, which generated ambivalence from the YPC members. Later I learned that undergirding this ambivalence was the question of my sexual identity. The youth, understandably, perceived me as straight, and although my referencing of my partner called this perception into question, it didn't disconfirm it entirely. Whether I was LGBTQ mattered to them, but they were not allowed to ask. I entered wanting to be a researcher, but after my conversation with the committee that day, I left committed to be a volunteer. Several days later I returned to the Attic with my partner to be an adult presence and queer participant in a Queer Youth Take Back the Night parade. Youth who were diverse in terms of race, class, gender expression, and sexual identity rallied around huge puppets they had constructed in collaboration with community activists. They pulled us in to walk with them through the streets of the Gayborhood in Philadelphia as they chanted, "We're here, we're queer, our parents think we're in Wildwood!" (Wildwood is a nearby beach community with a boardwalk and amusement park. It is both close enough that young people could feasibly go there for an evening but far enough away to explain why a young person might not be home until quite late.) I was struck by the diversity, the warmth, the confidence, the leadership, the activism, the humor, and the humanity of the youth. This was a group I wanted to learn with.

I volunteered at the Attic for a year and worked there as an employee for two more years. For those two years, my official job title was Women's Project Coordinator. I was a researcher across all three years. It was not always easy balancing the simultaneous roles of volunteer or employee and researcher. I grappled with this as I read and wrote about research and ethics, as I talked with my peers about our field-based ethical dilemmas, as I rode the bus and walked to and from the Attic, and as I spent time with youth at the Attic. Ultimately, I made peace with the imbalance with a general rule of thumb: Every decision I made had to be made first as a volunteer or employee and second as a researcher. If ever I came to decision for which I could not make myself live by that rule, I would consult Carrie for advice. Such a consultation never came to pass. Once I set the rule for myself, I could live with it.

Here I draw from my work as both an employee and researcher as I explore the notion of humanizing research.

Humanizing Fieldwork: Listening, Learning, and Mentoring With Youth

As the Women's Project Coordinator, I worked with Dara, an older youth staff member, to start and facilitate a weekly social and support group for women who love women. The group started during a summer when there was a big influx of youth both in the group and in the center more broadly. These new youth had come home to the Philadelphia area from various colleges just for the summer. Early in the autumn, though, the group thinned out to youth who had known one another for longer periods of time. It was during this time that conversation moved from acknowledging the diverse desires among group members to seeking out and watching videos that were pitched to me as "safer sex" videos—and thus educational—to eventually planning and going on what I understood at the time as a field trip to several local erotica/fetish boutiques.

It is probably worth mentioning at this point that I was born and raised in a southern, Catholic, Republican, suburban family and community. I had learned that women were not sexual or that to be sexual was not ladylike. Intellectually, as an adult living outside of my parents' home, this idea repulsed me; still, I found myself running into it in the forms of my discomfort and judgment, repeatedly. Increasingly, after leaving my parents' home when I was 18, I knew, intellectually and personally, that women were sexual and that that was something to value. But I also knew that gay adults were often understood as predators of youth. At best, gay adults were accused of trying to recruit youth into being gay as well, and at worst, they were accused of being pedophiles trying to have nonconsensual sex with youth, or, in short, to rape them. I don't recall hearing someone say that outright, but I had that sense, a sense constructed from a collection of media, friends, and family, a sense that came from living in a pervasively homophobic community. I don't recall either embracing or rejecting these notions; I just remember the subtle ubiquity of them. In this context, though, as a recently out lesbian working with young women who loved women, I was vulnerable to them in ways I had never been previously. I feared being recognized by my peers or the parents of these young women as a predator of queer youth. Still, I knew that my intention was to value and support these young women as women who love women, not just emotionally but sexually as well. I struggled with my own discomfort and fear in my efforts to fulfill my intention. The struggle included reading, writing, contemplating, and ongoing conversations—with youth, peers, and mentors—about the experiences of LGBTQ youth, their need for adult advocates, and the ways I could embody such advocacy. This struggle was not unlike the one I'd had while serving simultaneously as a volunteer or employee and researcher. In truth, it is how I generally function in this world: reading, writing, thinking, talking, some might say perseverating, to untangle the knots, if possible, or, if not, to come to know them intimately so I understand where and why I stand among the intricate tangles.

It was late in our first summer of meeting that someone in the group suggested going to a workshop held in a local bar that was designed for lesbians interested in sadomasochism. Perhaps in a subconscious reaction to this suggestion, almost six weeks later, I decided to bring a video that I understood to be about safer sex for women who love women. My selection was considered too boring by the young women, and the group decided not to watch it at all. Faced with their outright rejection of my choice, I asked Justine to accompany me in picking a video. I asked her partly because she was a younger member of the group and I was a little concerned about her comfort level (unnecessarily, as it turned out), and also because I was not very trusting of my own comfort level as a basis for judgment. Together we walked to a locally run video store that catered to the surrounding LGBTQ community and that donated all video rentals to the center. We asked where we might find lesbian safer-sex videos and were directed to an area labeled "of interest to lesbians." We perused, sometimes laughing a bit nervously, and Justine selected *She's Well.*[1] When we rejoined the group, Dara stated that this was not the film she had in mind, and the video went unwatched. Instead, we talked about how lesbians meet one another, and how they need fake identification so that they can get into bars to meet one another (not to drink underage). Several weeks later, Trish, another young woman in the group, explained that she was reading a Rita Mae Brown book, *In Her Day*, which Justine had recommended when Trish said she was looking for a book about lesbians with some but not too much sex. Another, and older, adult employee in the center was visiting the group at the time, and she talked about the difference between love and lust. It was a couple of weeks after that that the suggestion was made that we visit, as a group, one of the local erotica/fetish boutiques. The very next week a group of us deliberated over the possible field trip, but had no clear resolution. Two weeks later we continued the deliberations, this time among a smaller group that included two of the older youth, another adult volunteer, and me. We decided to plan the trip and set a date. It was on this day, just after deciding to plan the field trip, that we watched a safer-sex video that Dara had selected and the group had endorsed.

This video was the closest thing to pornography I had ever watched. I had *seen* porn on televisions in bars catering to gay men, but this film featured women, and I was *watching* it, not walking by it. As I sat stiff and startled in my seat, watching along with the young women, I was overwhelmed by embarrassment and conflict. The other adult volunteer in the group that day was also an academic mentor of mine from my university. As if this were not awkward enough, Carrie joined the group for a bit as well. I felt as I had back in middle school, watching an R-rated movie on HBO, when my mom walked into the room. As a middle schooler, I would keep my finger on the remote control, and as soon as I heard the squeak of floorboards, I would press the button to change the channel to something mundane and innocuous. I longed for such an option in this context, but this was not my decision to make. In this situation, among these young women who love women, I sat still, watched the video, and tried to remind myself, with something not unlike a mantra, that women, even young women, are in fact sexual, and that that is something to be celebrated rather than suppressed.

The field trip was scheduled to happen in two weeks. Now, in retrospect, I can see some things that might have gone really wrong with this trip, things that I'm sure Carrie had in mind when she asked me whether this was really a good idea, things that I was unable to attend to because I was so busy suppressing discomfort and fear—things like a young person feeling vulnerable or even being threatened in one way or another while in one of the shops, or like a parent vehemently or even violently disapproving. But those things didn't happen. This trip was a lovely autumn walk through the South Street area and Gayborhood of Philadelphia in which a group of around eight young women who love women chatted nervously together. Some stayed in the fronts of stores, pointing to things, giggling and talking. One flirted with a cashier. Others walked bravely into the backs of stores, returning to the front when they were ready to leave. Nothing all that eventful occurred. After five stops, including one at a convenience store, we walked confidently back to the Attic.

We talked about which store we liked best. We talked about the things that surprised us; for instance, someone expected there to be more toys and did not expect at all that there would be costumes. Justine talked about going back to purchase a collection of toys. When she mentioned the cost, Kira recommended the Good Vibrations catalog, which she said had better prices. The next week, though, when we met again, the conversation was decidedly less focused on sex. We talked about Justine's getting back together with her girlfriend and Kira's going on a "domestic shopping spree," which included the purchase of a new brand-name shower curtain. We talked about our grandmothers and music we listened to when we were in particular kinds of moods. I asked about the field trip; they said it was fine, but overall the intense focus on sex seemed to dissipate.

It was as if a curiosity had been satisfied, and to discuss the sexual was perfectly acceptable but not quite so essential.

Over the course of this first fall of the women's group, these young women who love women taught me in a thoroughly embodied way to "listen [to], learn from, and mentor" (Bartolome, 2010, p. 189) the young people with whom I work. I understand listening and learning together as being about dialogic communication. Roberts (2000) argues, based on his reading of Freire, that dialogic communication involves "'love' of the works and of other human beings" (p. 44), humility, "faith in the ability of others to 'name the world,' together with trust between participants, and a hope that dehumanization can be overcome" (p. 44). However, Roberts further claims that dialogic communication is humanizing only if it is also critical, or in Paris's terms, "consciousness-raising." I understand this in relationship to Bartolome's idea of mentoring, although I understand it in less unidirectional ways than those Bartolome suggests and in a more omnidirectional sense, as Paris suggests.

In this case, I had to listen to the young women in the group as they talked about their sexuality and desires. I had to listen lovingly, with faith in these women as they described their lives as young women who love women, and with hope in changing a generally misogynist and homophobic context. But I also had to listen with humility, knowing that I had learned false and harmful messages not only about women and our sexuality and desires but also about all people who are attracted to people of the same gender, lessons that I needed to unlearn for myself as well as the young people with whom I worked. Through this listening and learning, which I would do as a volunteer and employee but, to be totally honest, I allocated significantly more time to doing as a researcher, I became more critical of misogyny and homophobia and more aware of their impact on young women who love women. Such consciousness raising provoked me to serve as a stronger mentor, not one who just sat stiff and startled, embarrassed and conflicted, but one who walked and talked nervously but confidently with young women who love women in their exploration of their sexuality and desire.

Dehumanizing Fieldwork: Recognizing, Reflecting, and Revising

During my first summer of conducting fieldwork with the newly formed women's group, the members talked a lot about how to name and describe the group to those outside of it. Youth group members consistently used the phrase "women who love women" because it served to include everyone in the group. The word "love" was ambiguous enough to include women who had shared sexual relationships with other women without excluding those who had not been in sexual relationships with women thus far in their lives. The phrase as a whole included women who loved women and identified as lesbian or gay but also those who identified as dyke or queer. It also included women who loved women even if they also loved men, such as bisexual women. Just as the phrase included some, it excluded others—most obviously men. This was, in part, the purpose of the group—that is, to create a space separate from men, who dominated the Attic in many ways, always in their numbers but often by speaking first, most, and loudest about topics that could most easily be understood as of unique interest to same-sex-attracted men. There were women in the group who embodied masculinity, no doubt, but there were no group members who had ever been assigned or actively assumed a male identity.

While men were explicitly excluded, the exclusion of transgender people was implicit. The phrase did not explicitly limit the invitation to biological or anatomical women or people who were assigned such a gender at birth. However, the trans youth at the Attic were, to my knowledge, heterosexual. Those who were male-to-female identified as women but loved men, and those who were female-to-male loved women but identified as men. Because of these particular circumstances, the group avoided, at least early in the first summer, the question of who counted as women and who did not.

One day later that summer, though, the women in the group were taking photos of the group for a flyer they were working on. Shania, an African American male-to-female transsexual youth at the center, hung around as we took the photos. She expressed interest in being in the pictures. We all but dismissed her interest. In a weak attempt to include her, I took a picture of her but not as a part of the group. I rationalized that she really was not part of the group because she had never attended a meeting. We developed the photographs and brought them to the group, except for the photograph of Shania, which I gave to her. Here the group was confronted with the question of who counted as women and who did not, and when it came down to it, we deliberately excluded a transgender woman. We decided that she did not count.

Then, in the early fall, on a beautiful day, we decided to meet outside in the courtyard. There were three people in the group whom I had not met previously. I interpreted them all as women until, during introductions, one introduced himself as Jorge. During the discussion, Jorge told a very long story about his ex-boyfriend. I did nothing to curb his participation in the group. The next week I explained to the group that I had been grappling with what I should have done and solicited advice. They suggested that next time we allow him to stay but explain to him that the discussion was for women only.

Later that fall, Steve, a White female-to-male transsexual youth at the center, walked right into one of the women's group meetings. Dara and I made eye contact, shrugged, and went with it. I reflect back on this moment with great curiosity. I think the race and gender dynamics in the group played some role in our allowing Steve to stay. Dara is an African American masculine lesbian, and I am a White closer-to-femme lesbian. Steve, as a White man, albeit trans-man, felt entitled to make the decision and did not ask whether he could attend the group. Moreover, like Jorge, he asserted this sense of entitlement throughout the meeting. He spoke first, loudest, and most often. He even made comments about some group members' appearances appealing to him and made judgments about which women in the group he'd like to get to know better. Although this could have been a dynamic in any same-sex lesbian, gay, or bisexual group, it had not been in this group thus far. Dara and I were stunned, and it appeared as if many group members were. We took a break, which we rarely did, during which Steve left and did not return to the group.

Although race and gender dynamics played a role in our allowing Steve to stay in the group, initially, so too did our ignorance of transgender people. You see, Dara and I, as well as several others in the group, remembered Steve as Jane. It was the previous summer that he had come to the Attic and introduced himself as Jane. He quickly became a significant part of the community and slowly transitioned from female to male. So, even though he both identified and represented himself as a man, we remembered and even thought of him as a woman who loved women. This way of interacting with a transsexual person is offensive in that it disregards what the person knows to be true about himself. In other words, the acceptance of Steve was no less transphobic than the rejection of Shania.

Bartolome (2010), in her work on humanizing pedagogy, talks about the importance of people (in her case teachers and students, but here researchers and participants) "breaking away from . . . unspoken antagonism and negative beliefs about each other" (p. 177) so that we can eliminate the "hostility that often confronts" these young people. The women's group had much to learn about and from our transgender siblings. This is not learning that happened in women's group, per se, but it happened among women's group members in a variety of ways. For example, several group members were also part of a Speakers' Bureau, which solicited and received trainings on issues pertinent to transgender youth. This group began consulting trans youth about the ways they represented them and eventually recruited and hired trans youth, Shania and Steve among others, to represent themselves at the outreaches conducted by the Speakers' Bureau. Independently, and as a part of my research, I worked with Shania extensively to learn her story. For example, I learned about how, when she found school intolerable, she would dress as a woman and ride public transportation to the public library to study books about public transportation, a real passion for her. And how she was most vulnerable in her neighborhood, where someone might recognize her, and most confident in the library, where no one seemed to question her gender expression at all. She taught me about the tricky terrain she negotiated in schools, her family, and community, and my learning has continued in myriad ways in the years since. According to Roberts (2000), "Given an ever-changing world, humanization is a continuous, unfinished process, with new problems to be addressed as each epoch unfolds" (p. 51). Shania, Steve, and the women's group remind us that the process is one with starts and stops and struggles. Even when we strive to engage in humanizing research with some youth, it may have the unintended effect of dehumanizing others. Then we must broaden the scope of our efforts; we must embrace our humility, listen with love, strive to raise our consciousness, and act.

Later, toward the end of that calendar year, a young transsexual woman expressed interest in the group but wanted to make sure she was welcome. I agreed to check in with the group, all of whom said that if she loved women, she was welcome.

HUMANIZING ANALYSIS: FILLING IN GAPS

Justine, the young woman who helped me pick out a safer-sex video, is an African American lesbian. We connected two years before the women's group was initiated, early in her high school career and early in my volunteering at the Attic. Over the course of my three years at the Attic, we developed a friendship that has continued in the decade since I left. But maybe a year into our friendship, Justine and I got into a conversation about the journaling each of us had done in middle school. We both knew where our middle school journals were and agreed to exchange them. The day I gave her my journal, a three-ring binder, maybe 2 inches thick, with worn (even torn, in some places) bland blue fabric covering it, I wrote this in my field notes:

> I struggle with handing over my journal. I should have made a copy. But I remember that she handed hers to me yesterday, and I need to trust her as much as she trusts me, and I hand it over. She starts reading it. She laughs. I realize I am very nervous. No one else has read this ever, as far as I know.

Pragmatically, I was afraid she might lose the notebook; personally, I was afraid of how her reading might alter her perception of me and our friendship. She had already brought me her journal a few days before, and she had said I could keep it and read it for a while. It was a black-and-white composition notebook; the cover was worn and had stickers on it—one representing the Attic and the other a Spice Girl. Having her journal may have been the only reason I was able to give mine to her, but even so, it was difficult for me. However, the exchange enabled me to understand her vulnerability, experiences, and identities better. Because of the exchange, I read Justine's journal with the kind of love, humility, faith, trust, and hope that is integral to dialogic communication. This love, humility, faith, trust, and hope created a foundation for a friendship that continues to this day, across over a decade and hundreds of miles. Still, when I read her journal, there was consciousness raising work I had yet to do, and work that I ultimately did in the analysis of this journal.

I noticed that Justine didn't self-identify in terms of sexuality until her affinities shifted from Michael Jackson to Melissa Etheridge. It was as if, as long as her attractions were for men, her sexuality need not be named, but as soon as her attractions included women, they had to be named, or rather, *she* had to be named, as either bisexual or lesbian. In other words, as soon as she did not fit into the hegemonic norm, she had to name herself because it was inevitable that she would be named (Lather, 1991). This is what stood out to me as I analyzed Justine's journal with a focus on our common point of marginalization: sexuality.

Hooks (1990) argues that the margins are sites of resistance, creativity, and power. It seems to me they are also sites of insight. There are things I understood about Justine as a participant and the data that represented her because I am lesbian.

But there are also things about Justine I did not understand, insights I lacked because of our discrepant positionalities, particularly those defined by race—that is, because I am White and she is Black. As a White researcher, I will never have the insights about youth of color that a researcher of color will have. However, this does not mean I should limit my research to participants who mirror me. Rather, it is imperative to work across differences toward social justice. To compensate for our limitations, researchers must assume responsibility for learning as much as they can about experiences beyond their own so that they better understand the people represented in their data. We owe this to our participants. Of course, this means conducting member checks and paying particular attention to critiques offered by people of color, but it also means immersing oneself in the work of scholars of color, in this case. Hurtado and Stewart (1997) call this "academic 'walking in others' shoes'—reading, taking seriously, citing, and quoting—the scholarship by people of Color about race" (p. 309). They argue that actively seeking out literature written from perspectives other than your own is "one technique for addressing the limitations of one's own standpoint" (p. 309). Making a commitment to a body of literature defined, in part, by the racial identities of the authors does not mean reading for some monolithic perspective from these scholars, but paying attention to the multiple and variable perspectives of the scholars. Moreover, it does not mean reading to identify and attempt to fill gaps or holes in the literature. Instead, it means reading to recognize and attempt to fill gaps or holes in our understandings—and in this case, gaps in my understandings of race, racism, and the youth with whom I worked. The same is true, though, for straight allies, or any straight-identified researchers, I suppose, working with LGBTQ communities. Even the most well-intentioned straight allies must immerse themselves in the research and theory of LGBTQ scholars, authors, and artists to conduct insightful research focused on LGBTQ communities.

While I was analyzing Justine's journal, then, I was also reading the scholarship and literature and watching films by and about lesbians of color, which, of course, shaped my analysis. I noticed that just as Justine did not need to name herself in terms of her sexual identity as long as she was heterosexual, in my middle school journal I, as a White person, did not find the need to name myself in racial terms. In contrast, race was the first thing that Justine wrote about in her middle school journal. Here is her first entry:

> I believe there [is] no such thing as a 'oreo.' Your either black or white. Me and Michael have that in commin. Just because I might like rock or country doesn't make me white. Mother fuckers who would dare say that to me or that about Michael because he looks different better look out.

Since then, Justine has explained to me that, in middle school, she was often accused of acting White because she did well in school, and that she was called an "oreo" because people said that she was Black on the outside and White on the inside. Here, in this entry, Justine not only articulated her knowledge of the implications of race and racialized behavior, but also named herself in terms of race. She said that people were either Black or White and that she, quite definitively, and fervently, was Black.

According to Cisneros (1987), there is a certain need to write about experiences of institutionalized marginalization. She writes,

> Recently, talking with fellow writer and friend Norma Alarcón, we agreed there is no luxury or leisure in our lives for us to write of landscapes and sunsets and tulips in a vase. Instead of writing by inspiration, it seems we write by obsession, of that which is most violently tugging at our psyche. . . . Perhaps later there will be time to write by inspiration. In the meantime, in my writing as well as that of other Chicanas and other women, there is the necessary phase of dealing with those ghosts and voices most urgently haunting us, day by day. (p. 73)

Justine, like Cisneros, prioritized writing about issues that were important to her above writing about what she called "pretty things." In fact, Justine and I talked about the differences between such writings, and she effectively dismissed writing about "pretty things" as frivolous. Moreover, on her high school journal she had a sticker on which she had written, "Whatever happened to poems about roses?" When I asked her about it, she explained to me that in one of her classes at school several students shared their poetry, to which one student responded by saying that she usually wrote about "pretty things" and that she wondered, "Whatever happened to poems about roses?" Justine laughed at the student, as evidenced by the mocking sticker, and claimed there were more important things to write about.

Clearly, Justine's experiences that were shaped by race and racism were among these more important things. It seemed to me that she *had* to write about race in her middle school journal, because it was "most urgently haunting [her] day by day," to use Cisneros's words, in a way that it had not been for me when I wrote my middle school journal. Justine, as an African American lesbian, *had* to write about sexuality, just as I had to write about sexuality once I came to understand myself as something other than heterosexual. In other words, a writer is obliged, both personally and politically, to write about, and thus to name, that which others use to oppress us.

Thus, Cisneros was part of a larger body of literature that helped me work against my own ignorance and provided me with one way of better understanding Justine as a lesbian of color. Taking an academic walk in the shoes of lesbians of color served as a sort of consciousness raising that I needed in order to conduct humanizing analysis.

BECOMING MORE FULLY HUMAN THROUGH ACTION

Through dialogic communication with and consciousness raising about oppressed populations, we can come to hear stories and come to know situations that can be downright paralyzing. According to Freire (1996), though, action is just as integral to humanizing as dialogic communication and consciousness raising are. Action, he explains—combined with reflection, which is fundamental to both dialogic communication and consciousness raising—is praxis. And undergirding praxis is the aim to transform the world. According to Freire, because praxis is a uniquely human capability, it can be uniquely humanizing. Researchers who strive to conduct humanizing research, then, are challenged to act. We must overcome paralysis.

Action must not be understood narrowly, however. Action might look like a highly visible and audible march through city streets, but it may not. Action often happens at personal and communal levels but has consequences at institutional and societal levels. Consider the acts embedded in the stories I've told in this chapter. Sharing significant and intimate parts of our histories with each other, as Justine and I did in sharing our journals, is a personal act with humanizing consequences in that we serve as "worthy witnesses" for each other (Winn & Ubiles, 2011). This personal act between Justine and me worked to combat both homophobia and racism as it took shape in our lives. Also, preparing youth (e.g., Dara, Shania, and Steve) to take over jobs that draw on and compensate them for their strengths and contributions (e.g., facilitating the women's group or working on the Speakers' Bureau) is a personal act with humanizing consequences. Such personal acts work to dispel transphobia and make the world a better place for young people who do not conform to gender rules and regulations.

Communal acts, such as watching safer-sex videos for women who love women and taking field trips to local erotica/fetish boutiques, are humanizing in that they create safe environments in which young women who love women can strive to understand themselves as sexual beings in the larger contexts of their lives. In this way, such communal acts work to dispel misogyny and homophobia. The act of uncovering and working against the biases of any community (in our case, disclosing the transphobic values among the women's group and educating members through the training provided by the Speakers' Bureau) is also a communal act, or collection of them, that has institutional and societal consequences. Institutionally, at the Attic, these acts brought to the foreground the need for many of us to learn more about the issues pertinent to trans youth. The education provoked by this revelation gave rise to a group of peer and adult educators more competent to fight transphobia in the world beyond the Attic. Thus, these personal and communal acts promoted social transformation by working on behalf of LGBTQ youth and against misogyny, homophobia, and transphobia. And each of these interrelated acts was embedded in my research—it made the learning both worthy and worthwhile.

Of course, there were related acts that I haven't captured in this collection of stories, infinite acts that should or at least could have come out of the stories presented here. The possibilities are endless. The challenge, though, is to remember the action. Remember to act. Strive to act in ways that resonate with what you've learned in dialogic communication with youth and your efforts at consciousness raising, but don't get lost in these. Don't forget to act. For it is the action grounded in reflection, it is the praxis, that will transform the world, on behalf of these youth, at the hands of these youth, as well as many others. The possibilities are endless.

REFLECTIVE QUESTIONS

1. Reflecting on your life, identify situations in which you experienced and rejected dehumanizing forces and, in turn, asserted your humanity. Did your actions impact others? In what ways? How have you taken up, or how might you take up, these experiences in your stance toward and practice of research?

2. What might be some of the risks of failing to talk about controversial subjects, such as sexual activity, with young people in your research?

3. In whose shoes do you most need to take an academic walk? How might you fulfill this need? How might such a walk change your research practices?

4. Reflecting on your life, identify situations in which you experienced and were paralyzed by dehumanizing forces. What personal actions might you have taken to assert your humanity? What communal actions might have been taken? How have you taken up, or how might you take up, these experiences in your stance toward and practice of research?

NOTE

1. This title is based on my field notes, although I cannot find anything online by this title to cite this film.

REFERENCES

Bartolome, L. I. (2010). Beyond the methods fetish: Toward a humanizing pedagogy. *Harvard Educational Review, 64*(2), 173–194.

Blackburn, M. V. (2002–2003). Disrupting the (hetero)normative: Exploring literacy performances and identity work with queer youth. *Journal of Adolescent and Adult Literacy, 46*(4), 312–324.

Blackburn, M. V. (2003a). Exploring literacy performances and power dynamics at The Loft: Queer youth reading the world and word. *Research in the Teaching of English, 37*(4), 467–490.

Blackburn, M. V. (2003b). Losing, finding, and making space for activism through literacy performances and identity work. *Penn GSE Perspectives on Urban Education, 2*(1). Retrieved from http://www.urbanedjournal.org/articles/article0008.html

Blackburn, M. V. (2005a). Agency in borderland discourses: Examining language use in a community center with Black queer youth. *Teachers College Record, 107*(1), 89–113.

Blackburn, M. V. (2005b). Co-constructing space for literacy and identity work with LGBTQ youth. *Afterschool Matters, 4,* 17–23.

Cisneros, S. (1987). Ghosts and voices: Writing from obsession. *The Americas Review,*
    15(1), 69–73.

Freire, P. (1996). *Pedagogy of the oppressed* (Rev. 20th anniversary ed.). New York, NY:
    Continuum.

Freire, P. (1998). *Politics and education.* Los Angeles, CA: UCLA Latin American Center
    Publications.

hooks, b. (1990). Marginality as a site of resistance. In R. Ferguson, M. Gever,
    T. T. Minh-ha, & C. West (Eds.), *Out there: Marginalization and contemporary cultures.*
    New York, NY: New Museum of Contemporary Art.

Hurtado, A., & Stewart, A. J. (1997). Through the looking glass: Implications of studying
    whiteness for feminist methods. In M. Fine, L. Weis, L. C. Powell, & L. M. Wong
    (Eds.), *Off white: Readings on race, power, and society* (pp. 297–311). New York, NY:
    Routledge.

Lather, P. (1991). *Getting smart: Feminist research and pedagogy within/in the postmod-*
    ern. New York, NY: Routledge.

Paris, D. (2011). "A friend who understand fully": Notes on humanizing research in a
    multiethnic youth community. *International Journal of Qualitative Studies in Education,*
    24(2), 137–149.

Roberts, P. (2000). *Education, literacy, and humanization: Exploring the work of Paulo*
    Freire. Westport, CT: Bergin & Garvey.

Winn, M. T., & Ubiles, J. R. (2011). Worthy witnessing: Collaborative research in urban
    classrooms. In A. Ball & C. Tyson (Eds.), *Studying diversity in teacher education.*
    New York, NY: Rowman & Littlefield.

PART II

Navigating Institutions and Communities as Participatory Activist Researchers: Tensions, Possibilities, and Transformations

Maisha T. Winn

One of the questions I grapple with in my work is how do educators "teach freedom" in confined spaces. In my work as a participant observer and co-teacher with formerly incarcerated girls who write and perform plays both inside and outside youth detention centers, I have learned that girls use playwriting and performances to create and sustain literate identities. Many girls I worked with believed these plays and performances were the first time anyone had really listened to and *heard* them. While the women teaching the girls in the theatre program, Girl Time, hoped to teach these student artists how language and performing literacy are potentially liberating, the student artists did not always see this manifested in their lives outside of their participation in the program. There were often times when my colleagues and I would ask whether or not it was irresponsible to "teach freedom" when there was not always a clear roadmap for where the youth we worked with would go next. One teaching artist, Kaya, talked about the privilege teaching artists had to leave the detention centers or the Department of Juvenile Justice multi-service center, where workshops were held, and return to comfortable living conditions, while it was uncertain how or even where the girls we worked with would sleep (Winn, 2010, 2011). Similarly, researchers and scholars return to their silos, labs, offices, or cafés with free wireless where they can read, write, and think for countless hours, while youth return to spaces that cannot always support them in becoming their whole selves. Scholars in Part II ask similar questions while showing both the promises and perils of youth-centered work, as well as how an "activist stance"—to borrow from McCarty, Wyman, and Nicholas (Chapter 5)—is essential when doing collaborative work with youth and communities.

In Chapter 4, Irizarry and Brown provide a roadmap for Participatory Action Research (PAR)—what it should look like and what it could look like—while also offering a portraiture of vulnerability in their own work as they show what PAR often looks like in real time in real schools where there are testing climates and cultures of power reign. When the new principal at the site where Brown worked on the SSP project expressed, "It's just not a good time. Maybe we can try again next year" (p. 76), the principal sent a clear message that youth participatory work is dangerous—at best—and that youth asking difficult questions about inequities in education were unwelcome to the school staff and administration. When youth are given the space and opportunity to become critically literate and raise questions, it becomes difficult for school personnel to ignore their findings. Noguera (2007) raised this issue in his straightforward study, "How Listening to Students Can Help Schools Improve," in which 150 tenth-grade students from Boston Public Schools shared their ideas about school safety, high-stakes testing, and relationships between students and teachers. Jonathan, who we meet and get an opportunity to listen to "with ears to hear" in McCarty, Wyman, and Nicholas's chapter, underscores why researchers who are committed to activist research must listen to youth. McCarty recalls, "I was not prepared for the deep commitment to land and language Jonathan expressed," marveling over their two-and-a-half-hour "in-depth ethnographic interview" that traversed topics ranging from heritage language politics to environmental politics (p. 87). Listening to Jonathan revealed that he had thought critically about language loss and reclamation and understood his relationship to learning English as "having to learn how to cope and adjust in this colonial world that we live in" (p. 86). In this "colonial world," young people have found other ways to amplify their voices. In her work as a critical media ethnographer, Jocson demonstrates that our young people from all over the world are using music, poetry, and media to transform lives.

There is nothing youth-centered scholars would like more than to be able to say that a youth-led inquiry process went well, that the youth owned the process (and product), and, finally, that someone (preferably someone who could influence policies and practices that touch these young lives the most) listened to these young people and acted. Scholars committed to activist research agendas have the responsibility to get these stories and projects into the hands of various stakeholders who influence young people's (and their families') lives and hold them accountable. The authors in this section challenge us to consider: What does this commitment from scholars look like in schools? In communities? In colleges and universities?

REFERENCES

Noguera, P. A. (2007). How listening to students can help schools improve. *Theory Into Practice, 46*(3), 205–211.

Winn, M. T. (2010). "Betwixt and between": Literacy, liminality, and the "celling" of Black girls. *Race, Ethnicity, and Education, 13*(4), 425–447.

Winn, M. T. (2011). *Girl Time: Literacy, justice, and the school-to-prison pipeline* (Teaching for Social Justice Series). New York, NY: Teachers College Press.

Humanizing Research in Dehumanizing Spaces

The Challenges and Opportunities of Conducting Participatory Action Research With Youth in Schools

Jason G. Irizarry and Tara M. Brown

4

Schools have been lauded by some as the "great equalizer," offering opportunities for individuals to become educated and participate more fully in society, regardless of their race, ethnicity, cultural background, or socioeconomic status. However, for many youth of color, particularly those attending high-poverty urban schools, schooling has also served a social reproductive function, often doing more to stratify society based on race and class than to ameliorate group-based inequities. The disparate educational opportunities offered to students based on race and class are evident in the "achievement gap," discrepancies in test scores between students of color and White students and between students from low-income and more affluent families. Efforts of policy makers and educators to close this gap have led schools to intensify discipline and control, narrow the focus and flexibility of the curriculum, and focus on test preparation in a way that equates becoming educated with performance on standardized tests rather than meaningfully engaging in quality learning experiences (Brown, 2007; Rodriguez, 2011). In short, the education offered to many youth of color, who will soon compose the majority of students in public schools, can be aptly described as dehumanizing and oppressive. In the face of these challenges, liberatory approaches to research, teaching, and learning are sorely needed but unfortunately rare in urban schools.

A growing body of research documents the liberatory potential of Participatory Action Research (PAR) with youth in K–12 schools (Brown & Rodriguez, 2009b; Cammarota & Fine, 2008; Irizarry, 2011). While this research illustrates the possibilities of PAR, it often does not address the many everyday challenges that researchers face when working in schools. Situating PAR projects inside schools is a vital yet complex endeavor, as PAR researchers often strive to conduct investigations that directly disrupt the ways formal schooling reproduces social inequality. Drawing on our own experiences of conducting school-based PAR projects over the last five years, in this chapter we highlight two realms of challenge—pedagogical and political—that can arise in such projects. We argue that customary ways in which K–12 schools (and universities) are organized around these two realms put pressure on researchers to subvert the liberatory and transformative goals of PAR to the very structures that they are critiquing. We discuss some of these challenges, the pressures they create, and ways that university and youth researchers can work against the subjugation of PAR in K–12 schools. It is our hope that this chapter will serve as a resource to researchers who strive to conduct humanizing research in schools that challenges social injustice and educational inequity.

METHODOLOGICAL AND EPISTEMOLOGICAL FOUNDATIONS OF PAR

Moving beyond a vision of research as the sole domain of officially credentialed university researchers in the ivory tower, PAR is an empirical research methodology in which representatives of the focus population(s) participate as co-researchers. PAR projects can utilize qualitative, quantitative, and/or less traditional data collection and analysis methods. PAR has an explicit goal of "action" or intervention into the problems being studied.

In the United States, PAR was popularized during the 1960s and 1970s amid social movements and rising contestations about systems of oppression and marginalized people's lack of participation in creating official knowledge about their own experiences. Specifically, it "originated as a challenge to positivist research paradigms as carried out largely by university researchers" (Hall, 1993, p. xviii). PAR draws on the work of critical theorists like Antonio Gramsci, Paulo Freire, and others who shed light on the production and control of knowledge as a primary means through which dominant groups maintain and exercise power over subjugated groups. Such scholars assert that oppressed peoples must identify, interrogate, and intervene into the conditions of their own lives. In his classic text *Pedagogy of the Oppressed*, Freire (1970) referenced the unique vantage point of marginalized people, asking, "Who better than the oppressed to understand the terrible significance of an oppressive society? Who can better understand the need for liberation?" (p. 45).

Unlike traditional social science research, in which university researchers are presumed to be best positioned to discern the problems and needs of local people, "PAR is grounded in the epistemological belief that authentic understandings of [and solutions to] social problems require the knowledge of those directly affected by them" (Brown & Rodriguez, 2009a, p. 1). PAR researchers hold that local people possess expert knowledge about the conditions of their lives that outsiders cannot access on their own. While university researchers typically initiate and lead PAR projects, they commit to power sharing and to directly addressing social boundaries (e.g., race/ethnicity, age, socioeconomic status, and education) between themselves and local researchers, which might subvert democratic research processes. While power cannot be completely equalized, PAR researchers work toward this ideal and work to ensure that power is not used in suppressive or coercive ways—that is, that power is used "with" and not "over" others.

Ideally, local researchers participate in every stage of the PAR process: identifying problems; designing the study and instruments; collecting, analyzing, and presenting data; and carrying out action. Through action, PAR researchers implement strategic interventions into the problem(s) under study. Action can take different forms (e.g., teach-ins, workshops, symposia, rallies, and art exhibits) but should be authentic and relevant to the study objectives and findings and to the community's needs, concerns, interests, and ways of knowing and communicating. Action is also a means of examining and enhancing the validity of the research findings, through testing strategies and gathering further evidence. Building on Freire's (1970) notion of praxis—reflection and action on the world in order to change it—the outcomes of action are folded back into the research as data used to further the refine research process (Brown, 2010).

PAR is premised on principles of sociopolitical justice and equity. It is based on the conviction that all people's knowledge is valuable and that all have the right to self-determination and to have their perspectives accounted for. PAR provides a means for disenfranchised people to better understand and address the social, structural, and cultural forces that shape their lives. It provides a means for them to enter into discourses of power, (re)frame their experiences, and challenge the ways in which social science research has historically excluded and denigrated them. In these ways, PAR methodology is humanizing research, creating a space in which individuals and communities can work collaboratively toward more fully realizing their human potential.

PAR, PEDAGOGY, AND K–12 EDUCATION

PAR's effectiveness as a tool for individual and collective development speaks directly to the learning processes inherent in this approach. For example, as a part of the research process, local researchers learn how their experiences have been understood by others as well as the theory and practice of research. University researchers learn the perspectives of local community members and the on-the-ground nuances and implications of the problem(s) under study. Further, all research team members must develop mutual trust and respect and the ability to communicate, teach, learn, and collaborate effectively in order for PAR projects to be successful.

PAR, as a pedagogical approach, is problem-based and learner-centered, as researchers identify, conceptualize, and investigate problems. PAR projects capitalize on researchers' existing knowledge while building new knowledge and skills, and they are guided by the needs, interests, perspectives, and experiences of local researchers. Thus, PAR reflects the principles of culturally relevant and multicultural pedagogy (Irizarry, 2009). Further drawing on Freire's (1970, 1973, 1998) notions of critical consciousness and liberatory education, PAR researchers work to better understand and confront "the situations which limit" (Freire, 1970, p. 99) opportunities for success among local researchers and their communities.

Given PAR's pedagogical approach and liberatory objectives, in our own work we have employed this methodology in K–12 schools to investigate schooling conditions among historically marginalized youth (Brown & Galeas, 2011; Irizarry, 2009). Our research highlights the benefits of collaborating with youth in understanding and addressing the educational challenges they face. It brings the oft-silenced perspectives of youth into the discourse on school policy and reform and the pedagogical practices that affect their daily pursuit of quality education.

Young people provide unique and vital insights into the perceptions and actions of students and school personnel and the everyday conditions of schooling. This includes how school policies and practices, institutional structures, and interpersonal interactions can, and often do, impede student success. Capitalizing on these important emic perspectives increases the relevance and applicability of research and interventions to the local school context. Further, as a form of praxis in which research, theory, and pedagogical practice are developed concomitantly, PAR directly addresses the "theory-practice gap," often cited as a drawback of educational research. PAR studies also show that youth can gain valuable competencies through their engagement in formal research. These include enhanced skills in empirical research, critical analysis, leadership, reading, writing, mathematics, and presentation (Brown, 2010; Morrell, 2004; Yang, 2009). Thus, PAR itself is a form of intervention that can foster personal and academic growth and development among marginalized youth.

As we will discuss later in the chapter, the aspects of PAR which make it a powerful pedagogical and methodological approach are often at odds with the way that schools are organized and run. This is particularly true in schools that serve predominantly students of color from urban communities that have strict mechanisms for social control, and where student learning is highly remediated and regimented. Such schools are often dehumanizing spaces, where students of color are unduly punished and excluded (Brown, 2007): where their intellectual potential is discounted and their cultures and identities are disparaged (Irizarry, 2011), and where school personnel's resistance to addressing these realities "cuts [students] off from home, from heritage, and from lived experience, and ultimately severs [them] from their educational process" (Fine, 1991, p. 35).

These are the schools in which we do our work. In working within these institutions, in the midst of these challenges, we are uniquely positioned to humanize educational practice and research. In the following section we describe four PAR projects that we coordinated to highlight the challenges as well as the unique opportunities this approach to research offers to those committed to educational equity and social justice.

OUR PAR PROJECT DESCRIPTIONS

Here we describe the settings, participants, goals, and methodological approaches of four school-based PAR projects that we have conducted over the past five years. We draw examples of challenges and opportunities of school-based PAR from these four projects.

Project FUERTE (Future Urban Educators Conducting Research to Transform Teacher Education)

Fuerte, meaning "strong" in Spanish, was a multiyear participatory action research project that engaged students in urban schools in meaningful, co-constructed research while enhancing their academic skills. FUERTE was designed specifically to inform the students' personal and professional trajectories by addressing sociocultural and sociopolitical issues that impacted their lives. A primary goal of the project was to familiarize the students with the conventions of PAR as a means of examining the educational experiences of Latino, African American, and other youth who have been historically underserved by schools. Although a wealth of research explores urban teacher preparation, very little seriously considers the perspectives of youth or heeds their recommendations. Rather than being positioned as responsible for poor academic outcomes, participants in FUERTE served as researchers of their schooling experiences, developing and disseminating recommendations to improve the practice of teachers and other school personnel working with African American and Latino students.

Project FUERTE was embedded in the course, Action Research and Social Change, which Jason offered at two high schools in the northeastern United States. The project aimed to improve student achievement as well as teacher professional development. The project addressed the significant academic challenges faced by Latino students by fostering the development of the critical thinking, literacy, numeracy, and analytical skills necessary for postsecondary education. Further, by engaging students in the study of urban education and how to improve it, Project FUERTE sought to address the underrepresentation of teachers of color by attracting youth of color into the profession in an effort to diversify the teaching force by "home growing" teachers of color for urban schools (see Irizarry, 2007). Project FUERTE also aimed to contribute to teacher preparation by generating scholarship that was directly informed by youth of color and that could be utilized in professional development efforts. Finally, this project sought to help teachers and researchers better understand the educational needs of Latino youth.

Project FUERTE at Metro High School

During the 2007–2008 academic year, FUERTE was implemented in Metro High School (MHS), an interdistrict magnet school whose student population was 80% youth of color. It was a relatively new school attracting a large number of Latino and African American students from several urban communities, as well as a small number of White suburban students. Students were selected for admission into MHS through a lottery system, and once accepted, they were transported to and from the school by private school buses.

The research team consisted of seven 12th-graders who volunteered to participate and committed to meeting for a minimum of two class periods per week for the entire school year. Four of the students self-identified as Latino (Puerto Rican) and three as African American or Black. They all came from urban communities with schools categorized by the state as "underachieving." They applied to the magnet school in hopes of escaping to a system where learning opportunities were more abundant than in their home districts. The students were acutely aware of the unequal opportunities offered across the two settings, and these comparisons became a focal point of our research as we critically examined the students' educational experiences and the factors that impact the availability of quality educational opportunities for urban youth of color. The students contributed to all aspects of the research process and presented findings emanating from their work at various conferences and professional meetings.

Project FUERTE at Rana High School

From 2008 to 2010, the Action Research and Social Change course was offered at Rana High School (RHS), a more traditional, comprehensive public high school where Latino youth represented approximately half of the student population. The school was one of the poorest and lowest-performing in the state, and the student population was divided fairly evenly between Latino and White students, who each represented a little less than half. The cohort completion rate for Latino students was approximately 50%, meaning that about half of all Latinos that began the ninth grade at RHS did not graduate in four years.

At RHS, Action Research and Social Change was open to any student at RHS who articulated an interest in improving the quality of the education offered to Latino students. Twelve students registered for the course, but after meeting with guidance counselors to review their schedules, several students were forced to drop in order to take other required courses necessary for graduation. The seven students who remained joined the Project FUERTE team as student-researchers, collaborating with Jason and two graduate students from the University of Connecticut.

Six of the seven students were juniors at RHS at the outset of the project, and one was a senior. They varied in age from 15 to 18 at the beginning of the study.

Three of the students had (im)migrated to the mainland United States, two coming from Mexico as young children and one from Puerto Rico at the age of 14. The remaining participants had completed all of their formal education, up to that point, in Rana city schools. All of the students articulated a desire to attend college, but only two were enrolled in prerequisite courses, such as Algebra 1 and 2, for admission into four-year institutions of higher education.

Reflecting the demographic shifts occurring in many U.S. communities, RHS was experiencing a surge in the Latino population, and the majority of teachers, administrators, and professional staff were unprepared to meet the needs of these students. As part of one of the lowest-performing and most economically depressed districts in the state, the school was under increased pressure to improve student performance and graduation rates while also facing significant economic constraints. In this phase of Project FUERTE, the students focused their research on the undereducation of Latino students in urban schools and how administrators and educators within those settings were responding to the surge in the Latino population.

Action Research Into School Exclusion (ARISE)

The focus of ARISE, a two-year PAR study, was to better understand and to improve the schooling experiences of adolescents excluded from mainstream public schools, largely through disciplinary action. The project took place in an urban alternative school in the Mid-Atlantic. All of its students were Black and Latina/o and designated as having special needs. The research team included Tara, nine 11th- and 12th-graders, and two doctoral, graduate assistants (GAs), Thurman Bridges and Summer Clark. Much of the work of the project took place at the Social Action Research Seminar, led by Tara and the GAs. The seminar, which met for four hours per week, was offered during the 2006–2007 and 2007–2008 school years as a for-credit elective class.

All of the youth researchers in ARISE had experienced significant academic and/or disciplinary troubles and multiple school transitions throughout their schooling careers. Although all had been labeled with a documented disability, the research team did not use a disability framework to understand the experiences of the researchers or our student participants. Rather, we examined how particular experiences, beliefs, and actions, which are logical responses to economic, sociopolitical, and educational marginalization, get interpreted as "disordered." This perspective was in stark contrast to how urban schools most often frame the challenges facing these students, as resulting from individual and familial deficiencies.

The ARISE team collected data primarily through interviews and document analyses, and the youth researchers were trained in qualitative study design and data collection, analysis, and presentation. The research team examined school disciplinary policies at the local and national levels to contextualize the study. We interviewed 30 students in Grades 9 through 12 and six teachers at the school about their in-school experiences and topics related to school exclusion and school discipline. As action steps, the research team used data and findings to design and conduct six workshops for preservice teachers at the University of Maryland, College Park. The team also presented their work at several local and national research conferences and symposia, including the American Educational Research Association's annual meeting.

Student Solidarity Project (SSP)

SSP was implemented in the fall of 2009 in James Barker High School (JBS), a racially/ ethnically diverse, urban public high school in the Northeast. Due to poor performance, the school had been designated a "turnaround" school, and that year it had a new principal and faced the layoff of 50% of its teaching staff. SSP focused on relationships between race/ethnicity and immigration status and students' social and academic experiences; improving interethnic relations among students at the school was also a primarily goal. The research team included Tara; Ambrizeth Lima, a classroom at the school; Daren Graves, a faculty member at a nearby university; and seventeen 11th- and 12th-graders attending the school. The project took place in a for-credit elective class, which met four times per week for approximately one hour and was led by the three adult researchers. Although the class was intended to meet for the full 2009–2010 academic year, it was held only during the fall semester, for reasons that we will explain later.

We collected data for the project primarily through interviews and document analyses. Youth researchers analyzed texts pertaining to the experiences of immigrant students and students of color in urban schools, and they were trained in qualitative study design and data collection, analysis, and presentation. The youth researchers conducted 34 interviews with students in Grades 10 through 12 about their social and academic experiences and interactions with teachers and other students. As an action step, the research team presented their findings at a mandatory professional development session at the school, which was attended by teachers and administrators at the school.

THE CHALLENGES AND OPPORTUNITIES OF OUR PAR PROJECTS

To illustrate the complexities of implementing PAR projects in urban schools, in this section we examine some of the challenges and opportunities we and our research teams faced in the PAR projects described above. They are organized into two subsections reflecting the (a) pedagogical and (b) political realms. In each subsection, we begin by describing how K–12 schooling (and, in some cases, academia) is organized in ways that conflict with the goals and principles of PAR. Next, drawing from our experiences, we provide examples of how those conflicts played out in our projects and to what effect. We summarize each subsection by reflecting more theoretically on the challenges and the possibilities—both realized and missed of PAR research can bring about in each respective realm.

The Pedagogical Realm

Pervasive low expectations of low-income youth of color create both challenges and opportunities for PAR projects. Students who are struggling academically may not be seen as worthy of rich and complex learning experiences such as PAR. Because they have received poor academic preparation, they require much support in gaining the skills they will need to conduct and present academic research. On the other hand, schools that believe there is little they can do with these young people to help them to be academically successful may be more willing to let them participate in a school-based PAR project, especially if it keeps them engaged. This section explores the pedagogical implications of PAR as humanizing research in urban schools.

"Teachers Don't Want to Hear That!"
The Pedagogical Implications of Humanizing Research

As noted in the introduction, dehumanizing pedagogies dominate the landscape of urban schools, creating learning environments that are often disconnected from the lived experiences, needs, and learning preferences of youth of color. RHS was no exception. Implemented under the guise of raising achievement, the school's policies and practices were often experienced by the students as restrictive and punitive. Teachers were under increased pressure to improve standardized test scores, and to meet this goal, they used scripted curricula and narrowly constructed lessons that were disconnected from the students' lived experiences. As a turnaround school, JBS faced similar pressures, and both students' and teachers' performances were intensely controlled and scrutinized.

In contrast, PAR, with its focus on the lived experiences of local researchers, "interrogate[s] conditions of social injustice through social theory with a dedicated commitment to social action" (Fine, 2008, p. 213). PAR speaks directly to the sociopolitical contexts in which students are educated, builds on what they already know, and is centered on their experiences and concerns. This represents a sharp departure from the pedagogies most prevalent in urban schools, which are centered on curricular standards derived from prescribed learning objectives. PAR challenges the banking method of education (Freire, 1970), in which students are taught discrete facts and expected to regurgitate them on tests without making connections between their learning and their daily lives. For many students, this lack of connection fuels an exodus from schools that is evidenced in the alarmingly high dropout/pushout rates in urban schools.

Once students begin to feel affirmed and engaged with learning through the PAR process, they become more critical of the teaching methods employed in other classes. This is highlighted in the following excerpt from a conversation among students in Project FUERTE at RHS during the end of the first year of the project:

Taina: Like, this is the way education should be. We are learning a lot, but we want to learn because it is connected to us. We see that connection. You know what I mean?

Alberto: I feel you. But what makes me mad at the same time is that now I see what it could be like, you know if teachers taught different, like, changed the way they teach us. I don't know; it's, like, frustrating, more frustrating now because for the first time I see what is out there, what is possible.

Jasmine: I tried to tell Mr. [Smith] and another teacher about what we are doing and how we are learning and doing high-level work without [the teacher] lecturing or worksheets and yelling all the time . . . all the stuff that they do. But teachers don't want to hear that! That means more work for them. The teachers here, they don't want to get to know us. They don't believe in us like that.

Taina: Word.

Because the social reproductive function of schools has remained largely unexamined by school and district personnel, pedagogical practices that aim to make students critical consumers of schooling are often met with hostility. This was also reflected in the SSP project in which teachers refused requests to be interviewed by the research team and complained to administrators about what they saw as the project's threat to their authority.

In the PAR projects, students' growing awareness of school quality not only validates PAR as a pedagogical approach with the potential to increase student engagement and achievement, but also illustrates some of the complexities that arise when youth experience humanizing approaches juxtaposed with dehumanizing experiences within a school setting. Narrow approaches to teaching that fail to meaningfully engage youth and examine issues of power can dim sensibilities and metaphorically lull students (and their teachers) into helplessness, hopelessness, and conformity. In contrast, the youth researchers who participated in the PAR project shifted the gaze of critique from students' behavior and performance on tests to the institutions that shape them. This created the conditions through which students could assert agency and become increasingly conscious about their schools, their communities, and the world around them. They entered a state of "wide-awakeness" (Greene, 1988), moving from feeling powerless to finding power through their search for self-determination.

Despite the fact that PAR projects can directly and effectively address problems facing urban schools and their students, PAR is most often conducted outside K–12 schools in institutions of higher education or in community-based organizations. If schools are to become spaces for critical consciousness raising and liberation for marginalized youth, the pedagogical practices of educators must become more humanizing. In the following section we describe some of the challenges and opportunities associated with such efforts.

Reflections on Pedagogical Challenges and Opportunities

Students in both Projects FUERTE, ARISE, and SSP, like many urban youth, were being educated under what Haberman (1994) refers to as the "contract": an implicit understanding between teachers and students that neither will expect much from the other, and that as long as order is kept, students will be passed along to the next grade. One of the most formidable challenges we encountered was the dissonance between students' experiences with PAR pedagogy and those with draconian "drill-and-skill" approaches to teaching. As discussed, students became less willing to be passive recipients of education and demanded more from their teachers. After experiencing active participation in humanistic research and educational practice, students expanded their thinking about the learning opportunities available to them. They became increasingly critical of the educational opportunities offered to them, and as they developed a burgeoning sense of critical consciousness, they sometimes critiqued the practices of their teachers. These critiques were often not warmly embraced by educators and administrators in their schools. This reflects one of the significant challenges of grounding PAR in the very institutions that are being critiqued; conflict can and often does emerge when educators seek to maintain the status quo while students begin to assert their voices to demand more from the institutions entrusted with their education. Students' newfound thirst for knowledge was manifested in ways that made many teachers uncomfortable. The humanistic approaches to research and teaching in our PAR project were often met with contempt by educators who refused to believe that the students, who were consistently marginalized and thus often underperformed, were capable of high-level work. The programs were blamed for inciting students, "causing problems where there were none," as a teacher at RHS said, and "stirring up trouble," as a teacher at JBS charged.

Moreover, when the student researchers named and challenged the multiple forms of institutional oppression that narrowed the opportunity structure available to them at their schools, many teachers fired back, questioning the value of the class and the credentials of the university researchers to teach high school students. In one case, teachers went so far as to file an IRB grievance, demanding access to the data that was collected so that they could reanalyze it themselves and disprove the group's findings. In all of the projects, there were individual teachers and administrators who were supportive allies. However, generally speaking, the responses of teachers were often characterized by rancor and suspicion, creating a formidable obstacle in institutionalizing this work and extending the pedagogical benefits of engaging in humanistic research to other spaces and students within the buildings.

While the pedagogical challenges are formidable, there are also unique opportunities offered by grounding PAR projects in schools. Perhaps most significant, PAR represents a chance for teachers to engage in a process of liberation—engaging with urban youth as they struggle to liberate themselves from an oppressive education and social system and liberating themselves from the shackles of short-sighted school reform efforts that treat urban youth and their communities as objects to be fixed rather than as meaningful partners in the teaching and learning process. Teachers and students, we argue, should be natural allies in the struggle for educational equity and social justice. PAR represents a means to that end.

The Political Realm

K–12 schools are inherently political. That is, they play a key role, as aptly described by Gee (2005), in "how social goods are thought about, argued over, and distributed in society (p. 2). Social goods, as characterized by Gee, include "anything that a group of people believes to be a source of power, status, value, or worth, whether this be . . . academic intelligence, money, control . . . wisdom, knowledge, technology, literacy . . ." (p. 2). Importantly, K–12 schooling is a mechanism through which particular types of knowledge that can beget power, status, resources, and opportunity are determined, imparted, and withheld.

A primary way in which access to knowledge is manipulated in schools is through the hierarchy of power. For example, what must and can be learned, how it must and can be taught, and to whom, is prescribed through a clear chain of command in which, at each descending level (i.e., the federal and state departments of education → school administrators → classroom teachers → students), power is diminished. As Fine (1991) describes, "The compulsion to control from the top trickles down to a common institutional fetish with power" (p. 185). This leads to "struggles of power asymmetries" (p. 185) in schools that take on a "zero-sum" quality in which power is predicated upon relative powerless at the lower level(s). Thus, power is secured by exercising control over and, thereby, limiting the power of others, and through the threat and use of sanctions which can be levied against those who fail to acquiesce (e.g., loss of resources and autonomy, pink slips, and disciplinary action).

The field of academic research is also political, influencing the production of, access to, and discourses about knowledge. And like K–12 education, it is governed by hierarchies of power and mechanisms of social control. PAR with youth in schools—specifically, research focusing on the schooling experiences of educationally marginalized youth—directly challenges the political hierarchy of K–12 schools in at least two important and interrelated ways. First, it challenges traditional, school-based conventions around how and what knowledge is produced, valued, and used. In youth-led PAR projects, this is determined largely by students rather than by teachers or administrators. Through the research process, students gain a better practical and theoretical understanding of their schooling experiences. They build their capacity to identify problems, systematically collect and analyze data, and articulate their claims and support them with evidence. This provides them with the means of communicating their experiences in more "official," more compelling, and more public ways.

Second, students can use this power over knowledge to legitimize critiques of the role of schools and school adults in the production of school-based social and academic inequities. In schools serving low-income students of color, where equalitarian ideals stand in stark relief against a background of race- and class-based injustices, control over students' learning and the suppression of their critiques can be particularly intense. In such contexts, students' ability to produce official knowledge about their experiences, and to make claims about the illegitimacy or misuse of power in schools, can be seen as particularly threatening.

In the example below, we describe how PAR projects can come into conflict with the political organization of schools, in which students are, arguably, the least powerful constituency. In doing so, we also describe school personnel's attempts to subvert the objectives of the projects to minimize their potential to disrupt established hierarchies of power.

When in Doubt, Shut It Down:
The Political Implications of Humanizing Research

The focus of the SSP project was the role of ethnicity and immigrant status in students' academic and social experiences. Of particular concern to the youth researchers was the apparent segregation of students within the school building. Initial observations revealed that students of particular ethnicities and immigrant statuses tended to occupy particular tables in the lunchroom and certain hallways and classrooms on particular floors of the school. At the time, the school community was experiencing interethnic conflict, particularly between Black U.S.-born and immigrant students, resulting in teasing, harassment, and fights both in and out of school. The research team, made up of African Americans and Black immigrants and native and nonnative speakers of English, was interested in how the lack of integration within the school might be related to alienation and antagonism between these two groups.

Through data gathered in observations and interviews with students, the SSP team learned that group segregation had both interpersonal and structural dimensions. Some students socialized primarily with those in their own ethnic group because they were comfortable with others who shared their nationality or language. Segregation between Black U.S.-born and immigrant students also occurred due to room and locker assignments and course placements. For example, immigrant students' classes and lockers tended to be located on the same floor as the office for English Language Learning (ELL). Looking further into class placement, the team discovered that mainstream (non-ELL) classes were often segregated by race/ethnicity; lower-level classes were disproportionately African American and higher-level classes disproportionately immigrant. Following these discoveries, the team scheduled a meeting with the principal, who corroborated the findings and expressed support for the team's further investigation of the origins of social and academic segregation in the school.

The racial/ethnic dimensions of academic disparities led to discussions among the youth researchers about the nature of students' academic and social experiences with, particularly, teachers. Resolved to better understand this, the team crafted student and teacher interview protocols and then began interviewing students and devising a schedule for teacher interviews. By this point in the project, as we were nearing the winter break, teachers in the building had heard about and were talking among themselves about the project. Importantly, this was occurring in an extremely uneasy political environment in which teachers' jobs hung in the balance and staff morale was low. The new principal confided in the adult researchers that some teachers were construing the project as her "pet project" to expose teacher bias and incompetence. Not surprisingly, we could find only a handful of teachers who were willing to be interviewed, so we tabled the teacher interviews and focused on the students.

About two weeks before the break, the principal broke the news that the project would end that semester. She informed us (the adult researchers) that school administrators had expressed opposition to the project, and that perceptions of the research were inhibiting staff morale and her ability to gain their trust and cooperation. "It's just not a good time," she told us. "Maybe we can try again next year." What was supposed to be a yearlong project was shut down after the first semester. The youth researchers were angry and dismayed at the news. As one youth researcher wrote in her reflection on the project,

> Because of this experience, I started learning about the school system and what we were going through, because no one ever explained to the students what was going on. To make things worse, instead of trying to work with students to help them be more active in school, the school system decided to take away our project. This was not fair.

Ironically, most of the teachers and administrators at the school had little understanding of the SSP project, whose primary goal was to build solidarity among students through an understanding of how students' disparate social and academic experiences might contribute to divisions and antagonisms among them. Consequently, virtually all student interviewees, even those that held negative views of others, expressed a desire for more solidarity across the different student groups. As voiced by one student participant,

> There no point in segregating students. The American students won't be able to interact with immigrant students and the immigrant students won't be able to learn from the English speakers. This breaks down communication so they cannot unite their voice. The school needs to encourage good relationships between all the students.

Reflections on Political Challenges and Opportunities

While our projects were embedded in the structure of the school, we, as university-based faculty researchers, were not. Therefore, although we both spent a substantial amount of time in the schools in which we worked, we were not always on site to support students as they navigated institutions that they perceived as hostile. Operating somewhat independently of the schools (i.e., we were not employed by the school district) offered us some freedom and autonomy in our work. However, at times, it also made it difficult to navigate the highly politicized organizational structures of the institution and develop relationships with potential allies on the faculty. This is evidenced in the SSP example, which describes how the project was terminated due to resistance from the faculty and staff. With limited power in these spaces, stemming at least in part from our positionality as outside researchers, we experienced difficulties in getting the PAR projects off the ground and bringing them to culmination. In the cases of FUERTE and ARISE, the research spanned two years, through the students' graduation, but the projects were constantly criticized and scrutinized by various school personnel. The highly political nature of urban schools makes PAR and other approaches to humanizing research simultaneously difficult and necessary.

The sociopolitical contexts in which efforts at humanizing research take place also offer unique opportunities. By engaging in research designed to address "limit situations" faced in the schools, students are well positioned to replicate these efforts in the future, making more informed decisions and becoming increasingly critically conscious. The skills that emerge through participation in PAR have not only pedagogical but political implications, engendering more politically savvy individuals armed with an array of data collection and analysis tools that can be applied across a variety of contexts.

"I AM SMART, A RESEARCHER, A STUDENT": FINAL THOUGHTS ON POSSIBILITIES

PAR has emerged as an exciting and effective approach to engaging youth in transformational resistance, a struggle to simultaneously transform oneself and the educational system. A variety of studies have recently documented the benefits of PAR with youth and other marginalized populations (Cammarota & Romero, 2009; Duncan-Andrade & Morrell, 2008; Fine & Torre, 2006; Morrell, 2004; Payne & Brown, 2010). Grounding PAR in the educational context the students must navigate on a daily basis is necessary if the social reproductive function of schools is to be disrupted and replaced with a more humanizing model of teaching and learning that facilitates academic and personal success for all students.

Youth researchers in all projects observed that conducting research can be intimidating, as empirical research is typically viewed as the domain of a highly credentialed knowledge elite. Historically, researchers have sought to maintain a distance from their "subjects" to preserve presumed objectivity in learning more about the issue or individuals under investigation. PAR represents a departure from this rigid, detached, and often oppressive approach to research by meaningfully integrating and placing value on the emic (or "insider") perspectives of those most directly impacted by the problem under investigation. While much traditional research on the schooling experiences of youth underserved by schools is done with students positioned as the objects of research, PAR includes students as co-researchers as well as informants with important insights that can inform all aspects of the research process. Stressing the intersections of valuable emic perspectives and collective investment in social change, Jeff Duncan-Andrade and Ernest Morrell (2008) note,

> Participatory action research is valuable because it brings in populations that are often alienated within the traditional research paradigm, but it is also important because these populations often have the best vantage point and the greatest vested interest in the work itself. (p. 108)

PAR is not solely a research methodology that constitutes a systematic and rigorous approach to empirical inquiry. It is also useful as an ideology that represents a paradigmatic shift in thinking about researchers' relationships to their study participants. That is, PAR represents a more humanizing approach to research in that it attempts to honor local knowledge and the perspectives of participants. Moreover, PAR explicitly uses the research to inform actions aimed at challenging and dismantling oppressive conditions. PAR, then, is not solely focused on the academic goal of generating publications to inform a particular body of research literature, although a wealth of important scholarship, typically co-authored with youth members of the collaborative, has emerged from these efforts. Rather, in the hands of youth themselves, PAR can serve as an unapologetic tool for social change. In this sense, research is reclaimed as an indelible right of all people as a tool that they can use to transform the conditions of their lives. While other approaches to research may claim a liberatory focus, the development of multigenerational collaboratives connected by an explicit commitment to social action is unique to PAR as it has developed in recent years.

The humanizing aspects of PAR and the importance of implementing such research and pedagogical approaches in spaces such as urban schools, which can be extremely oppressive, were captured by Carmen, a student participant in Project FUERTE. She beautifully articulated the impact of participating in the project during an interview at the culmination of the project, and her words are a fitting end to this chapter:

> Doing this research here in this school, where I never feel like a real person, like, makes me see for the first time what is possible in my life. I never thought anything about being treated bad by teachers and being made to think I'm dumb, that kids like me are dumb. I thought it was my fault, like something I did to deserve to be treated bad. Now I realize that I am smart, a researcher, a student. But more important, doing that research made me feel like a full person.

REFLECTIVE QUESTIONS

1. What beliefs about and dispositions toward youth must adults have in order to effectively conduct PAR with K–12 students?

2. Given the political and structural constraints of schools (and other institutions where you might do research), what is the potential of PAR as a strategy for school reform (or reform of the institutions at which you do your research)?

3. Is it possible for students to research the negative effects of teachers' practices and beliefs in ways that do not alienate teachers but help them to improve? If so, how might that be done?

4. How can universities better support faculty who conduct PAR with youth in schools?

5. What do teachers and administrators need in order to invest in the empowerment of students through PAR?

REFERENCES

Brown, T. M. (2007). Lost and turned out: Academic, social and emotional experiences of students excluded from school. *Urban Education, 42*(5), 432–455.

Brown, T. M. (2010). ARISE to the challenge: Partnering with urban youth to improve educational research and learning. *Penn GSE Perspectives on Urban Education, 7*(1), 4–14.

Brown, T. M., & Galeas, K. (2011). Confronting "limit situations" in a youth/adult educational research collaborative. In B. Schultz (Ed.), *Learning from students* (pp. 7–13). Charlotte, NC: Information Age.

Brown, T. M., & Rodriguez, L. F. (2009a, Fall). Editors' notes. *New Directions for Youth Development*, pp. 1–9.

Brown, T. M., & Rodriguez, L. F. (Eds.). (2009b). *Youth in Participatory Action Research*. San Francisco, CA: Jossey-Bass.

Cammarota, J., & Fine, M. (Eds.). (2008). *Revolutionizing education: Youth Participatory Action Research*. New York, NY: Routledge.

Cammarota, J., & Romero, A. F. (2009, Fall). A social justice epistemology and pedagogy. *New Directions for Youth Development*, pp. 53–65.

Duncan-Andrade, J., & Morrell, E. (2008). *The art of critical pedagogy*. New York, NY: Peter Lang.

Fine, M. (1991). *Framing dropouts: Notes on the politics of an urban public high school*. Albany, NY: State University of New York Press.

Fine, M. (2008). An epilogue, of sorts. In J. Cammarota & M. Fine (Eds.), *Revolutionizing education: Youth Participatory Action Research*. New York, NY: Routledge.

Fine, M., & Torre, M. E. (2006). Intimate details: Participatory Action Research in prison. *Action Research, 4*(3), 253–269.

Freire, P. (1970). *Pedagogy of the oppressed*. New York, NY: Seabury Press.

Freire, P. (1973). *Education for critical consciousness*. New York, NY: Seabury Press.

Freire, P. (1998). Learning to question: A pedagogy for liberation. In A. A. Freire & D. Macedo (Eds.), *The Paulo Freire reader* (pp. 186–230). New York, NY: Continuum.

Gee, J. (2005). *Discourse analysis: An introduction to theory and methods*. New York, NY: Routledge.

Greene, M. (1988). *The dialectic of freedom*. New York, NY: Teachers College Press.

Haberman, M. (1994). The pedagogy of poverty versus good teaching. In J. Kretovics & E. J. Nussell (Eds.), *Transforming urban education*. Boston, MA: Allyn & Bacon.

Hall, B. (1993). Introduction. In P. Park, M. Brydon-Miller, B. Hall, & T. Jackson (Eds.), *Voices of change: Participatory research in the United States and Canada* (pp. xiii–xxii). Toronto, Ontario, Canada: Ontario Institute for Studies in Education.

Irizarry, J. G. (2007). Home-growing teachers of color for urban schools: Lessons learned from a town-gown partnership. *Teacher Education Quarterly, 34*(4), 87–102.

Irizarry, J. G. (2009). Reinvigorating multicultural education through youth Participatory Action Research. *Multicultural Perspectives, 11*(4), 194–199.

Irizarry, J. G. (2011). *The Latinization of U.S. schools: Successful teaching and learning in shifting cultural contexts*. Boulder, CO: Paradigm.

Morrell, E. (2004). *Becoming critical researchers: Literacy and empowerment for urban youth*. New York, NY: Peter Lang.

Payne, Y. A., & Brown, T. M. (2010). Contextualizing Black boys' use of a street identity: Why Black boys use street life as a site of resiliency in high school. *Journal of Contemporary Criminal Justice, 26*(3), 316–338.

Rodriguez, L. F. (2011). Challenging test-prep pedagogy: Urban high school students educate pre-service teachers using liberatory pedagogy. In B. Schultz (Ed.), *Learning from students* (pp. 87–100). Charlotte, NC: Information Age.

Yang, W. (2009, Fall). Mathematics, critical literacy, and youth Participatory Action Research. *New Directions for Youth Development*, pp. 99–118.

5

Activist Ethnography With Indigenous Youth

Lessons From Humanizing Research on Language and Education

Teresa L. McCarty, Leisy T. Wyman, and Sheilah E. Nicholas

*I just want to learn my cultural language. . . . [I]t is a big
important part of my life if I am going to be Native.*

—Youth interview, June 2004

Indigenous youth in endangered-language settings face multiple challenges as they negotiate their linguistic, cultural, and academic identities under pressure from both inside and outside their communities. On the one hand, they may be viewed as the "last line of defense" in maintaining community-specific linguistic and cultural continuity. On the other hand, they are likely to have incomplete knowledge of their heritage language as a consequence of their parents' experience with punitive English-only schooling and parental desires to protect their children from the humiliation and suffering they endured in school. Nor are youth immune to wider racializing discourses that stigmatize their heritage language as backward and lacking mobility in globalizing linguistic ecologies.

In this chapter we share insights and experiences from researching language and education with Indigenous youth in endangered-language communities. Language is both a repository and a carrier of a people's heritage and knowledge, and is thus central to the humanistic enterprise. How do we humanize our work with youth around this deeply felt core capacity? Why is youth research in Indigenous communities significant for understanding issues of language endangerment and education—and why is an activist stance in youth language research significant to youth researchers across diverse communities and academic disciplines? How can we, as insider-outsider activist researchers, negotiate our journeys into Indigenous youth research?

We begin by contextualizing our project in the wider literature on youth language research, focusing on recent research with Indigenous youth in North America.

We then illuminate key questions that have arisen in our own research, grounding these questions in ethnographic vignettes from our work with Navajo, Hopi, and Yup'ik youth. In presenting the vignettes, we speak with our individual researcher voices, but collectively we employ the vignettes to consider (a) how we can listen to youth with "ears to hear" their testimony (Nietzche, 1883/2006, p. 258), (b) how we may learn more about strengths than losses when researching with youth in endangered-language communities, and (c) how we can humanize insider-outsider roles with regard to language use in these settings. We then draw upon all three vignettes to reflect on lessons learned from our wider research experiences in situations of language shift—contexts in which intergenerational transmission of the heritage language has broken down—and with community-driven efforts to reclaim heritage languages. In dynamic situations of language shift, how can we take youth language opportunities and resources into account when analyzing their language ideologies and practices? How can we work in an activist stance with both youth and adults to directly benefit community-driven language reclamation? How can we ensure that youth shape these research and language planning processes and products? We conclude by highlighting the importance of researcher commitment in work with Indigenous youth, arguing for research as a form of praxis that proactively contributes to communities' language development goals.

SITUATING INDIGENOUS YOUTH LANGUAGE RESEARCH[1]

Historically, researchers have tended to position youth as inconsequential to adult concerns or as "not yet" adults. Recent research on youth language and peer culture, however, engages youth as interpreters and shapers of society, with an emphasis on youth agency, youth stylistic performance, and youth as ethnographers of communication (see, e.g., Alim, 2007; Bucholtz, 2002; Mendoza-Denton, 2008). Current youth researchers highlight the role of larger social, economic, and political systems in structuring inequalities, focusing on youth culture to examine "the production of cultural centers or margins" and discursive styles that are "privileged, condemned, or overlooked" (Maira & Soep, 2005, p. xix). This research explicitly recognizes that, like adults, youth "act as agents, resignifying and articulating the different and conflicting messages" they receive (Szulc, 2009, p. 144). Many youth researchers also see the potential for engaging youth in addressing educational and social inequities (see, e.g., McCarty & Wyman, 2009, for ethnographic cases with Indigenous youth).

As suggested above, much of this recent research centers on youth language ideologies and practices. Multiple scholars have shown how youth use diverse languages and language varieties to perform identities within local peer cultures and to position themselves in emerging interactional moments in classrooms, families, and other extra-school spaces. The communicative repertoires of heritage language learners can also vary dramatically within communities, peer groups, and families. As our own work has shown, Indigenous youth often express feelings of linguistic insecurity, especially if they have been teased or criticized for their language use. Youth also may "cloak" or "hide" their linguistic competencies depending on the social context (McCarty, Romero-Little, Warhol, & Zepeda, 2009; Mendoza-Denton, 2008).

It has only been fairly recently that these issues—and an activist stance—have been systematically taken up with regard to Indigenous youth. Based on a survey and interview study of 215 Navajo high school students, Diné-Lakota scholar Tiffany Lee (2007) notes the respect with which Navajo youth hold their heritage language, even as they contend with demeaning stereotypes that associate speaking Navajo with "backwardness" and traditionalism. In subsequent research with Navajo and Pueblo college students, Lee documents youth agency and intervention as they developed a "critical Indigenous consciousness" about language shift and began to "intervene through their own research, language practices . . . , and personal efforts to learn their heritage language" (Lee, 2009, p. 317). Similarly, in ethnographic research with Native youth in five southwestern U.S. communities, McCarty, Romero-Little, Warhol, and Zepeda (2009, 2011) examine the conflicting language ideologies that position Indigenous languages as highly valued by youth—"my cultural language . . . my blood language"—and simultaneously as "just the past" (2011, pp. 41–42).

Looking specifically at Hopi youth, Nicholas (2009, 2011) examines the family-, community-, and school-based dynamics in which these ideologies are nurtured and expressed. In this research, although Hopi youth indicated a desire to learn the Hopi language, they often expressed fear of being ridiculed for linguistic errors. As the vignette we present in the following section shows, Nicholas posits that Hopi oral tradition—"song words, prayer, teachings, ritual performances, religious ceremonies, and cultural institutions"—constitutes a powerful language transmission mechanism that gives rise to "an emotional commitment to the ideals of a communal society" (2009, pp. 337–338).

In a longitudinal study of a Yup'ik village with the pseudonym "Piniq," Wyman (forthcoming) traced how youth brokered changing schooling and migration practices, diffuse language socialization processes, and language ideologies, "tipping" from using mostly Yup'ik to using mostly English in local peer culture, and transforming family and community linguistic practices in 5 to 10 years' time. Youth in the study struggled with linguistic insecurity and painful local claims that they wanted to be White by speaking English. Yet the study also highlighted Indigenous people's *linguistic survivance*, showing how both youth and adults in Piniq used wide-ranging language practices to maintain a unique subarctic way of life, co-construct local knowledge, and creatively express and adapt unique identities under challenging circumstances (Wyman, forthcoming; for more on Indigenous youth in the Far North, see Tulloch's [2004] work with Inuit youth and Meek's [2007] work with Kaska youth, both in Canada).

In a study of Cucapá youth in northern Mexico, Shailah Muehlmann (2008) documents how, in a context in which "only a handful of elders still speak the

Cucapá language" (p. 34), a national policy shift valorizing Indigenous-language use calls into question both youths' and adults' identity claims. Youth strategically deploy Cucapá swearwords in the presence of outsiders to "negotiate claims to indigeneity" (p. 43). According to Muehlmann, this constitutes a discourse of resistance to a long (and continuing) history of racial, economic, and social injustice.

Finally, an emerging set of studies from around the world evidence how Indigenous youth can use new media skills to play important roles in Indigenous language and knowledge documentation efforts (see, e.g., Kral, 2011), as well as the ways that some youth are bringing Indigenous languages forward through new cultural forms such as hip-hop (Hornberger & Swinehart, in press; Mitchell, 2004). Each of these studies raises challenging questions about the ways in which young people's existing choices, hybridities, and linguistic strategies relate to the future of their heritage languages as part of unique Indigenous knowledge systems, even as they highlight the importance of youth voices and contributions to Indigenous movements. Many youth express what Wilson and Kamanä (2009, p. 375) call "great yearnings" to maintain their heritage languages as links to specific identities and community practices. Many also provide evidence that today's language learners want to use their ancestral languages for reasons "deeply rooted within local relationships, practices, knowledge systems, and geographical places" (Wyman, 2009, p. 346). Should their circumstances and language-learning opportunities change, youth in these varied discursive contexts may activate their heritage languages to productive levels and become the authorizing agents moving their languages forward in the future. As a growing body of research shows, they may also become actively involved in movements to support Indigenous languages.

Ultimately, this research on Indigenous language ideologies and practices positions youth as part of broader communities of practice that are situated historically within processes of marginalization and countermovements. Desanitizing, humanizing, and creatively employing these histories remain central to fostering bilingualism and multilingualism within Indigenous communities. As we show in the following sections, this work contains important insights for young people's ability to "bring their languages forward" (Hornberger & King, 1996) while learning languages of wider communication. Further, the work contains important questions for all youth researchers to consider. To ground these insights and questions, we turn now to our three ethnographic vignettes.

PRESENTING THE ETHNOGRAPHIC VIGNETTES

Listening "With Ears to Hear"
Youth Testimony: Teresa's Vignette

Jonathan gazed at me intently, his Gothic-style contact lenses mimicking the amber eyes of a cat. A 16-year-old ninth grader at a pre-K–12 Navajo community school, Jonathan had been excused from class by his teacher—a co-researcher on our multisite research project—to participate in what the project proposal described as an "in-depth ethnographic interview."[2] He and I sat next to each other in an otherwise empty classroom, a tape recorder whirring quietly between us. Sunlight streamed through the single classroom window, lighting up the canyon crevasses that crisscrossed nearby "Beautiful Mountain," a pseudonym for the Diné (Navajo) sacred site for which we had named Jonathan's school. His heavy long-sleeve black shirt and red-zippered vest belied the warmth of the brilliant May afternoon scene outside.

I came to this ethnographic moment as a vested outsider, what Julie Kaomea (2004) calls the "allied other." I had never met Jonathan, though I knew his community and teachers well, having worked within the Navajo Nation and in Indigenous education for nearly 25 years at the time. I felt comfortable and welcomed by the educators and families in this place, yet I realized that to Jonathan, I was very much a stranger—a White woman from the university "down there" in the city, whom he had seen in his school hallways and classrooms but did not really know. Despite my longstanding alliances and friendships with older community members, I knew that in this exchange with Jonathan—and more generally with our team's research with youth—I was starting anew.

"So you were saying," I continued gently, "that your early school experiences with a Native-speaking teacher didn't instill in you a good feeling about your language . . ."

"No they didn't," Jonathan replied. "That [teacher] didn't know how to . . . bring out that kind of—I don't know, that kind of pride and the continuation of the language in a positive sense. . . . And she was mainly forcing us to learn English. . . . I don't know, it was a real confusing time, I guess."

A little later in the interview Jonathan related these early language-learning experiences to "what I like to call the Long Walk Syndrome," a reference to the forcible removal of Diné in the late 19th century to a federal concentration camp, where thousands of Navajo people were incarcerated and died. Not long after the Navajos' release from federal imprisonment, the government turned to schools as the primary vehicle for coercive assimilation. "Having all this boarding school stuff and the government trying to force English upon them," Jonathan explained. "And a lot of people are still recovering from that." Gazing downward, he continued in a soft, steady voice, "They [government officials] took the children away from their families at a young age, and they instilled this image that is still alive—this image of self-hate. To be ashamed of who you are. . . . It's all about survival since 1492. . . . It's all about how far will you go to—to survive."

I recalled the words of my late colleague and friend, Galena Sells Dick, who had attended a Navajo reservation boarding school during the 1950s and 1960s. "We were forced and pressured to learn English," she told me. "We had to struggle. . . . Students were punished for speaking their native language. This punishment was inflicted even by Navajo matrons in the dorm. This shows that even for Navajo adults like the dorm matrons, school was not a place for Navajos to be Navajos" (cited in McCarty, 2002, p. 45). Galena's account of her schooling experience more than a generation before echoed in young Jonathan's words.

The purpose of this interview, as of the 61 others our research team conducted with youth from five Native American communities, was to go beyond the bleak projections of Indigenous-language death to understand how language loss and reclamation are experienced in young people's everyday lives. When, where, and for what purposes do youth use the Indigenous language and English? What attitudes and ideologies do youth hold toward their heritage language and English? How do these ideologies shape their developing linguistic, ethnic, and academic identities? The interview protocol had been carefully prepared in collaboration with Indigenous teacher-researchers at each site, and we characterized this as participatory action research (for details, see McCarty, Romero, & Zepeda, 2006; McCarty et al., 2009; Romero-Little, McCarty, Warhol, & Zepeda, 2007). The interview questions asked about language. But for Jonathan and many youth in our study—just as for Galena Sells Dick in an earlier generation—questions about language could not be divorced from issues of race, history, land, self-determination, and cultural survival.

"I just . . . it's just a meaning of survival," Jonathan reiterated when I asked him about his memories of learning English, "having to learn how to cope and adjust in this colonial world that we live in. Both sides, no? So mainly I was forced into that out of my own will."

I asked Jonathan whether he felt knowing Navajo was helpful to him now.

"Yes, it helps me, having that as my first language," he replied. "Like, y'know, it helps not lose the identity of who I am, of where I come from, of how . . . that's all linked with survival, y'know."

Jonathan again returned to the theme of the Long Walk Syndrome. His words urged up those from another interview I had conducted eight years before with my longtime Diné colleague, Fred Bia. I had asked Fred what speaking Navajo meant to him. "My language, to me, . . . that's what makes me unique, that's what makes me Navajo, that's what makes me who I am," he reflected. "That's what going to Fort Sumner and coming back, and all that—it was *worth* it. The language, my language" (cited in McCarty, 2002, p. 179).

For Jonathan—of age to be Fred Bia's son—the Long Walk seemed to hold a different kind of meaning. Jonathan spoke of the "inherited trauma" of that historic time, which "has to do with the psyche" and "goes from generation to generation." Internalized colonization, he said, had left an indelible psychological imprint: "You forsake who you are, you give up having to learn Navajo in order to accommodate the mainstream life. It goes back to survival."

"But it goes far deeper than that," Jonathan added. "It has to do with the loss of our homes, having to be removed from here and there and switched around." Turning his gaze out the window to the mountain beyond, he said, "Having to see something so beautiful and so perfect, like the mountain up there, being destroyed [by coal mining] for all eternity. It eats away at your soul."

I wondered if the survivability of the Navajo language was like that mountain. "You were saying how there are economic practices that could destroy this beautiful [mountain] for eternity," I said. "I was thinking that the Navajo language is in that same sort of situation."

"It is," Jonathan responded. "We are so much a part of the land. It is hard for me to see the trash littering the highways, the coal being dug up, all the radio-activity, all the dumping. It really hurts me. It's not a physical pain; it's more of a spiritual anguish."

It was well into the more-than-two-hour interview before I fully "heard" the connections between land, language, and personal and communal survival Jonathan was making. His reflections on language repeatedly returned to the integrity of the human and physical landscape in which Diné identity is rooted—the place where his umbilical cord, following Diné tradition, had been buried. "Everything as a human being [is about] being a child of this earth," he explained. "That's why we don't have floors in our *hooghan* [a traditional family dwelling]. We want to feel the earth, and we want to feel the heartbeat, the power that's within it. We don't want to be separate from it."

Finally it seemed appropriate to ask the last question in our interview protocol. "Forty years from now, when you are a middle-aged person like your parents, do you think people will still be speaking Navajo?"

Jonathan paused, looked down at his hands, sighed. "A part of myself likes to think there would be, but you never know. Yeah, I have some hope; that is all I can say, I have hope. Hope that someday we can go back to living with the sacred-ness a little longer. To continue, carrying on longer who we are, as a people."

* * * * *

When I first met Jonathan, I did not anticipate the thoughtful, two-and-a-half-hour conversation (in research terms, "in-depth ethnographic interview") that would ensue. I did not expect to be discussing coal mine slurrying, depletion of the aquifer, and environmental racism—all topics he raised in connection with language loss and recovery. And, given portrayals of youth indifference by many adults we had interviewed, as well as by the popular media, I was not prepared for the deep commitment to land and language Jonathan expressed, or for the bold moves of personal vulnerability he evinced—especially in light of the fact that he had just met me for the first time. Moreover, Jonathan was not alone in these expressions. Our interview database is replete with youths' testimonials of their concern and desire to be deserving participants in their heritage language communities—desires they related directly to language, peoplehood, and place (McCarty et al., 2006, 2009).

As researchers and human beings, how do we respond to these deeply felt youth sentiments? How can we be "worthy witnesses" (Winn & Ubiles, 2011) to their sociolinguistic testimony?

Affirming Strength Amid Loss: Sheilah's Vignette

Sheilah: Do you speak Hopi?

Justin: Yeah.

S: Was that your first language?

J: Well, I would say my first because . . . I would mostly speak it until I got into school, and then I started learning English.

S: . . . How old were you when you started school?

J: Head Start [preschool].

S: That means about three or . . .

J: Three or four, yeah.

S: What language did you speak in Head Start?

J: They would mostly teach us some Hopi, and then just regular, regular English.

S: Then when you went to regular . . .

J: Kindergarten, we kinda changed. . . . That most of all, you just dropped, you know, learning about the Hopi language.

S: Who were your teachers? Were they mostly *Pahaanas* [Anglos]?

J: Well, no. They were Hopi, but it's not just that they don't talk it. They wouldn't teach us [Hopi]. . . . From then on [we were taught only in English] until I learned about the Hopi class in high school. . . . until I got to Hopi class and somebody was willing to teach us. That's when I jumped to it.

This ethnographic interview with Justin illustrates the style of interaction—direct question, brief and direct response—between adult and youth, researcher and study participant, that marked the opening to the initial interviews with each of the three youth participants of my study. This particular interaction style also masked a sense of apprehension for both researcher and youth on discussing the vitality of the Hopi language—a heritage language we all shared and to which we each brought a personal, often painful, history of experience. The apprehension lessened as the interviews continued and we recognized the significance of our individual roles in the project: to ascertain the role of the Hopi language in the lives of contemporary Hopi youth and how youth define and assert their personal and social identities as Hopi citizens and members of Hopi society (Nicholas, 2009).

My interest in this work grew out of my personal experience with Hopi language loss at an early age, and my subsequent arduous journey as an adult to reclaim my Hopi speaking ability (Nicholas, 2009, 2011). Investigating language shift among Hopi youth came about through my involvement in providing Hopi literacy lessons to Hopi students in reservation schools. I was compelled to understand why these students, immersed and active participants in Hopi culture since birth, had neither acquired a receptive ability nor become speaker-users of the language. The increasing enrollment of Hopi students in Hopi language classes at the junior and high school levels spurred in me a sense of urgency to address this linguistic situation for the present youth generation—including my own children.

Elsewhere I have described Justin's shy, soft-spoken demeanor as projecting a gentle and sensitive nature while veiling a strong sense of family and communal responsibility and self-discipline (Nicholas, 2009). At the first interview in April 2003, Justin was 19 years of age, a high school graduate of one year and on the cusp of young adulthood. Early in this interview, I learned that he understood and spoke Hopi, describing his proficiency at "about 75 percent" fluency. This immediately countered my own assumptions and those of elder speakers of Hopi, who perceive and characterize community youth as non-speakers of Hopi. A self-identified fluent Hopi speaker, Justin was unique among his peer-age group and as a study participant.

Fast forward to the topic of Hopi language classes:

S: . . . you took Hopi language as an elective?

J: Hopi language, yeah.

S: How come you decided to take Hopi language [class]?

J: 'Cuz, nobody *teached* [emphasis added] me. I mean, I learned [Hopi] here at home and from my grandma and them [other significant kin], but I just wanted to keep learning . . . more of what's in the Hopi language.

In the introductory dialogue, Justin describes acquiring Hopi as his first language in his home from significant kin, and continuing this trajectory as his Hopi teachers used or "taught" with Hopi during his Head Start experience. He carried this expectation into kindergarten, where things changed abruptly and dramatically; the Hopi teachers in his classroom "dropped" the Hopi language. These teachers may have been Hopi individuals employed as classroom assistants, who, while highly visible in the classroom and school, have a marginal position in the classroom curriculum. What Justin recounts in his expression, "You just dropped . . . learning about the Hopi language," is a seriously distressing experience at an early age associated with schooling. That as a young adult he recalled this memory with these words indicated to me that he remained perplexed and troubled by this experience. This was heightened by the fact that it was only as a high school student that he could learn "more of what's in the Hopi language" in language classes offered as an elective.

S: . . . you went to that class and you already spoke Hopi and understood it.

J: Yeah.

S: How about the rest of your classmates?

J: Yeah, they could understand and speak most of it. . . . I guess we were all shy [about] how we said it. I guess we were scared about people making fun of us and saying, "That's not how to say it . . . ." But I think we got over that feeling.

S: . . . Did you ever take that Hopi out of class and start talking Hopi to other people?

J: No. . . . I wouldn't go out and speak Hopi to my friends because I was too shy to speak to them in Hopi; I thought they would make fun of me.

This dialogue revealed to me that even among peer speakers of Hopi, Hopi was not a peer-culture language. Instead, youth in the study anticipated and were subjected to peer teasing and criticism of their emerging but limited linguistic competency, an experience widely noted as extremely detrimental to language learners (Lee, 2007, 2009).

S: Did you ever experience a time when the people did make fun of your Hopi?

J: Yeah, lots of times. . . . by my friends, or other people. But, I wouldn't say they were making fun of me. I would say that they're just, you know, laughing 'cuz, you know, a little kid as I was [was] talking Hopi, and they [adults] thought that was the way to do it. They wish they could teach their kids like that. I wouldn't say it was teasing or making fun or nothing, it was just encouragement to do, learn more [build proficiency].

S: Was it [teasing] mostly from family, elders, or . . . ?

J: Well, it would be mostly the friends, the students' friends, and they would be criticizing or laughing at them 'cuz they're talking in Hopi [emphasis added], not because their parents and their grandmas and them, they don't teach 'em. And that's why they think it's kind of funny. But when you learn it [to speak Hopi], it's not funny.

What Justin conveys in this excerpt is that using Hopi as a language of everyday interaction and communication is a practice reserved for adult and elder speakers. Among peers, using the Hopi language is atypical and unnatural. Attempts to use it elicit embarrassment and discomfort; teasing and laughter, the visible responses, are coping mechanisms employed to ease the tension and lessen linguistic insecurities. These behaviors are perceived by older Hopi as disrespectful toward the Hopi culture and language, a misunderstanding by older Hopi about the profound impact of language shift on youth.

S: You use it [the Hopi language] now. If you use it now, who do you use it with?

J: I would say [with] my uncles, and my dad and them, and everybody when we're out at the field, or in the house, or even at the *kivas* [ceremonial chambers]; that's where I mostly use it, in the kivas.

S: How often do you go to the kiva?

J: I say, all the time, if there's dances down here [at my village] . . . I go to help my dad at his village. I also go to my kwa'a's [grandfather's], so I go to all three of 'em [village kiva activities].

S: You said too that most of the time you hear or speak Hopi is when you're planting?

J: Yeah. And then, you know, if you can, you talk to the plants. They're just like your children, you know. You talk to 'em and they hear you, and they'll grow.

S: Do you hear your dad and your grandpa doing those things too?

J: Yeah. And they'll be singing to them, and we just sing all different kinds of songs as we're planting.

S: . . . Why is it that you get involved in those things?

J: It's just that I was born and raised [in] how to do it and I don't want to let it go.

The study asked: When Hopi youth are no longer socialized through their heritage language, are they still learning the culturally appropriate social knowledge—the important principles and values—of Hopi citizenship? Justin poignantly expresses that being "born [into] and raised" in the Hopi way of life instills a strong cultural identity and resilient sense of responsibility for cultural and linguistic continuity. My in-depth conversations with Justin and two other youth study participants confirmed that most youth continue to be active participants in the Hopi culture transmitted through myriad forms of the Hopi oral tradition, including spoken language. More important, I discerned, these youth affirm that the vitality of the Hopi language and culture is captured in the notion of "language as cultural practice" (Nicholas, 2009, 2011).

* * * * *

The purpose of these youth interviews—part of a larger study that included ethnographic interviews with parents and grandparents of the three youth participants—was to determine the impact of language shift on contemporary Hopi society. While confirming an upheaval in the cultural and community dynamics of Hopi society, the study also affirmed the strength of Hopi culture. These youth elucidate *what* of the traditions, practices, and religion remains salient and *why*, and perhaps *which* will remain salient in future generations.

Humanizing "Insider-Outsider" Language Use in Endangered-Language Settings: Leisy's Vignette

My interest in Indigenous youth language grew out of early experiences as a young teacher-researcher and later experiences as a graduate student studying language shift in Piniq (a pseudonym), a small Yup'ik village of 600 in southwestern Alaska. From 1992 to 2001, I compared how two consecutive cohorts of youth negotiated a rapid shift to English. Youth in the older group spoke Yup'ik as their main language of peer culture and were described by community members as the last "real speakers" of Yup'ik. Most youth in the younger group spoke English, but also used bilingualism to "get by," as community members put it, with adults and one another.

Between the two groups, the local school changed its primary language of elementary instruction from Yup'ik to English. As schooling and increased migration placed pressure on young people's language learning networks, dynamics of family language maintenance and shift began to mirror those found in immigrant communities in urban contexts. While adults and older youth verbally valued Yup'ik and voiced strong concerns about language endangerment, youth described increasing insecurities about speaking Yup'ik. Still the potential remained for young people to take up new positions as Indigenous language speakers (Wyman, forthcoming).

Language is an important way researchers impact the situations they study. Between 1992 and 2001 my ability to understand and use local "village English"—which incorporated different generational styles and code-switching patterns—changed dramatically. Here, however, I will briefly discuss how my own learning and use of Yup'ik, in particular, helped me humanize local youth in language research, and helped adults and youth humanize me as a White outsider working in an Indigenous community marked by historically rooted language ideologies and racialized dynamics of distrust.

The Yup'ik term for English, *kassa-tun*, translates literally as "like a White person/outsider," while the term for the Yup'ik language, *Yug-tun*, translates as "like a human." In my early teaching days, Piniq youth and adults were most comfortable speaking Yup'ik as an everyday language; learning Yup'ik seemed like an obvious way to connect to my students' linguistic strengths. As a young teacher I petitioned for and attended a beginning Yup'ik videoconference class for teachers. Participating in the local church, a hub of village life and Yup'ik use, I also worked on my Yup'ik singing in the choir and performing requested duets and solos. Elders thanked me after my early attempts to sing Yup'ik, and as individual students moved beyond postures of resistance to schooling, and from being *takaryuk*—self-conscious—in my classroom, they often declared, smiling, "I saw you sing in church the other night." Within a year, village friends were taking me to intervillage songfests, where they would tease me by saying they were showing off their "Yup'ik-singing *kass'aq* [Whitey]." From the time I learned to use common Yup'ik phrases, friends also used the fact that I spoke Yup'ik to assure others, especially wary elders or visitors from neighboring villages, that I was not like White teachers of the past who had punished them for speaking their language, or some other contemporary White teachers who denigrated Yup'ik language and culture.

Five years after I left Piniq for graduate school, I moved back to Piniq as a young, married mother of a small child. As a graduate student, I had the luxury of studying Yup'ik with a tutor and worked my way through a Yup'ik grammar book. During 14 months of fieldwork, I continued to learn Yup'ik in nightly steams with a local friend. While I never attained fluency, I understood and told stories and interacted in Yup'ik as I participated in daily activities. I also spoke Yup'ik with adults and strong Yup'ik speakers in the younger group of youth in the study. In my time away, however, language shift had progressed quickly and unevenly. Many youth in the "get by" group expressed insecurity about "speaking Yup'ik wrong" and negotiated painful accusations from adults that they wanted to "be like *kass'aqs*" (Whites) by speaking English.

Working with the younger group in the study, I paid extra attention to the rapidly changing sociolinguistic dynamics and tailored my language use accordingly. Following young people's linguistic lead, I used Yup'ik as much as possible with the few students who spoke Yup'ik regularly to peers, mirrored local patterns of code-switching with many others, and switched to the local variety of English when working with youth who spoke primarily English.

Language ideologies in Alaska Native communities are shaped by complicated histories and ongoing racial dynamics. Most Piniq youth spoke a local variety of village English, yet many parents had been punished for using Yup'ik in school and associated English with colonization and damaging experiences with outsider White teachers. Many youth voiced strong connections to Yup'ik and fears that "English is taking over our culture." As changes in local youth culture became a driving force of language shift, I was struck by the ways Piniq youth continued to value and use token Yup'ik as a marker of identity. I also noted how my own Yup'ik use made space for youth to position themselves as knowledgeable Yup'ik speakers and teachers. Many youth in the younger group, for instance, were curious about my efforts to learn and teach my child Yup'ik, and would watch me, taking the initiative to correct and encourage me. In one study hall, for instance, I alternated between Yup'ik and English as I talked with a boy about a speech contest. When the boy commented that the speech contest "was fun," a girl I didn't know joined us and commanded, "Say *anglanarquq* [It's fun]." As the girl supervised me, I repeated the phrase, wrote it down, and double-checked how to say *Mamterillermun ayallemni anglanarq-ell-ruq* ("When I went to Bethel it was fun"). After I checked more complicated statements with the students, another boy I didn't know came over and asked if I knew Yup'ik, to which I responded, "*Naspaqatartua* [I'm going to try]; *elicupiartua* [I really want to learn]."

"*Qaillun?* [How?]" he asked, smiling.

"*Eli-cu-piar-tua* [literally, Learn-want-really-I]," I repeated a little more slowly.

"Gee, you came over to the school in this?" another girl I'll call Mary asked, also smiling, gesturing to my light clothes on the chilly rainy day as she moved toward our growing group.

"Yeah."

"Say *eli-cug-yari-qua*—I really want to learn," Mary encouraged, coaching me how to swap in a new post-base while adding a necessary proceeding phoneme. "It's the same as *eli-cu-piar-tua*."

As I finished, a third high school boy in the room commented, "You should be a Yup'ik *kass'aq* [White person]."

"She *is* already," Mary declared. "She was born that way."

In this and similar instances, I was struck by the ways that youth in an endangered-language setting came together to talk enthusiastically about their heritage language, and to voice strong positive associations with Yup'ik. Throughout my research, young people's spontaneous comments about *kass'aq*s and Yup'ik also reminded me of my complicated positioning as a White outsider-insider researcher in an Indigenous setting. In another interview, for instance, I asked a pair of boys about their future hopes for Piniq. One boy initially responded with the familiar echo, "All *kass'aq*s out of Piniq," then quickly glanced at me and followed up with, "except those *kass'aq*s who speak Yup'ik." In my work, I and others encourage teachers to move beyond defensive postures to hear in such statements young people's critique of systemic racism, and their longing for teachers who could use schooling to support Yup'ik language and culture (Wyman & Kashatok, 2008).

It is tricky to position oneself through language crossing as a teacher and researcher in an endangered-language setting, or as a White researcher in an Indigenous community. Throughout my research, many educators voiced assumptions about Yup'ik as an unlearnable language. As I gained Yup'ik proficiency, some local adults and youth would also point to my language use, critiquing the ways that outside teachers or even local Yup'ik spouses and children had failed to learn Yup'ik. In these instances, individuals might say directly to others in front of me, "See, even [though] she only taught here for three years, she speaks Yup'ik." Such instances were uncomfortable, since I knew other valued White teachers and researchers who had developed strong local relationships and promoted equity in schooling without learning Yup'ik. I was also learning how youths' and adults' linguistic insecurities often stemmed from circumstances beyond their control, such as childhood migration to urban settings. Many accommodations were afforded me as a Yup'ik-learning *kass'aq*, while villagers often assumed youth should simply be able to speak it well.

* * * * *

Today only a small number of youth speak Yup'ik, and multiple Yup'ik teachers have used my unusual Yup'ik language use to stress to youth learners that Yup'ik is learnable. I worry that youth may hear teachers' claims that "*She* learned to speak Yup'ik" as an implicit critique: "If this *kass'aq* can do it, why can't you?" I know that to humanize Yup'ik youth in my research, I must find ways to help educators understand how schooling and everyday interactions can inadvertently deny youth the opportunities they need to learn to speak their Indigenous languages comfortably, and how young people's seemingly simple language "choices" are anything but simple. I must also remain attuned to the ways young people respond to a multiply privileged Yup'ik-speaking *kass'aq* university researcher.

LESSONS LEARNED IN WORKING WITH INDIGENOUS
YOUTH IN ENDANGERED-LANGUAGE SETTINGS

Each of the vignettes above illuminates facets of humanizing research—what Paris (2011) describes as "a certain stance and methodology, working with students in contexts of oppression and marginalization" (p. 137). Within this social context and methodological stance, "the researchers' efforts must coincide with the students,' as both the researcher and participants seek mutual humanization through understanding" (Paris, 2011, p. 137). These attempts to listen to youth with "ears to hear" their narratives, counternarratives, and claims about language can elicit meanings that are at once immensely joyful and painful, discomfiting and reassuring, perplexing and edifying. Above all they are teaching moments, and it is to the lessons learned from this work that we now turn.

While our individual experiences, contexts, subjectivities, and positionalities vary, taken together our extensive research experiences point to key areas in which we can humanize research with Indigenous youth in endangered-language settings. First and foremost, researchers should recognize and be sensitive to the commonplace ways that Indigenous youth are positioned vis-à-vis language endangerment. In each of our cases, young people's words highlight the sometimes overwhelming, damaging, and contradictory language ideologies circulating in settings of rapid language shift. In many Indigenous communities, local Englishes are relatively recent, ambiguous emblems of local identities. In contrast, ancestral languages in Indigenous and other communities that value connections to traditions of historical persistence can provide a high degree of focus, or instantiation of mutually constituted beliefs, since, through "long-accumulated convention," the groups who use them develop links among language, community identity, and norms of use over the course of multiple generations (Woodbury, 1993). As Native Hawaiian scholar-activist K. Laiana Wong writes of his own language learning journey, "Learning Hawaiian became an avenue whereby one might access the wealth of [language learning] materials left to us by our forebears" (2011, p. 5). At the same time, as the vignettes above reveal, Indigenous youth in endangered-language communities today are continuously negotiating their linguistic identities amid eroding resources for Indigenous language learning and crosscurrents of local and dominant language ideologies. In such contexts, it is imperative that researchers take youth language opportunities and resources into account when analyzing their language ideologies and practices.

Deeply engaging with young people's perspectives, and paying close attention to young people's circumstances and everyday language use, has helped us—as researchers, language activists, and friends or members of the communities with whom we work—to begin to counter damaging, pervasive assumptions that Indigenous youth are simply abandoning their ancestral languages by "choice." To the contrary, even when they do not claim to be proficient speakers of their ancestral language, the youth in our studies repeatedly express strong attachments to it, referring to the community language—as in the epigraph that introduces this chapter—as "my cultural language" (McCarty et al., 2009, 2011).

Yet youth face challenging social positionings vis-à-vis their heritage language and heritage community. On the one hand, youth may be viewed as "losers of the language." As Jonathan's Long Walk narrative poignantly illustrates, youth are also receivers of unerasable histories of linguistic and cultural genocide. Further, youth may be viewed as critical carriers of endangered languages while simultaneously being shouldered with this responsibility without sufficient support from local adults, schools, and other social institutions. As Jonathan told Teresa in explaining the tendency of bilingual youth to "hide" their Native-language proficiency, many "teachers don't have any [personal] involvement with the students, so it's hard to bring it [the Native language] out within them."

As Sheilah's and Leisy's vignettes show, youth language use may also be overly scrutinized by both adults and peers. When youth speak primarily English, outsiders and even some local adults may accuse youth of "not caring" about language maintenance and identity issues, yet young people's "choices" to speak English are not necessarily freely made. Alternately, when youth voice Indigenous languages that haven't been spoken by children for decades, their language use can be an especially moving and powerful symbol of decolonization for community members.

Secondly, as Leisy's vignette demonstrates, it is important that everyone in the language learning-teaching-researching enterprise—language speakers and nonspeakers, adults and youth, and various types of insiders and outsiders—pays close attention to how their own language use and language ideologies shape research relationships with youth in settings of language shift and endangerment. Community and noncommunity members must also attend to the circumstances in which specific language uses, ideologies, and interactions in the research process help youth interact as language *knowers and users*, as opposed to language losers, hiders, and forgetters (Wyman, 2009). Learning and using a heritage language in culturally acceptable ways can be one of the most effective avenues for demonstrating respect and developing humanizing relationships with youth and adults in language-minoritized communities. Researcher language use, language learning, and youth language sharing can also serve as fertile ground upon which researchers and youth negotiate subjectivities and language ideologies in the research process. At the same time, outsiders' use of a heritage language, especially in cases of lesser-used languages (i.e., Indigenous languages), is also an attention-drawing act—one that may be received with confusion and feelings of loss, suspicion, or anger.

There are many ways, of course, that outside researchers' language crossing, no matter what the intention, could be deeply *de*humanizing, especially if the researcher's lack of fluency undermines accuracy and understanding in the research process, or if community members interpret researchers' use of a heritage language as an act of unwelcome heritage language appropriation. As Sheilah's research shows, even Indigenous researchers studying their own communities must be careful in how they talk about and use Indigenous languages in the research process with youth who may have been criticized for not speaking their heritage language, or for speaking their language "incorrectly." Youth who feel insecure about their heritage language skills or critical of the lack of local language learning opportunities may not want to use their community language with researchers, or may feel resentful when outsiders learn it. Power dynamics around language in academia and schooling often contribute to heritage language devaluing and loss, making the linguistic interactions between educational researchers and language minority youth complex. As such, researchers in endangered-language contexts must stay attuned to how their words and acts of crossing, and young people's acts of language sharing, are being perceived in light of the intense emotional dynamics of language shift.

Similarly, researchers should take youth language learning opportunities into account when analyzing youth language ideologies and practices. In each of our studies, by listening to youth, attending to their actions, and paying close attention to educational processes and struggles in and out of school, we have highlighted how Indigenous language learning resources can become eroded through changing circumstances in and out of school in "vicious cycles of *doubts about*, and *reduced resources for* bilingualism" (Wyman, 2009, forthcoming). This erosion of resources places Indigenous youth in deeply challenging positions vis-à-vis their languages, communities, and heritages.

Youth also cannot be expected to reclaim Indigenous languages on their own, since they require the support of a larger nexus of authorizing agents—their families, to be sure, but also educators and the schools in which they spend much of their lives. When youth are held responsible for transforming histories of linguistic oppression, they and the adults around them need a deep understanding of the forces and processes at work that created the shift in the first place. The eminent sociolinguist Joshua Fishman (1991) refers to this as "ideological clarification." Scholar-activists Nora Marks Dauenhauer and Richard Dauenhauer write of this process for Tlingit communities in southeast Alaska:

> All of us now inherit the legacy of this unpleasant and even genocidal history, one component of which is that Native languages are on the verge of extinction, and at this point we ask, "What to make of a diminished thing?" (1998, p. 60)

This necessary question asking and dialogic process can in turn open up "ideological and implementational spaces" (Hornberger, 2006) for intergenerational language reclamation. Like a growing number of researchers with longstanding commitments to Indigenous communities, each of us has combined our youth work with a parallel strand of action research focused on opening such spaces in the communities we serve.

This brings us to the final lessons—and questions—we pose for ourselves and our readers: How can we work in an activist stance with both youth and adults to directly benefit endangered-language communities? How can we ensure that youth shape these research and language planning processes and products?

Each of us continues to answer *to* this question in distinct but complementary ways. A core response has been to work in collaboration with Indigenous communities from an activist and co-researcher stance. In the case of Teresa's multisited ethnography undertaken with university colleagues Mary Eunice Romero-Little, Larisa Warhol, and Ofelia Zepeda, this has involved ongoing partnerships with teams of Indigenous educators identified as community research collaborators (CRCs). Originally recruited based on self-nominations and the recommendations of other local site personnel, the CRCs have become the critical change agents positioned to apply research findings to local language planning and education efforts. In several of the study sites, the CRCs are heading up language revitalization initiatives, founding and staffing heritage-language immersion programs, and leading in-school and out-of-school language learning and teaching efforts (McCarty et al., 2009, 2011). In some cases, youth participants from the study—now young adults—are co-leading these initiatives as well. McCarty and her colleagues continue to work with the CRCs, their communities, and schools as this action research evolves in response to ever-changing cultural and sociolinguistic conditions.

For Sheilah, long-term work on Hopi language revitalization led to the creation of the Hopilavayi Summer Language Institute to assist Hopi teacher assistants (TAs) responsible for language and culture teaching in schools. Over seven years, one cohort of language educators has attained a critical understanding of contemporary Hopi linguistic and cultural ecology and the language teaching skills necessary to carrying out tribal mandates for language revitalization. Yet these accomplishments are played out against a backdrop of entrenched ideologies about the viability of Indigenous languages, their place within a history of institutional exclusion, and current policies of high-stakes testing and English-only. In this context, the Hopilavayi Institute has created a space for TAs to redefine themselves as language teachers—an expression of empowerment as they reconcile their own sense of the language's viability, their conception of schools as appropriate sites for Hopi language and culture, and their notions of professionalism with their personal histories of linguistic punishment and a reemerging sense of language pride. In the following quote, institute participants voice a collective understanding of their role in "bringing forward" the Hopi language for contemporary youth:

> We need to prioritize helping our youth; they cannot do this alone. They have found us to be the needed help they have been seeking. Language learners are in need of a comfort zone. We as caretakers of the language can be the ones to offer this space. (cited in McCarty, Nicholas, and Wyman, in press)

For Leisy, in-depth follow-up discussions of youth research findings helped lead to the development of a new, collaborative action research project examining and supporting bilingual programs with Yup'ik educators and "allied others" (Kaomea, 2004). Over multiple trips to the Yup'ik region, Wyman vetted her research findings, presenting and discussing summaries to incorporate feedback from youth, adults, educators and community leaders in Piniq, and inviting individuals to review and edit their quotes in context. Wyman also visited an array of Yup'ik-serving schools, projects, and university programs, discussing her findings with Yup'ik language educators, activists, and scholars to situate her research in one village within regional dynamics of language maintenance and shift. This process, described elsewhere (Wyman, forthcoming), took years. Yet over time, the process helped Wyman understand how her research might inform, and be informed by, broader efforts at Yup'ik language reclamation. It also helped her build the relationships to work alongside experienced Yup'ik educators Yurrliq Nita Rearden, Ciquyak Fannie Andrew, and Cikigaq Rachel Nicholai, as well as school district leader Gayle Miller and university colleague Patrick Marlow, in language planning research and program development in a school district serving 22 Yup'ik villages (Wyman et al., 2010a, 2010b).

In these and other ways, each of us has worked to approach youth as members of communities engaged in ongoing, generational decolonization struggles. To humanize work with youth, researchers must invest in developing relationships with young people themselves, holding their own assumptions and positionalities at bay in order to carefully consider young people's positionalities, critical perspectives, and forms of agency. As an increasing number of youth researchers currently emphasize, researchers should also bring their research goals into some kind of alignment with youth concerns in new forms of humanized and action youth research. At the same time, Indigenous communities rightfully demand that researchers recognize and contribute to the ongoing decolonizing efforts of Indigenous adults, which will have profound implications for research (Smith, 1999).

If we take the demands of both youth researchers and Indigenous communities into account, this means that youth researchers in Indigenous and, we would argue, all marginalized and linguistically oppressed communities must develop a form of *triple vision* that recognizes and forwards academic, youth, and broader community projects. In developing such a triple vision, academics must invest considerable effort in understanding and valuing not only youth perspectives, but also the ways that youth practices are shaped by the historical circumstances and ongoing struggles of specific communities. Such a stance takes much longer to develop than the classic ethnographic year, since it requires researchers to develop the relationships necessary to consider their research goals, processes, and products in light of youth and adult community members' concerns. Still, by developing research trajectories within long-running dialogic conversations with Indigenous community members, and by connecting youth research to broader community-focused work, youth researchers can begin to meet Indigenous-inspired demands for a new level of reflexive and careful attention to research ethics in the academy (Lomawaima, 2000; Smith, 1999). Importantly, youth researchers can also use their work to support and foster humanized, intergenerational relationships within communities experiencing profound and rapid societal changes and the reverberations of oppressive histories. We hope the activist ethnography profiled here will be an important step in that direction.

REFLECTIVE QUESTIONS

1. Given your reading of the Indigenous youth accounts in this chapter, why is youth research on language, in particular, such a sensitive and challenging endeavor? How would you position yourself as a researcher working with the youth in the ethnographic vignettes presented here?

2. In thinking of a potential research project with youth, how might we envision a process in which we take a critical view of our researcher positionalities and identities that locates youth vulnerability at the heart of our projects? How might this process further help us define and locate ourselves as worthy witnesses to and in the process?

3. In embarking on youth research, how can we pursue "authenticating" and "validating" the ways in which youth attempt to "make sense of a diminished thing"? How can we support their efforts to engage in cultural survivance through their own agency?

4. Thinking of an existing or potential research project with youth, what languages, language varieties, and/or mixes of languages would you try to use in the research process? With whom, and for what purpose? How might your own language choices invite youth to position themselves as language knowers and users? What language uses might be tricky to navigate, or potentially problematic, and why?

5. Considering an existing or potential research project, how might you work toward developing the "triple vision" described by the authors in this chapter? What of your own preconceptions would you embrace or put aside in order to engage youth perspectives? What community histories and enduring struggles would you need to keep in perspective, and how might you take these into account in the research process?

6. What does it mean to take an "activist stance" as a qualitative researcher? What are the challenges and possibilities entailed by taking such a stance?

NOTES

1. This section is adapted from McCarty and Wyman (2009).

2. The Native Language Shift and Retention Study was supported by the U.S. Department of Education Institute for Education Sciences. Co-principle investigators with Teresa McCarty were Mary Eunice Romero-Little and Ofelia Zepeda; Larisa Warhol served as the study's data manager. At the request of the Internal Review Board that sanctioned the research, we include this disclaimer: "All data, statements, opinions, and conclusions or

implications in this discussion of the study solely reflect the view of the authors and research participants, and do not necessarily reflect the views of the funding agency, tribes or their tribal councils, the Arizona Board of Regents or Arizona State University. This information is presented in the pursuit of academic research and is published here solely for educational research purposes."

REFERENCES

Alim, H. S. (2007). Critical hip-hop pedagogies: Combat, consciousness, and the cultural politics of communication. *Journal of Language, Identity, and Education, 6*(2), 161–176.

Bucholtz, M. (2002). Youth and cultural practice. *Annual Review of Anthropology*, *31*, 525–552.

Dauenhauer, N. M., & Dauenhauer, R. (1998). Technical, emotional, and ideological issues in reversing language shift: Examples from southeast Alaska. In L. A. Grenoble & L. A. Whaley (Eds.), *Endangered languages: Language loss and community response* (pp. 57–98). Cambridge, UK: Cambridge University Press.

Fishman, J. A. (1991). *Reversing language shift: Theoretical and empirical foundations of assistance to threatened languages*. Clevedon, UK: Multilingual Matters.

Hornberger, N. H. (2006). *Nichols* to *NCLB*: Local and global perspectives on US language education policy. In O. García, T. Skutnabb-Kangas & M. E. Torres-Guzmán (Eds.), *Imagining multilingual schools: Languages in education and glocalization* (pp. 223–237). Clevedon, UK: Multilingual Matters.

Hornberger, N. H., & King, K. A. (1996). Bringing the language forward: School-based initiatives for Quechua language revitalization in Ecuador and Bolivia. In N. H. Hornberger (Ed.), *Indigenous literacies in the Americas: Language planning from the bottom up* (pp. 299–319). Berlin, Germany: Mouton de Gruyter.

Hornberger, N., & Swinehart, K. (in press). Not just *situaciones de la vida*: Professionalization and Indigenous language revitalization in the Andes. *International Multilingual Research Journal*.

Kaomea, J. (2004). Dilemmas of an Indigenous academic: A Native Hawaiian story. In K. Mutua & B. B. Swadener (Eds.), *Decolonizing research in cross-cultural contexts: Critical personal narratives* (pp. 27–44). Albany: State University of New York Press.

Kral, I. (2011). Youth media as cultural practice: Remote Indigenous youth speaking out loud. *Australian Aboriginal Studies*, *2011*(1), 4–16.

Lee, T. S. (2007, Spring). "If they want Navajo to be learned, then they should require it in all schools": Navajo teenagers' experiences, choices, and demands regarding Navajo language. *Wicazo Sa Review,* pp. 7–33.

Lee, T. S. (2009). Language, identity, and power: Navajo and Pueblo young adults' perspectives and experiences with competing language ideologies. *Journal of Language, Identity, and Education, 8*(5), 307–320.

Lomawaima, K. T. (2000). Tribal sovereigns: Reclaiming research in American Indian education. *Harvard Educational Review, 70*(1), 1–23.

Maira, S., & Soep, E. (Eds.). (2005). *Youthscapes: The popular, the national and the global*. Philadelphia: University of Pennsylvania Press.

McCarty, T. L. (2002). *A place to be Navajo: Rough Rock and the struggle for self-determination in Indigenous schooling*. Mahwah, NJ: Lawrence Erlbaum/Routledge.

McCarty, T. L., Nicholas, S. E., & Wyman, L. T. (in press). Re-emplacing place in the "global here and now": Critical ethnographic case studies of Native American language planning and policy. *International Multilingual Research Journal.*

McCarty, T. L., Romero, M. E., & Zepeda, O. (2006). Native American youth discourses on language shift and retention: Ideological cross-currents and their implications for language planning. *International Journal of Bilingual Education and Bilingualism, 9*(5), 659–677.

McCarty, T. L., Romero-Little, M. E., Warhol, L., & Zepeda, O. (2009). Indigenous youth as language policy makers. *Journal of Language, Identity, and Education, 8*(5), 291–306.

McCarty, T. L., Romero-Little, M. E., Warhol, L., & Zepeda, O. (2011). Critical ethnography and Indigenous language survival: Some new directions in language policy research and praxis. In T. L. McCarty (Ed.), *Ethnography and language policy* (pp. 31–51). New York, NY: Routledge.

McCarty, T. L., & Wyman, L. T. (2009). Indigenous youth and bilingualism: Theory, research, praxis. *Journal of Language, Identity, and Education, 8*(5), 279–290.

Meek, B. A. (2007). Respecting the language of elders: Ideological shift and linguistic discontinuity in a Northern Athapaskan community. *Journal of Linguistic Anthropology, 17*(1), 23–43.

Mendoza-Denton, N. (2008). *Homegirls: Language and cultural practice among Latina youth.* Malden, MA: Blackwell.

Mitchell, T. (2004). Doin' damage in my native language: The use of "resistance vernaculars" in hip hop in Europe and Aotearoa/New Zealand. In S. Whiteley, A. Bennett, & S. Hawkins (Eds.), *Music, space and place: Popular music and cultural identity* (pp. 108–123). Burlington, VT: Ashgate.

Muehlmann, S. (2008). "Spread your ass cheeks" and other things that should not be said in indigenous languages. *American Ethnologist, 35*(1), 34–48.

Nicholas, S. E. (2009). "I live Hopi, I just don't speak it": The critical intersection of language, culture, and identity in the lives of contemporary Hopi youth. *Journal of Language, Identity, and Education, 8*(5), 321–334.

Nicholas, S. E. (2011). "How are you Hopi if you can't speak it?" An ethnographic study of language as cultural practice among contemporary Hopi youth. In T. L. McCarty (Ed.), *Ethnography and language policy* (pp. 53–75). New York, NY: Routledge.

Nietzche, F. W. (2006). Thus spoke Zarathustra: A book for everyone and no one. In K. A. Pearson & D. Large (Eds.), *The Neitzche reader* (pp. 252–278). Malden, MA: Blackwell. (Original work published 1883)

Paris, D. (2011). "A friend who understand fully": Notes on humanizing research in a multiethnic youth community. *International Journal of Qualitative Studies in Education, 24*(2), 137–149.

Romero-Little, M. E., McCarty, T. L., Warhol, L., & Zepeda, O. (2007). Language policies in practice: Preliminary findings from a large-scale study of Native American language shift. *TESOL Quarterly, 41*(3), 607–618.

Smith, L. T. (1999). *Decolonizing methodologies: Research and Indigenous peoples.* New York, NY: Zed Books.

Szulc, A. (2009). Becoming *Neuquino* in Mapuzugun: Teaching Mapuche language and culture in the province of Neuquén, Argentina. *Anthropology and Education Quarterly, 40*(2), 129–149.

Tulloch, S. (2004). *Inuktitut and Inuit youth: Language attitudes as a basis for language planning*. Unpublished doctoral dissertation, Department de Langues, Linguistique et Traduction, University of Laval, Québec, Canada.

Wilson, W. H., & Kamanä, K. (2009). Indigenous youth bilingualism from a Hawaiian activist perspective. *Journal of Language, Identity, and Education, 8*(5), 369–375.

Winn, M. T., & Ubiles, J. R. (2011). Worthy witnessing: Collaborative research in urban classrooms. In A. F. Ball & C. A. Tyson (Eds.), *Studying diversity in teacher education* (pp. 293–306). Lanham, MD: Rowman & Littlefield.

Woodbury, A. (1993). A defense of the proposition, "When a language dies, a culture dies." *Proceedings of the First Annual Symposium about Language and Society–Austin (SALSA). Texas Linguistic Forum, 33*, 101–129.

Wong, K. L. (2011). Language, fruits, and vegetables. In M. E. Romero-Little, S. J. Ortiz, & T. L. McCarty (Eds.), *Indigenous languages across the generations: Strengthening families and communities* (pp. 3–16). Tempe: Arizona State University Center for Indian Education.

Wyman, L. (2009). Youth, linguistic ecology, and language endangerment: A Yup'ik example. *Journal of Language, Identity, and Education, 8*(5), 335–349.

Wyman, L. (forthcoming). *Youth culture and linguistic survivance*. Bristol, UK: Multilingual Matters.

Wyman, L., & Kashatok, G. (2008). Getting to know the communities of your students. In M. Pollock (Ed.), *Everyday antiracism: Getting real about race in school* (pp. 299–304). New York, NY: New Press.

Wyman, L., Marlow, P., Andrew, C. F., Miller, G., Nicholai, C. R., & Rearden, Y. N. (2010a). Focusing on long-term language goals in challenging times: Yup'ik examples. *Journal of American Indian Education*, *49*(1/2), 22–43.

Wyman, L., Marlow, P., Andrew, C. F., Miller, G., Nicholai, C. R., & Rearden, Y. N. (2010b). High-stakes testing, bilingual education and language endangerment: A Yup'ik example. *International Journal of Bilingual Education and Bilingualism*, *13*(6), 701–721.

Critical Media Ethnography

Researching Youth Media

Korina Jocson

6

Researching youth media is no exception from any critical inquiry that seeks to use research to combat forms of inequity. The inquiry entails a process of humanization that is mutually constitutive for participants and researchers. More important, the inquiry yields altered views of youth as knowledge producers and as active members of society enabled by today's media technologies. As Paris (2011) put it, the research act becomes humanizing as youth provide researchers access to understanding their world. The research act involves building relationships of dignity and care, and creating terrains of exchange to confront multiple borders of difference. That is, interactions between youth participants and researchers are shaped by their willingness to share life experiences uncommon in traditional research. In my own work, these interactions gifted me with a more informed lens to understand youth-produced media and other cultural texts created in school, in after-school programs, or on their own. Youth media is a growing cultural and educational movement; studying what young people create as linked to their everyday experience has implications for humanizing research.

In the past decades, critical ethnography has influenced the way educational researchers and other social scientists conduct studies in different communities, moving toward new historical moments in qualitative research. This chapter builds upon what critical ethnographers have put forth as doing research that seeks to better the social conditions of participants in particular settings. The focus is youth media, specifically multimedia writing and video production. In this sense, critical ethnography frames the approach the researcher takes, while multimedia writing and video production offer an area of inquiry through which to examine students' consumption, creation, and dissemination of cultural products. What follows is a discussion of critical media ethnography with examples from two studies based in northern California.[1]

Along with the researcher's role, key in the discussion are uses of digital media that attend to and challenge cultural representations of youth in new media times. I note the importance of visuality in youth's multimedia writing and video production. On one hand, the visual affords layered meanings in representation and allows creators to lace image with sound and printed text through the use of digital technologies. On the other, the visual implies transparency and identification that may reinforce the dominant gaze on nondominant populations—in this case, youth of color in low-income urban communities. Implications of digitality and visuality for humanizing research are included in the discussion. Before turning to the studies, I approximate the beginnings of my line of inquiry and how it has taken shape ever since.

BEGINNING AND EVOLVING INQUIRY

I was an undergraduate student majoring in ethnic studies when I first helped to produce a short film for submission in an African American studies course. It was an opportunity to explore race, ethnicity, and the underrepresentation of students of color at the university. It was a time for writing up an analysis beyond the format of a research paper; the film included a range of perspectives based on interactions and interviews with various groups of students on campus. My co-producers and I felt compelled to create something that would call attention to issues that mattered in our lives. Consistent with our academic and artistic interests, it was also a point in filmic history when media production forced us to edit our footage the conventional way (i.e., intricately splicing film and putting the pieces together during post-production). It was an exciting time for learning. Today, digital technology has made the editing process less grueling and more manageable through editing software such as Final Cut and iMovie, among others.

Since my early experimentation with film, I have continued to be interested in media production, for both my own purposes and those of students I serve at the high school and college level. In the past decade, I have been involved in research projects with high school teachers and students to investigate the use of digital media in the classroom. Part of my task has been to promote literacy learning while seeking culturally relevant ways of incorporating innovative approaches to better prepare students for 21st-century literacies. Additionally, the proliferation of youth media organizations such as Just Think and Youth Radio in the San Francisco Bay Area and the Educational Video Center in New York has increased the number of young people who participate in media production (Goodman, 2003; Halverson, Lowenhaupt, Gibbons, & Bass, 2009; Soep & Chavez, 2010). I often share information with high school teachers and students about specific organizations that surface in my research to incite ideas about possibilities in youth media work. I also utilize the organizations' websites to access youth-produced media to serve as models from which teachers, students, and I can learn. More recently, YouTube and other video sharing platforms have been popular among youth for distributing do-it-yourself media production. It is once again an exciting time for learning—to understand such cultural phenomena as shaped by a growing media-savvy generation. As a literacy researcher, paying attention to these developments in and out of school is important in rethinking the implications of researching youth media.

In the digital era, new technologies of communication continue to demand new literacies. New technologies such as computers and mobile phones not only have created different ways of interacting with others, but also have changed how individuals spend their time in particular spaces—whether physical, online, or both (e.g., video chat). This movement toward new(er) literacies marks the transformations in a post-typographic world (Reinking, McKenna, Labbo, & Kieffer, 1998). Within the area of literacy studies, Lankshear and Knobel (2003) point out that new literacies are inclusive of both existing and emerging forms of literacy. Similarly, Voithofer (2005) points to the importance of keeping in mind that "new" in "new literacies" doesn't mean better or best or that one form supersedes the other. He asserts that we are in a specific historical period—the new media age—in which production and reception are at the forefront of the discourse. That is, changes in technology beg us to ask questions about convergence of texts (the mixing of video, photo, audio) and presentation (using particular kinds of interfaces). Of most interest in this chapter is how youth media offers fresh ways of thinking about new literacies, convergence, and presentation.

TOWARD CRITICAL MEDIA ETHNOGRAPHY

Throughout my work in literacy and urban education, I have espoused a critical ethnographic approach. Critical ethnography is no different from conventional ethnography in that it relies on qualitative methods and interpretation of data. It is inductive in nature and often leads to the development of grounded theory (Glaser & Strauss, 1967). Critical ethnography, however, draws on critical methodology that resists the domestication of truth; it is based on critical epistemology, not on value orientation (Carspecken, 1996). It moves away from "what is" to "what could be" in the commitment to address processes of injustice within particular lived domains and toward human freedom. The art of fieldwork and the recognition of subjective human experience along with local knowledge and vernacular expressions adhere to the postmodern turn, or new movements in qualitative research (Denzin, 2001, 2003; Noblit, Flores, & Murrillo, 2004). For critical ethnographers, it is important to attend to one's positionality and dialogue with the Other (Fine, 1994; Madison, 2005). Critical ethnography is also about conducting rigorous research to invoke a call to action and to use knowledge for social change (Thomas, 1993).

As my interest in youth media grew, so did my approach to research. The demands of qualitative research made explicit my subjective role as a researcher, and often as a participant, doing critical ethnography. For this chapter, I draw on examples from two studies in which my positionality and dialogue with youth are embedded. While I have been attentive to this aspect of the research, it has been just as important to consider how processes of media production and meaning making construct as well as communicate particular narratives in a multimedia world.

I have begun to call this aspect of my work critical media ethnography. It is similar to current research in media studies (see Kearney, 2006), with more emphasis on discovering system relations that link to literacy, schooling, and education.

EXAMPLE 1: SYMBOLIC CREATIVITY IN YOUTH MEDIA

The first example illustrates how symbolic creativity shapes student writing. Willis (1990) suggests that the nature of symbolic creativity is in the everyday cultures of youth, from fashion styles to choices in music, film, television, and other media. He defines symbolic creativity as what all practices have in common or what drives them. These practices include language, the body, and other dramatic forms—in other words, raw materials and tools—that allow individuals to produce specific forms of human identity and capacity. I build on this definition in my analysis of Naier's "Wastes Away" based on an emulation writing exercise in June Jordan's Poetry for the People program. Briefly, Poetry for the People (P4P), as established by the late poet June Jordan in 1991, is a university program centered on redefining poetry to respond to the needs and struggles of marginalized populations. Its pedagogical objectives are as follows: (a) to create a safe medium for artistic and political empowerment, and (b) to democratize the medium of poetry to include "the people," or populations that have been historically denied access and representation. As I will point out, most significant for Naier was a unique encounter with poetic and musical texts. Naier derived inspiration from contemporary works and enacted what Bakhtin (1981, 1986) theorized as "ventriloquating" others' words to reflect a unique speech experience and to create something new. For Naier, this was an opportunity for a cultural and textual remix that resulted in a video poem.

Inquiry Through Participation

Research for the larger study on youth poetry was conducted over a period of 30 months (Jocson, 2008). Bellevue High, a racially diverse, comprehensive high school in northern California, served as the focal site.[2] For this larger study, I used various methods to collect data, including interviews, participant observations, student poetry and literacy artifacts, curricular materials, official student records, and video and audio recordings of class sessions and other related events. With students, interviews provided insights into their literacy practices in and outside of school as well as explanations about constructed meanings in their writing. With teachers, interviews provided a window into students' literacy and academic development in the context of their English classrooms. Participant observations occurred inside the classroom three days per week for four to six weeks; these observations allowed me as a researcher to actively participate in activities and take notes in the midst of them to record key episodes. Students' poems, including written drafts and completed assignments within the P4P program, were collected over time. Seeing these poems paired with their corresponding curricular materials shaped the ways I examined student writing.

Through purposeful sampling, seven students were selected based on teacher recommendation as well as grade level, ethnicity, and year of participation in P4P to provide a cross-section of the larger student population in the program. Naier's case is represented in this chapter. Naier is African (Nigerian) American and was a one-time participant in the program in the 10th grade, when he was one of six students in my writing workshop group.

For this particular study, I used an ethnographic case study approach to examine the various experiences of students as individuals and as part of a larger whole. My dual role as a researcher and student-teacher-poet in P4P allowed me to build a unique relationship with students, particularly through the co-facilitation of whole-group discussions, small-group writing workshops, and individual consultations. Student-teacher-poets were largely responsible for P4P's programmatic functions at the university and Bellevue High School. As a student-teacher-poet during the time of study, I had the privilege of working closely with high school students in English classrooms. But, as I realized along the way, my role as a student-teacher-poet for the P4P program manifested beyond the classroom, where I began to interact with high school students on school grounds during lunch and after school, and whenever we encountered each other on the street or at various community-related events. Our interactions eventually led me to discover a synergistic student-led discourse community named P4P2 (after the program that set off students' interests). Two sophomore students with whom I worked at Bellevue High initiated P4P2. At first, both students were invited as speakers to discuss their poetry and writing process at a midwinter conference sponsored by the National Council of Teachers of English. Not long after, a colleague and I, in collaboration with students, participated in a panel and performance session at the California Association for Teachers of English Annual Conference. The objective of sharing our work on youth poetry with a professional audience forced us to offer something more than just *our* words and to create an intellectual space where youth voice was at the center of the exchange. We thought, what better way than to have young people themselves share their perspectives on the topic—not simply as performers but as knowledge producers? The session consisted of three youth poets as presenters (two from P4P and one from Youth Speaks, a literary arts organization) and two adults as moderators (I was one of them). From this unique opportunity, which gave impetus to many more, the duo group from P4P gradually grew as six other junior and senior students joined to participate in classroom presentations held at several locations, including San Francisco City College, James Lick Elementary School, and the University of California at Berkeley. These high school students established time to convene voluntarily, to write and revise poems on their own, and to share their knowledge of poetry with different audiences. For two years P4P2 had a strong presence in various classroom settings. One evening, four students and I were on our way to a classroom presentation in

San Francisco. While in the car, we were discussing aspects of poetry and why writing poems was important in our lives. That spontaneous discussion led to the creation of P-O-E-T-R-Y, which all of us in that fleeting moment collaboratively expanded to "Power, Opportunity, Electricity, Transformation, Responsibility, Youth." We were ecstatic about our clever acronym, yet the dialogue did not stop there. Later that evening, the students began their classroom presentation with "P-O-E-T-R-Y!" They stood before an audience of prospective teachers and in unison declared their collective stance; then they each shared a poem of their choosing to demonstrate how words turn into action. As a student-teacher-poet, I was there to facilitate the presentation, but with the energy in the room I felt compelled to offer a poem in the end. Balancing this role with my role as a researcher, I interviewed students and documented part of their experience in P4P2 for a self-produced video documentary called *One Night.* The result was a deeper understanding of what and why young people write. This initial look at youth poetry as an emerging discourse community propelled me to ask specific questions about writing in the larger study. It also shaped my relationship with Naier, who was one of P4P2's original members.

Key questions that guided my investigation on youth poetry were as follows: (a) Who or what influences adolescent writing? (b) In what ways do these influences shape adolescent literacy development? (c) What tools are used to craft adolescent writing? To answer these questions, I used content and textual analysis to examine textual products of students. I began by identifying which weeks in the program coincided with emulation and which poems in the printed reader were used as examples for the writing exercise. Then I compared those printed poems in the reader with students' emulation poems as produced in the classroom, at home, or other places. To better understand the construction of emulation poems, I drew upon student interviews and notes from participation observations, data that added to the ethnographic content analysis of student writing (Huckin, 2004). In Naier's case, emulation also took the form of a multimedia production, offering a more complex look at adolescent writing across contexts in new media times.

Across five different time periods from 2000 to 2002, I observed that emulation was integral to P4P's curriculum and writing instruction. Emulation was always one of the writing exercises. However, to set apart emulation poems from others prompted by writing topics such as self-affirmation, love, ode, and profiling, or poetic forms such as a haiku or T'ang, I continued to use content analysis in my examination of students' poems in published anthologies. I again consulted the template poems in the printed readers used specifically during the emulation writing exercise. For example, I identified 18 emulation poems out of the 55 published poems in the Fall 2000 anthology, and 6 out of the 30 in the Spring 2002 anthology. This provided a representative set of student work. Upon a much closer look, however, I quickly discovered that all poems from each anthology were to some degree emulation poems. Embedded in these poems were sources of meanings used at face value or explicit social dramas that reflected those from prior texts we had studied in class. These poems contained either direct or indirect quotation, recognizable phrasing, and/or language forms that echoed certain ways of communicating—techniques of intertextuality "that represent[ed] the words and utterances of others" (Bazerman, 2004, p. 88). While they figured prominently in data analysis, emulation poems could not be easily identified and categorized as I had initially anticipated. On one hand, emulation served as an explicit writing assignment. On the other, given the use of prior texts in the writing instruction and the possible levels of intertextuality in the process, emulation poems offered a way to understanding the nuances in student writing. Given this overlap in the data, I turned to students themselves and examined, instead, what they had identified as their most favored poems produced in P4P: works that illustrated traces of emulation, not strictly those produced under the umbrella of an emulation writing assignment but also those created through their own volition. Methodologically, turning to students was key and led to a necessary dialogue about what each student found to be significant in their experience. How I was positioned both as a researcher and student-teacher-poet deepened the inquiry I was making. The following is an examination of Naier's writing that happened both in school and out of school.

The Case of Naier

Prior to his participation in the P4P program, Naier had taken interest in poetry in the eighth grade when a teacher positively commented on the very first poem he ever wrote. It was also at that time that he had discovered the works of Langston Hughes, who since then had been influential to his interest in reading and writing poetry. Additionally, Naier liked reading books, such as *The Assassination of the Black Male Image* by Earl Ofari Hutchinson, and magazines, such as *The Source*, *XXL*, and *Ebony*, among others. Naier listened to various types of music, from contemporary jazz to neo-soul, R&B, and rap, which he too considered poetry. Artists he followed at the time of the study included Najee, Jill Scott, Alicia Keys, Musiq Soulchild, Nas, Missy, CeeLo, Talib Kweli, Mos Def, and Goapele. One of these artists, as I will point out, was integral to the production of Naier's video poem. According to Naier, paying attention to his surroundings allowed him to better understand "what [he] was up against" as a young black male. He revealed what it was like "moving place to place" and riding the bus with a keen eye:

> I've lived in places where . . . blacks are very accepted . . . [and] aren't very accepted . . . the poorest of places. And it doesn't matter where you live, I've seen segregation. I've seen oppression or hidden aggression against all the races . . . I write about that. And I write about what I see. When you ride the bus all through the city . . . you see, through me, through your eyes. It's kind of like a photograph . . . you see people hanging on the corner. And, I mean, you see this 'hood atmosphere that you don't see in many other places. And it's kind of scared me in a sense, like, how was this happening?

To answer his own question, Naier found it essential to reflect on the importance of poetry in his life:

> If you drive down [name of] Street, in a sense you kind of feel like it's a burnt-out city . . . as if you were living in some other country, and where . . . they don't have any money and the buildings are all desecrated and burnt down or smoked out. . . . You see that, when you're sitting on the bus. And you know seeing it. And then I just rap about it. I rhyme about it. I write poetry about it because I want it to change.

These extemporaneous markings subsequently shaped the writing of "Wastes Away" in the 10th grade. For Naier, "Wastes Away" represented a critical response to his slain brother's lifestyle, a poem that paints a picture about violence and racism in a "'hood atmosphere." This response suggests what Kelley (1996) articulates as working-class black youth participating in forms of politics and acts of resistance, or as race rebels in postindustrial working-class communities. The writing—later turned into multimedia writing—served as a symbolic representation of his lived experiences. It had been nearly two years since Naier and I worked together inside his English classroom. However, we continued our communication through P4P2 along with other students. During his senior year, Naier expressed interest in an after-school program I started called Digital Video Poetry, or DV Poetry. So I invited him to participate. There, he revisited "Wastes Away" and combined it with two other poems (see Figure 6.1) to create a video poem.

Figure 6.1   Naier's Poem "Wastes Away" (extended version)

```
 1   as he twists and turns through life
     his soul turns from divine to unkind from time
     will he forever be punished for past sins of his lifetime
     as he dies, i see the whites of his eyes turn red from greed

 5   he feels the need to lie, cheat, and steal
     all to make that bill he thinks he needs so badly
     but doesn't he see that while he's a G
     his gun is destroying reality for you and me
     doesn't he realize that he's erased the tracks

10   made by the broken backs of his ancestors
     but as proceeds his family bleeds
     the pain which he causes
     and as time pauses he falls into a cycle of ill-begotten dreams
     that shatter like glass that last for a lifetime

15   he says that he loves his life
     but is cold enough to take another
     he wants his family to love each other
```

but cannot love his baby's mother
he is running for cover

20 as the cold hard wing of reality hits his face
and the sun rises up from the shadows
and shines the last hint of darkness away
he stays away from the light
afraid that his mask will decay

25 and dare i say
he wastes away
awww
look what happened to you
got shot like a fool

30 on life support
six inches from that basket called a casket
i heard shots fired, screeching of raw tires
i saw your body there
motionless and expired

35 why did you have to leave, why did you have to die
i never knew you, but i can't
cause some dumb niggas screwed you
as i lay a rose on your casket i pray to god
that one day i will meet you some day

40 hopefully
one day
you never saw the bite of the snake
until the venom killed you
and i prayed to god every day that he's with you

45 i miss you
i wish you could teach me all the things
like how to get that and hit that
and deal with the girls who never used to call back
i wish i could rewind back

50 tell you to solve your problems with liquor
they only make your problems come quicker
and make you sicker
because when death was knocking at your front door
you were too drunk to listen

55 you died by the gun, that's the way you went out
pouring liquor blazing the trigger with glory without a doubt
but whose glory
my story
ain't goin out like that

(Continued)

Figure 6.1 (Continued)

60 awww
    black brotha
    stripped from my mother
    too soon and broomed
    with brothers to an early tomb

65 society's poster child
    for destruction and gloom created for doom
    black brotha
    descended from slaves
    locked in iron chains

70 behind steel bar cages
    that lasted ages then to now
    black brotha
    spits bars in Cadillac cars
    behind school parking lots

75 showing

WHY HE DON'T GET SERVED

Content analysis of Naier's video poem yields visual representations of slaves and torturous acts to depict slavery, dollar bills to stand for capitalism, liquor and guns to portray drugs and crime, children and families to denote unity, open paths and meadows, and the cosmos to allude to the future or uncertainty (see Table 6.1). The sounds (voice and music) and images (words and photographs) on the edited timeline afford layered meanings that otherwise might have been circumvented by the written text (i.e., a printed poem). Editing effects such as zoom, dissolve, fade, and motion (31 in total), as well as the placement of words on the screen (24 in total) and the use of red color fonts (2 in total) for emphasis also give additional texture to the production. Indeed, features of multimodality contribute to the production's design and make hybrid discourses possible within a text. The making of Naier's five-minute video consisted of more than the lacing of words, images, voice, music, and transitional effects on a timeline. It involved structuring ideas and meanings to be represented with multimedia writing tools. At the very least, it involved manipulating 26 different images found on the Internet and corresponding them with multiple poetic verses. It points to the significance of multimodality and raises questions about what it takes to examine threaded written and visual literacies in multimedia composition. Gaining some understanding of the intertextualities within Naier's video poem was a result of our continued dialogue about his academic interests and

Table 6.1   Naier's Video "Wastes Away": Sample Analysis[3]

	2:00	:10	:20	:30	:40	:50	3:00
POEM	(Lines 38–66)						
VIDEO Words only Images	Lines 42 – 45 ...Red cosmos	Meadow	Shot glass	Dead President Tombstone Rifles	Corpse Liquor neon sign Man & Olde E.	Gun Corpse Red Cosmos Roses Man & Olde E.	Lines 61 – 66...
EFFECTS	...zoom out upper left, lower right upper left, lower right center – "I miss you" in red font cross dissolve zoom in	zoom in cross dissolve	zoom in cross dissolve cross dissolve cross dissolve	zoom out cross dissolve	cross dissolve black screen zoom in/pan down—right	black screen black screen black screen upper left, upper right, center, lower left, upper right, lower right	
AUDIO 1 (voice)	38 as i l ay you on your casket i pray to god 39 that one day I will meet you some day 40 hopefully 41 one day 42 you never saw the bite of the snake 43 until the venom killed you 44 and i prayed to god every day that he's with you 45 i miss you 46 i wish you could teach me all the things 47 like how to get that and hit that 48 and deal with the girls who never used to call back 49 i wish i could rewind back 50 tell you to solve your problems with liquor 51 they only make your problems come quicker 52 and make you sicker 53 because when death was knocking at your front door 54 you were too drunk to listen 55 you died by the gun, that's the way you went out 56 pouring liquor blazing the trigger with glory without a doubt 57 but whose glory 58 my story 59 ain't goin out like that						
AUDIO 2 (music)	(Cont. - Nas Instrumental)						

cultural practices. This dialogue was key to understanding more fully his writing in relation to his everyday experiences. The time Naier and I spent working together through P4P, P4P2, and DV Poetry allowed me as a researcher to learn from him with a more informed lens. To deepen our relationship, I felt compelled to share some of my own experiences through multimedia writing as well. I had written several poems that year and chose one of them as the basis for a video poem. I produced "Rest," a three-minute installment about the demands and complexity of teaching in multicultural environments. I used this video poem to model possibilities in the DV Poetry after-school program; more important, the video poem was my way of sharing a personal story with students who were expected to produce video poems based on their interests. During the process of production, I was privileged to create with students, discuss their work, ask about choices they made, and become a "worthy witness" (Winn & Ubiles, 2011) to the interlacing of words, images, and sounds that represented their worlds.

While techniques of intertextuality are present in the writing, stemming from Naier's participation in P4P, there were also others present in the multimedia composition that related to multivoicedness, temporality, and politics of difference (Jocson, 2010). For instance, Naier's use of Nas's instrumental song reflects his affinity for rap music and rap artists as part of his literacy practice; it also represents an emulation of style and form to produce another text. Nas's song

"Nas Is Like" from the 1999 album *I Am* addresses similar social conditions as in Naier's poem. The first verse of the song, for example, contains references to freedom, pain, struggle, drugs, guns, and survival. According to Naier, it was a conscious choice to use only the instrumental version of the song in order to lay a new voiceover (his own) and create a multimedia text from the perspective of another young black male (his). Lacing his words with carefully selected images from the Internet afforded him a means to communicate his message about social inequities with more precision.

Symbolic creativity, from writing poetry in the 10th grade to media production in the 12th, provides a glimpse into what shapes adolescent writing. Upon high school graduation, Naier went on to attend a historically Black university on the East Coast, where he continued to engage in similar interests. To further consider implications of researching youth media, I draw on another study with questions about visuality in critical media ethnography.

EXAMPLE 2: POLYCENTRISM IN YOUTH MEDIA

The second example builds on my former study to suggest polycentrism in youth media. According to Shohat and Stam (2002), polycentrism is the multiplicity of perspectives in visual culture that historically has been defined by a Eurocentric narrative. I will point out that polycentrism is key in do-it-yourself production and has implications for humanizing research. The example described here stems from an examination of youth media in and out school. As part of a larger study conducted from 2005 to 2007, I built on existing professional networks, attended and observed various community media arts events, and accessed media texts online or through copies provided by artists themselves. I was also active in a Web sphere search, an approach to studying Web objects and mediated patterns (Schneider & Foot, 2005), to follow the dissemination of local youth-made media regionally and nationally. Based on this approach and my level of access to media texts, I discovered a well-circulated poem called "Slip of the Tongue" that had been performed widely by a local poet in the San Francisco Bay Area; later, it was produced into a video poem by a novice filmmaker who at the time was a high school student. (Note: The reader may access "Slip of the Tongue" on YouTube; viewing it beforehand may be helpful for grasping the extent of the analysis.) In addition to the poem (written and multimedia in form), other data sources included semistructured interviews with the poet/writer and producer/filmmaker, field notes from participant observations, and filmmaker/director commentary on the completed production. I used content and visual analysis to make sense of the collected data. For the purposes of this article, I discuss the idiosyncratic uptakes of the producer/filmmaker rendered in the video. The uptakes illustrate how youth contribute to visual culture as part of a growing remix culture in youth media arts (Jocson, under review). An analysis of "Slip of the Tongue" suggests an epistemological shift in the construction of multiple perspectives (i.e., whose narratives count or should be told, by whom, and with what tools). As a critical ethnographer, I was attentive to those epistemological shifts that along the way raised questions about the use of written, performative, and visual tools in multimedia writing and video production. This aspect of the research is worth exploring here.

The Case of Adriel and Karen

The Poet/Writer. In 2002, spoken word artist Adriel Luis wrote "Slip of the Tongue." He was a freshman at a four-year public university when he first wrote the poem, admittedly "to impress a girl." He was a senior at a racially and ethnically diverse urban high school in northern California when his interest in spoken word poetry took shape. As a high school student, he joined Youth Speaks, a literary arts organization based in San Francisco, where he began to perform on stage, compete in slams, and form alliances with other spoken word artists, including a group that later became iLL-Literacy (http://ill-literacy.com). As a college student, Adriel began to get involved in social activism as well as take courses in Asian American studies and women's studies. In light of his new experiences, Adriel was intrigued by the concept of makeup (i.e., beauty products) and subsequently wrote a poem from the perspective of an Asian American woman. The result was "Slip of the Tongue." According to Adriel, the original poem "Slip of the Tongue" took various forms—in print (chapbook), on stage (live performance), and in the studio (recorded for a CD album). The changes to the original poem over a period of four years (2003–2006) suggest a recurring practice of revision with purpose, format, and audience in mind. Adriel noted that he had eventually put the poem to rest until it started to receive attention through the video.

The Producer/Filmmaker. The poem evolved into the video "Slip of the Tongue," produced by Karen Lum. At the time of production, Karen was in the ninth grade attending an urban high school in northern California. She witnessed one of Adriel's performances of "Slip of the Tongue" at a local slam event and took notice of its message. Soon after, she realized the poem's potential for a multimedia public service announcement (PSA) project. Karen was an active member of an after-school program called Youth Sounds/The Factory (now merged with the Bay Area Video Coalition, or BAVC), a place where young people can access media technologies and gain various media production skills. The following is an excerpt from Karen's explanation of the project's beginnings:

> Slip of the Tongue originated when I was asked to participate in a filmmakers conference in Connecticut in 2005. In order to go, I had to produce a one-minute PSA that incorporated the theme of how youth are making a difference. Being a lover of spoken word, I wrote out a vague treatment about how many youth utilize poetry to change the world through self-expression. The organizers of the conference immediately

rejected my treatment and told me that I needed to have a solid story line. Then one day, the idea suddenly came to me. I would take a poetry recording and apply images to it. The slam poem "Slip of the Tongue" by my friend Adriel Luis stood out to me since it actually told a story and was structured just like a film with an introduction, conflict, climax and resolution. And so after 2 weeks, I finished my 1 minute PSA, and eventually, it turned into a complete 4 minute short. (Media That Matters Film Festival, 2007)

The video "Slip of the Tongue" (total running time 4:06 minutes) is based on Adriel's live performance of the poem. The tagline "Girl meets boy at a bus stop" captures the opening scene of a rather complex stance on race, ethnicity, gender, and media culture. By 2008, the video had been screened in over 50 film festivals and garnered numerous awards, including the Northern California Emmy Award for Best Youth Film and the Jury Award from the Media That Matters Film Festival. The video also became available for streaming online through UthTV, ListenUp!, Independent Movie Database, and YouTube. According to Karen, the editing software program, Final Cut Pro, was key in making the video "Slip of the Tongue." Do-it-yourself production proved to be significant as Karen appeared in and shot most of the scenes. In an interview, Karen noted,

It's funny. I basically made the film by myself. I shot a lot of those scenes whenever I could do it myself. I had a tripod, so I just set it up and hit record and ran in front of the camera and did something and then ran back and hit record again. I had some help, though. Some of my friends at Youth Sounds, they helped me with some shots I couldn't do by myself, but I did the editing. I did the editing myself. It was a one-person crew because initially I didn't expect anyone to see the film, so I treated it like a small little project, and then it blew up.

Locality of Uptakes. Evident in the video "Slip of the Tongue" are similarities and differences in Adriel's and Karen's experiences that merged into one text. A comparative textual analysis yields insights into each artist's use of pastiche, parody, irony, and hyperbole. In light of polycentricism, it is important to highlight the references to race, ethnicity, gender, culture, body, and place to suggest the locality of uptakes. Karen described at length how the poem resonated with her:

My mentor at Youth Sounds always tells me to put a little bit of myself into my films; well, in this one, I put myself entirely in it. But, the premise is a moment. I used to take the bus all the time, like what goes on in the poem. So when I listened to the poem, I imagined it at a bus stop because that's totally me. That's what I do, that's very Oakland, taking the AC transit, and I wanted to include that aspect of my life and my culture into the film. So, I just brainstormed. Adriel is talking about makeup or reading through magazines and stuff, and the thing is the poem really affected me because I totally related to it. I grew up in a majority white area . . . I thought being white was beautiful. Listening to the poem kind of affected how I feel about my beauty and my self-esteem. So, I just included things [in the film] that felt natural to me, like looking through magazines, seeing white models as pretty, brunette as pretty, but never seeing Asian girls, and to me that was my standard of beauty. Things weren't attainable through these standards. Over time, I overcame that and now I'm proud of who I am. That's how "Slip of the Tongue" really affected me and that's why I chose the poem, to reach a lot of people.

These experiences in Karen's life shaped the video as text, where new meanings were constructed. The video "Slip of the Tongue," carefully sequenced through editing, pays tribute to Adriel's performance and represents Karen's social worlds. A closer look at the video signals stylistic choices in multimedia writing made possible by do-it-yourself production. For example, locations in "Slip of the Tongue" included Oakland's Chinatown and downtown areas (sidewalks of stores, street signs, a bus stop, café, and restaurant); Karen's house (bedroom, bathroom, living room, kitchen and breakfast table, patio/balcony); Karen's family-owned video store (aisles and shelves); and the Youth Sounds building (elevator and hallway). Wide-angle shots were common to capture the physical environment. To emphasize particular signs, Karen used close-ups of street names, female images in magazines and other media, body curves, family portraits, and a Confucian quote. Depictions of a young female Chinese American and her social worlds reveal complex negotiations with American society, negotiations primed by race, ethnicity, gender, culture, body, and place.

Since its release, the video has reached various audiences across the globe. The film festivals provided official venues to further legitimize the work of youth media artists. The distribution of "Slip of the Tongue" online via YouTube and social media sites has also expanded the possibilities for reaching an even wider audience. "Slip of the Tongue" is indicative of a do-it-yourself production that provides the consumer, and in this case also the producer/filmmaker, with the ability to appropriate, tinker, and repurpose meaning from existing texts (de Certeau, 1984). The real names of the poet/writer and producer/filmmaker appear in the beginning and end credits of the video to recognize them for their creative contributions.[4] As in other media productions (Soep & Chavez, 2010), it is challenging enough for youth to fight for recognition in a high-powered field. The inclusion of real names is deliberate and invokes questions about humanizing research.

DIGITALITY, VISUALITY, AND HUMANIZING RESEARCH

The two examples above illustrate the opportunities afforded by new literacies to construct narratives mediated by youth's experiences. However, there are several limitations within each study. First, the video projects were produced by youth from a specific urban school and metropolitan context. It is important to consider how results of the studies might be further informed by a multisited approach or by scaling up to include more participants in similar settings. Second, and just as important, the nature of the video projects identified, documented, and represented intricate aspects of youths' lives. It is possible that their likenesses, reified through photographs, video sequences, and texts branded with real names, may yield unintended effects. This has been particularly significant in my research, where concerns about digitality and visuality have surfaced (see Jocson, 2012). In historically marginalized communities, the penetration into the private lives of students and their families as a potential outcome of research must be taken with serious consideration. In my view as a critical ethnographer, revealing research participants' likenesses without consideration of potential risks would be irresponsible. In other words, it is essential to take into account *identification* (of names and locations)*, documentation* (of faces and bodies), and *representation* (of individuals and groups) in multimedia projects.

In writing up research findings, I make a conscious choice to share information in a careful manner. In the case of delicate subject matter, it is always necessary to be cognizant of real names appearing in beginning and ending credits, as well as photographs of home addresses, neighborhoods, landmarks, and street names. Is this concern for identification, documentation, and representation a new phenomenon in qualitative research? Or is it similar to what appeared in visual anthropology, only now with the use of more advanced technological tools, including computer hardware and do-it-yourself movie editing software? The issue is neither to note the changing nature of media technologies nor to disregard what the latter has to offer research. Researchers have anticipated these changes and now know some baseline trends in literacy and technology. Instead, the issue is about the careful attention and sensitivity to the research participants that the researcher must provide. The nature of digitality and visuality in youth media production is such that it often reveals the likeness of those involved. It is the responsibility of the researcher to further protect the identities and affiliations of participants involved in the study, particularly if the production poses potential risks to their academic (school), career (work), and social (family and peer network) life trajectories.

More and more educators are embracing the use of video and other types of media production in their classrooms. Based on the examples in this chapter, it is essential for researchers (including teacher-researchers) to consider the implications of representing student products depicting personal material as well as their likenesses on the page and on the screen. What potential harm does publication or public viewing of student products render? What is the purpose of the production? Who is the intended audience? Depending on the nature of the video composition, the representation of certain segments and sequences may be limited, for example, to purposeful abstractions through the blurring of faces or removal of names. In treating entire videos with sensitivity, it may be necessary to include representations in the analysis but exclude them in the visual reporting. Perhaps research studies that examine similar phenomena in youth media production may seek other types of analysis or ways of reporting, or may not require the level of attention and sensitivity I am noting.

As research in new literacies expands, so will our approaches, methods, and analyses. The following questions may benefit future studies: What methodologies should researchers employ in the digital era? Is critical media ethnography an emerging method of research within do-it-yourself production? How do value orientations play a part in the research process? What are the epistemological issues that must be considered? If full reporting cannot be achieved, then what can researchers offer the research community in terms of validity and transparency? In what ways can the objects of study involving multiple modes be known and inscribed? How does ideology influence the apprehension of meaning? As Leonardo and Allen (2008) point out, representations in qualitative research are partial, and ideological differences between researchers and participants may guide what is constructed and translated from the data. Despite the many possibilities in youth media, it has been just as important to consider these limitations and the implications for research. For humanizing research in particular, the research act must continue to build relationships of dignity and care (Paris, 2011). I am more conscientious of my role (and its impact) as a result of being gifted with unique opportunities to interact with youth participants in mutually constitutive ways. It is my hope that the examples in this chapter advance the conversation about critical media ethnography. Doing research that embraces digitality and visuality will require a more sophisticated lens through which to understand the human experience.[5]

REFLECTIVE QUESTIONS

1. What is critical media ethnography? How does the author use critical media ethnography to make sense of youth cultural practices in and out of school?

2. Given today's emerging technologies, what does critical media ethnography look like in your context?

3. What technological and cultural shifts should researchers, together with participants, consider to further shape critical media ethnography?

NOTES

1. Parts of this chapter have appeared in a different argument (Jocson, 2010, 2012).

2. All names of participants and sites in this study are pseudonyms.

3. This table is an altered version of a table previously published in *Review of Education, Pedagogy, and Cultural Studies* (see Jocson, 2010).

4. Both Karen Lum and Adriel Luis helped to construct this narrative. Elsewhere (Jocson, under review), I provide a fuller description of their artistic collaboration and an expanded analysis of "Slip of the Tongue."

5. I am grateful to editors Django Paris and Maisha Winn for their vision and commitment to humanizing research. Also, special thanks to the University of California All Campus Consortium on Research for Diversity (UC ACCORD) and the American Educational Research Association (AERA) for providing fellowships in support of the work represented in this chapter. Any and all errors are mine.

REFERENCES

Bakhtin, M. (1981). *The dialogic imagination: Four essays by M. Bakhtin.* Austin, TX: University of Texas Press.

Bakhtin, M. (1986). *Speech genres and other late essays.* Austin, TX: University of Texas Press.

Bazerman, C. (2004). Intertextuality: How texts rely on other texts. In C. Bazerman & P. Prior (Eds.), *What writing does and how it does it: An introduction to analyzing texts and textual practices* (pp. 83–96). Mahwah, NJ: Lawrence Erlbaum.

Carspecken, P. F. (1996). *Critical ethnography in educational research: A theoretical and practical guide.* New York, NY: Routledge.

de Certeau, M. (1984). *The practice of everyday life.* Berkeley: University of California Press.

Denzin, N. (2001). *Interpretive interactionism* (2nd ed.). Thousand Oaks, CA: SAGE.

Denzin, N. (2003). *Performance ethnography: Critical pedagogy and the politics of culture.* Thousand Oaks, CA: SAGE.

Fine, M. (1994). Dis-stance and other stances: Negotiations of power inside feminist research. In A. Gitlin (Ed.), *Power and methods* (pp. 13–55). New York, NY: Routledge.

Glaser, B. G., & Strauss, A. L. (1967). *The discovery of grounded theory: Strategies for qualitative research.* Chicago, IL: Aldine.

Goodman, S. (2003). *Teaching youth media: A critical guide to literacy, video production, and social change.* New York, NY: Teachers College Press.

Halverson, E., Lowenhaupt, R., Gibbons, D., & Bass, M. (2009). Conceptualizing Identity in youth media arts organizations: A comparative case study. *E–Learning, 6*(1), 23–42.

Huckin, T. (2004). Content analysis: What texts talk about. In C. Bazerman & P. Prior (Eds.), *What writing does and how it does it: An introduction to analyzing texts and textual practices* (pp. 13–32). Mahwah, NJ: Lawrence Erlbaum.

Jocson, K. M. (2008). *Youth poets: Empowering literacies in and out of schools.* New York, NY: Peter Lang.

Jocson, K. M. (2010). Unpacking symbolic creativities: Writing in school and across contexts. *Review of Education, Pedagogy, and Cultural Studies, 32*(2), 206–236.

Jocson, K. M. (2012). Youth media as narrative assemblage: Examining new literacies at an urban high school. *Pedagogies: An International Journal, 7*(4), 298–316.

Jocson, K. M. (under review). *Remix revisited: Critical solidarity in youth media arts.* [Submitted for publication]

Kearney, M. (2006). *Girls make media.* New York, NY: Routledge.

Kelley, R. (1996). *Race rebels: Culture, politics, and the Black working class.* New York, NY: Free Press.

Lankshear, C., & Knobel, M. (2003). *New literacies: Everyday practices and classroom learning.* Berkshire, UK: Open University Press/McGraw-Hill.

Leonardo, Z., & Allen, R. (2008). On ideology: An overview. In L. M. Given (Ed.), *The SAGE encyclopedia of qualitative research methods* (pp. 415–420). Thousand Oaks, CA: SAGE.

Madison, D. S. (2005). *Critical ethnography: Method, ethics, and performance.* Thousand Oaks, CA: SAGE.

Media That Matters Film Festival. (2007). *Slip of the Tongue.* Retrieved November 2, 2007, from http://www.mediathatmattersfest.org/6/slip_of_the_tongue/

Noblit, G. W., Flores, S. Y., & Murillo, E. G., Jr., (Eds.). (2004). *Postcritical ethnography: An introduction.* Cresskill, NJ: Hampton.

Paris, D. (2011). "A friend who understand fully": Notes on humanizing research in a multiethnic youth community. *International Journal of Qualitative Studies in Education, 24*(2), 137–149.

Reinking, D., McKenna, M., Labbo, L., & Kieffer, R. (1998). *Handbook of literacy and technology: Transformations in a post-typographic world.* Mahwah, NJ: Lawrence Erlbaum.

Schneider, S., & Foot, K. (2005). Web sphere analysis: An approach to studying online action. In C. Hine (Ed.), *Virtual methods: Issues in social science research on the Internet* (pp. 157–170). Oxford, UK: Berg.

Shohat, E., & Stam, R. (2002). Narrativizing visual culture: Towards a polycentric aesthetics. In N. Mirzoeff (Ed.), *The visual culture reader* (2nd ed., pp. 37–59). New York, NY: Routledge.

Soep, E., & Chavez, V. (2010). *Drop that knowledge: Youth radio stories.* Berkeley: University of California Press.

Thomas, J. (1993). *Doing critical ethnography.* Newbury Park, CA: SAGE.

Voithofer, R. (2005). Designing new media education research: The materiality of data, representation, and dissemination. *Educational Researcher, 34*(9), 3–14.

Willis, P. (1990). *Common culture: Symbolic work at play in the everyday cultures of the young.* Boulder, CO: Westview.

Winn, M., & Ubiles, J. (2011). Worthy witnessing: Collaborative research in urban classrooms. In A. Ball & C. Tyson (Eds.), *Studying diversity in teacher education* (pp. 295–308). Lanham, MD: Rowman & Littlefield.

PART III

The Complex Nature of Power, Relationships, and Responsibilities

Django Paris

Early in the lead chapter to this section Mangual Figueroa challenges us with two questions: "We might ask: Have we acknowledged and fulfilled our responsibility to the communities who have welcomed us? Have we—in both our own opinion and the opinion of the participants—fulfilled the commitments we made at the beginning of our study?" (p. 129). In many ways, these questions lay out the pressing ground explored by the three chapters in this section. These chapters trace the tensions between what is often talked about and taught in too-simple and problematically neutral terms as "exiting the field," "participant observation," "open-ended interviews," and "action-research."

In the first chapter Mangual Figueroa takes up the silence in research methods training around what is at stake when researchers exit the field after many months of relationships and trust built through ethnographic work. Mangual Figueroa offers seminal episodes of her work with Marta and Carlos, undocumented migrants who ask Mangual Figueroa to sign *la carta*, an agreement to legally adopt their children to protect them in the event that Marta and Carlos were detained or deported. There could not be a more powerful example of the complexities of human relationship, power, and responsibility in ethnographic inquiry than parents asking a researcher to adopt their children.

Reading this chapter I was reminded of Carla, an undocumented Latina youth in my study of language and ethnicity in South Vista (Paris, 2011), who after many months of our working together asked if I would become the godfather of her future child and consider legal paperwork that would grant the child citizenship. Carla did not have a child during our work together or in the year that followed, but I remember struggling with her question and all it implied about my responsibility and how I was utterly unprepared for such a request. I mention this ethnographic memory for three reasons: to show that such events are not uncommon in humanizing research, to mention how I was not trained to deal with them, and as a way of acknowledging that I have never formally written about Carla's request in publications about this research. All three of these speak to what Mangual Figueroa is after in this chapter when she asks, "Why did signing *la carta* seem like an impossible responsibility when I knew and cared for the family so deeply? I considered what steps I could take and wondered, was this just a question of my personal preference or were there scholarly guidelines to consider?" (p. 136).

In the second chapter, Green posits that "the qualitative research method of participant observation is like playing double dutch. . . . The good jumpers (read "researchers") will be skillful and agile enough to improvise and acquire an awareness of rhythm, knowing when and how to enter" (p. 148). In reflecting on Green's chapter, I recalled my own struggles with finding the balance between participating and observing, between being a member of activities and remaining peripheral to them. I was reminded of a recent social literacy case study I conducted in urban Arizona with Pedro (see Paris, 2012), in which I chose to march with him and his peers in protest of Arizona State Bill 1070 (a bill Pedro and his community felt was unjust). It was not until I had gained a sense of some of what mattered to Pedro and his community that I felt ready to attempt to, as Green terms it, "keep time and rhythm" with him and his peers as we marched around the state capitol. And yet even in this moment of impassioned participation in social protest, I was documenting with a camera and an audio recorder and was interpreting what this moment might mean to Pedro and what questions I might ask him in our follow-up conversations. This sort of participant observation is not something we are often equipped for or encouraged to do. Green's chapter pushes us to consider how such participation yields richer understanding about what matters to the people we research with, and why it matters.

The stakes could not be higher in Romero-Little, Sims, and Romero's account of collaborative research with Pueblo communities in the Southwest in the final chapter of this section. As they comment, humanizing and praxis-oriented research "can have an especially significant impact on sustaining a way of life for future generations of Indigenous people" (p. 162). The authors reflect on and historicize the Keres Study of giftedness among Pueblo peoples, showing what interviews and teacher-action research done by and with community members in the context of sustained ethnographic interaction can do to change dominant norms and notions as pervasive, damaging, and colonizing as intelligence and genius and special education.

As I read this chapter I was struck by the way Romero-Little the researcher took up new ideas of giftedness from her study and employed them in her role as Romero-Little the teacher-action-researcher, all in the service of her Pueblo students' senses of self. I was also struck by the current efforts of the authors to revisit and further collaborate with Pueblo youth and elders a full two decades after the original Keres Study was completed. Just last week, in the spring of 2012, I had lunch with Rahul, a young Fijian Indian man and hip-hop emcee who has been fundamental to my conceptions of humanizing research that are at the heart of this book. It was now five years after our research together in South Vista (Paris, 2011), and Rahul asked if I wanted to engage in more work together as a follow-up to the now-published book of research I was delivering to him. His question got at that nagging feeling that I did not do enough with and for the youth of South Vista. Romero-Little, Sims, and Romero offer a portrait of such sustained work and encourage me and all of us to keep up our relationships and inquiries with communities over time in the effort to sustain their cultural ways of being in the world. Thus, perhaps, we will be able to answer more affirmatively one of Mangual Figueroa's questions that opened this preface: "Have we acknowledged and fulfilled our responsibility to the communities who have welcomed us?"

REFERENCES

Paris, D. (2011). *Language across difference: Ethnicity, communication, and youth identities in changing urban schools*. Cambridge, UK: Cambridge University Press.

Paris, D. (2012). Become history: Learning from identity texts and youth activism in the wake of Arizona SB1070. *International Journal of Multicultural Education, 14*(2), 1–13.

La Carta de Responsabilidad

The Problem of Departure

Ariana Mangual Figueroa

7

ersonal narratives of researchers' entry into the field have become an integral part of ethnographic writing. In her essay on the development of the "arrival trope," Mary Louise Pratt explains that these narratives of entry serve three functions: proving that the researcher has gained the insider status needed to obtain the data presented, distinguishing between the roles of researcher and researched while enlisting the reader in the ethnographer's project of interpreting the scenes described, and demarcating the boundaries between the subjective opening anecdote and the scientific authority characteristic of the ethnographic report (1986, p. 42). This trope of arrival has carried over into a contemporary methodological focus on gaining access to the field and establishing relationships with key gatekeepers in the community being studied. According to Pratt, arrival stories are "worth looking at, especially, to people interested in countering the tendency toward alienation and dehumanization in much conventional ethnographic description" (p. 33). From this perspective, the arrival trope holds out the possibility for humanizing research because it is the place where the personal is permissible, before it is superseded by the scientific character demanded of the ethnographer.

In this essay, I take up Pratt's approach to humanizing ethnography by focusing attention on the implicit but often unacknowledged counterpart to arrival: departure. Narratives of entry presuppose that the research site is a bounded geographical location that the ethnographer can, and ultimately must, leave at the completion of the study. Our failure to account for how researchers leave the field—how they can responsibly extricate themselves from an ethnographic situation that binds the researcher and researched through ongoing processes of "colonialism, imperialism, missionization, multinational capital, global cultural flows, and travel"—is a troubling area of silence (see Gupta & Ferguson on Pratt, 1997, p. 13). Aside from occasionally observing that it's hard to leave the field, ethnographers rarely reflect on those issues we are best positioned to consider at the conclusion of our fieldwork (LeCompte, 2008, is a notable exception). We might ask, Have we acknowledged and fulfilled our responsibility to the communities who have welcomed us? Have we—in both our own opinion and the opinion of the participants—fulfilled the commitments we made at the beginning of our study?

Contemporary ethnographers are working to challenge the "conventional stereotype" of the detached ethnographer (LeCompte, 1999, p. 6) by moving beyond outdated notions of researcher neutrality and calling for reciprocity between the researcher and researched. Qualitative researchers have also argued against conventional standards for scientific research in the field of education that are founded upon positivist notions that reproduce the stereotype (Eisenhart & Towne, 2003). In the following pages I recount my own exit experience, demonstrating how silence about exit denies the complex forms of interrelation that we must confront if we are to humanize our research.

For 23 months, I lived and conducted ethnographic research in an emerging Latino community in Millvalley, Pennsylvania,[1] a city that forms part of the New Latino Diaspora (Wortham, Murillo, & Hamann, 2002) of the U.S. Rust Belt. I wanted to understand the ways that juridical categories of citizenship status shaped the language socialization and educational experiences of migrant families.[2] After months of working alongside members of Millvalley's Latino community as a simultaneous translator in grassroots mobilizations to protect migrants' rights locally and to advocate for immigration reform nationally, I invited four mixed-status Mexican families to participate in my study. Mixed-status families include a combination of undocumented migrant and U.S.-born members, as well as others in various stages of applying for U.S. citizenship (Fix & Zimmerman, 2001). The mixed-status families living in Millvalley were typical of those residing in emerging Latino communities—they included undocumented parents and an older undocumented sibling who had crossed the border from Mexico into the U.S., and younger siblings born in the U.S. (Passel & Cohn, 2009). These younger siblings had been granted U.S. citizenship by birth, also known as *jus soli* citizenship (Bloemraad, Korteweg, & Yurdakal, 2008).

This essay focuses on my interactions with one family, the Utuado-Alvarez family. Figure 7.1 depicts the kinship relations and migratory statuses of the parents and siblings at the time of the study. In this diagram, a triangle represents a female relative and a circle represents a male relative. Two horizontal lines indicate a marriage bond while a single vertical line denotes a descent bond. A single, solid horizontal line indicates a co-descent bond. In addition to these traditional notations (see O'Neil, 2008), I have added two symbols relevant to my study: First, a dotted vertical line signifies that the child still lived in Mexico while the parents lived in the U.S. Second, shading indicates citizenship: The shaded geometric symbols denote U.S.-born children, while the unshaded symbols indicate undocumented migrant family members born in Mexico. This mirrors the way that the family talked about migratory status: The term *ciudadano* ("citizen") implied American citizenship, and family members rarely, if ever, talked about being Mexican citizens. A person who was a Mexican citizen was almost always referred to as someone who lacked U.S. citizenship, who did not have papers, or who was not legal.

I came to know the Utuado-Alvarez family very well as a participant observer, and sometimes as an advocate, during routine after-school activities that took

Figure 7.1 The Utuado-Alvarez family

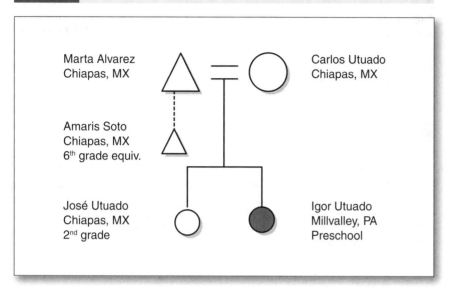

Marta Alvarez
Chiapas, MX

Carlos Utuado
Chiapas, MX

Amaris Soto
Chiapas, MX
6th grade equiv.

José Utuado
Chiapas, MX
2nd grade

Igor Utuado
Millvalley, PA
Preschool

place at home, in community settings, and in a variety of public spaces. On several occasions, Marta and Carlos, both undocumented parents, talked with me about something they referred to as *la carta* ("the letter"). This letter would itself become a symbolic site invested with all the challenges of departing from the domestic field of a mixed-status family living with the very real fear of deportation and family separation. At different points in the study, Marta and Carlos spoke about two versions of *la carta*: One was a document that migrant parents could draft in order to grant another adult temporary custody of José and Igor in the event of detention or deportation. Although this document would not be legally binding, the notarized letter would certify that Marta, Carlos, and the specified person had agreed that the person would care for the children until the parents were released from detention or would travel with the children to Mexico to reunite with the parents if they were deported. The other version of *la carta* involved finding a U.S. citizen who would consent to adopt the two boys legally; this would allow the adoptive parent to submit an application for José, their eldest undocumented child, to become a U.S. citizen. In this case, Marta and Carlos wanted to remain the primary caregivers for their sons, but hoped that the adoption would grant José access to the rights that U.S.-born Igor already possessed. The adoptive parent would become the brothers' temporary guardian in the event of detention or deportation.

With the occurrence of an increasing number of deportations leading to family separations in the Millvalley Latino community during the spring of 2009, community leaders began encouraging mixed-status families to develop a family plan that included provisions for childcare in the event of detention or deportation. The plan would include the notarized version of *la carta* that granted temporary custody of the children to a trusted adult. Figure 7.2 is a template of a "Descarga de Autorizaciones Para El Cuidado de Niños" ("Special Power of Attorney for Childcare") distributed at community meetings by local religious leaders and community organizers, who played a central role in advocating migrants' rights in and around Millvalley.[3]

Figure 7.2	*La carta* template

We are writing to designate, _____ (Name of Person) to serve as a Temporary caregiver for our children _____, _____, _____, _____, _____ in the event that we are unavailable for a short period of time (1-72 hours) to care for our children. The designation of _____as our temporary caregiver will not exceed a period of 72 hours.

Thank you in advance for your attention to this matter.

Sincerely, _____ and _____
(Name of Parent or Parents)

Date: _____

The Utuado-Alvarez parents hoped to find a trusted adult with U.S. citizenship that would agree to be named in a document like the one pictured here, or who would be willing to initiate the legal process of adopting José and Igor. As I will show, *la carta* calls all the bluffs of an ethnographer: objectivity, independence, and mobility. My wrestling with how to manage the request that I sign *la carta* and thus formalize a substantial role within the family after the conclusion of my research forced me to confront the question of ethnographic exit in deeply humanized ways—a question for which my academic training left me largely unprepared.

ENCOUNTERING *LA CARTA*

The first time that I heard about *la carta* was on a Saturday morning in February 2009, as I sat in Marta and Carlos's living room drinking coffee and debriefing after a visit to a nearby car dealership. I had translated between Marta and a salesman as she inquired about the possibility of buying a used minivan. Marta was eager to buy a vehicle because the brutal winter was taking its toll on the family; every day, they had to wait outside for Igor's bus to pick him up and drop him off from preschool, and they had to walk José to and from elementary school. The conversation was not unlike others I had translated for Marta. Once the salesman began listing the kinds of identification Marta would need to provide in order to complete the transaction (in this case, a Pennsylvania driver's license or international driver's license and visa), she turned to me and said, "*Ok, dile que lo pensamos y ya vamonos*" ("OK, tell him we'll think about it and let's go now"). As undocumented migrants, Marta and Carlos did not have these forms of identification; moreover, they were afraid of letting strangers find out about their migratory status. As we walked up the hill to their house, Marta called an undocumented friend who had purchased cars in neighboring Ohio to ask if he would drive the family to one of his trusted dealerships across the state border.

During our conversation about their possible trip to Ohio, Marta recounted an exchange that she, José, and Igor had recently had on one of their wintry walks home from José's elementary school (recall that Igor, their younger son, was a U.S.-born citizen). On this walk, Marta told the boys that she had a *carta que iba escribir con un abogado* (letter that she was going to draft with a lawyer). She told them that the letter *se trata de que va pasar a ustedes si algo nos pasa* ("has to do with what will happen to you both if something happens to us"). Igor asked what kinds of things could happen, and José answered, "*Si se mueren o si los agarra la policía*" ("If they die or if the police catches them"). Marta explained that "*como nosotros no tenemos papeles nos pueden devolver a México*" ("since we don't have papers, they can send us back to Mexico"). José added that if that happened, "*se tendría que ir a México porque la abuela es la única que nos cuida bien*" ("we would have to go to Mexico because Grandma is the only one who takes good care of us"). As they continued talking, José proposed, "*¿Por qué no le dices a la abuela que venga y nos cuide acá?*" ("Why don't you tell Grandma to come and take care of us here?") Marta had replied that some things were easier said than done. Igor, Marta recounted with a laugh, had one final plea: "*Pero si nosotros vamos a México, escribe en la carta que nos gusta pizza y dulces*" ("But if we have to go to Mexico, the letter should say that we like pizza and candy"). Carlos joined in the laughter, too.

I didn't know it at the time, but this first mention of *la carta* foreshadowed subsequent conversations in which Marta and Carlos would ask me to consider taking custody of José and Igor in the case of detention or deportation. What was immediately apparent in this exchange was how much the family thought about drafting *la carta*, and how involved José and Igor were in constructing the terms of this contingency plan. Although much of what we know about undocumented Latino youth indicates that they confront the realities of their undocumented status in adolescence when applying for driver's licenses or financial aid for college (Gonzalez, 2008), this exchange demonstrates that young undocumented and U.S.-born children of migrants are active participants in everyday conversations about migratory status (Bhimji, 2005; Mangual Figueroa, 2011). Children, along with their parents, express their fears about deportation and find ways to cope with the anxiety produced by knowing that undocumented family members are under the constant threat of state surveillance. Planning for *la carta* was a strategy that the Utuado-Alvarez family pursued in order to maintain their kinship ties and family cohesion in the face of state policies that threatened to separate them.

REVISITING *LA CARTA*

Over a year later, on a spring day in April 2010, I met Marta, Carlos, José, and Igor at the preschool that Igor attended. In the 14 months that had elapsed, I had accompanied the family to many other meetings, where they played an active role in Millvalley's public life. During these events, I often served as a simultaneous translator to help facilitate the family's participation in events such as parent-teacher conferences at José's school, grassroots meetings on migratory reform, and planning sessions for parents interested in founding Millvalley's first state-funded community-based social service agency for Latino families. We also spent many afternoons in the Utuado-Alvarez home sharing meals, completing school-related tasks, and talking about the everyday realities that the family members faced living and working in Millvalley.

As I had explained to them in previous conversations, this was one of the last times that I would visit with the family. I was traveling to California the following month to defend my dissertation and attend graduation and, although I would be returning to Millvalley briefly, I would soon be moving to New York City to begin a new academic position. Marta had invited me to join them for this month's parent meeting because she knew I would be interested in the immigration discussion on the agenda. She explained to me that Alexis, the program director, was hesitant about my coming because the topic was highly sensitive and the parents' migratory status was confidential; but Marta had assured her that I was a trusted friend. There were around 10 families present at this reunion. The undocumented Mexican and Central American mothers and fathers gathered in a room on the first floor of the center while childcare volunteers entertained the children in the upstairs classrooms. The meeting began when Alexis welcomed everyone and made several announcements about upcoming events, including the end-of-year celebration for the children moving on to kindergarten in the fall.

After making her opening remarks, Alexis quickly moved to the heart of the agenda. She explained that she had been thinking a lot about recent events in the Millvalley community in which Latino migrants had been detained and separated from their families in the process. She expressed concern about what would happen to the students enrolled in the program if their parents were deported. She strongly urged the parents to do two things: first, to find a trusted family member or friend who was a U.S. citizen and who would care for the children in the event that they were deported, and second, to have a lawyer draft a *carta de responsabilidad* ("letter of responsibility") that would give the U.S. citizen the power of attorney over the children's well-being in the event of deportation. The message was clear—the parents ought to have a plan in place so that someone could return their children to them in Mexico or Central America. Alexis asserted that the letter was one way to avoid having the children placed in the U.S. foster care system and to minimize the risk of not being reunited as a family.[4] Marta alternated between burying her head in her hands and looking up and despairingly asking, "*Pero ¿quién va hacer eso?*" ("But, who is going to do that?"). Marta and Carlos worried that no *ciudadanos americanos* (American citizens) would be willing to accept this responsibility; and yet, it was quite possible that their family's survival might depend on this act of goodwill.

When the meeting ended, the Utuado-Alvarez family and I exited the preschool and stood in the parking lot conversing. As the children played around us, Marta and Carlos thought out loud about who they could ask to be named in *la carta*. After listing several members of their church parish, they explained that someone like me would be a great fit. They enumerated the following reasons: They knew me and trusted me, I knew the children very well, I was familiar with U.S. systems like education and travel, and I was married and employed. It was entirely reasonable for Marta and Carlos to consider me for this role, given all of the reasons that they articulated; while I immediately began to wonder about the ethics of assuming this role as an ethnographer, they did not share the same concerns about what constituted appropriate boundaries between the researcher and researched.

I had often considered the relevance of the "participant-observer paradox"—how the presence of an ethnographer invariably influences the activities she observes (Duranti, 1997, p. 118)—to this project in which I intentionally defined participation as collaboration and advocacy, privileging reciprocity over objectivity. I had decided at the outset of the project that I would reciprocate the family's generous participation by serving as a translator whenever they asked me to; this helped the family in their interactions with service providers, teachers, and business owners whenever I was present. Translation was a form of exchange that remained inextricable from my study of language socialization; formed the basis for my first interaction with Marta at a grassroots meeting, where I translated as she spoke out in favor of migratory reform; and constituted a valued form of social capital that I could share. The request to be named in *la carta* went beyond reciprocity based on a series of ongoing but nonbinding exchanges; it attempted to formalize a commitment that would change the relationships between our families in a more permanent way.

I listened as Marta and Carlos spoke, but I did not respond to their implied question of whether I would be willing to assume this responsibility. Instead, I asked a lot of questions about other families they knew who had drafted *la carta*. The conversation remained unresolved that afternoon, but we decided to continue our visits once I returned from California. We all knew that my trip out west marked the beginning of my transition out of the field, and this meeting was a poignant reminder of the tension involved in doing so. The Utuado-Alvarez family had many accomplishments to celebrate—Igor was entering kindergarten next year, both boys were going to be baptized in the coming weeks, and Marta and Carlos were studying English. And yet, while they had successes to celebrate, they continued to live with the fears particular to being a mixed-status family. Meanwhile, I maintained the privilege of entering and exiting their lives at will; as a U.S. citizen and ethnographer, I had all the mobility their family lacked.

I continued to reflect on the question of *la carta* while in California. On the one hand, I felt assuming such a role would be inappropriate; on the other hand, I felt I might be failing the family. Why did signing *la carta* seem like an impossible responsibility when I knew and cared for the family so deeply? I considered what steps I could take and wondered, was this just a question of my personal preference or were there scholarly guidelines to consider? What would it mean if existing approaches to conducting educational research could not adequately address the exigencies of this ethnographic moment, and what would be the consequence of deviating from established practices?

REEXAMINING *LA CARTA*

When I returned to Millvalley in early June, I arranged to make one of my last field visits to the Utuado-Alvarez home. All of the family members were present that day; except for the weather, it was much like that visit in 2009 when I'd first heard of *la carta*. Over the course of the year, Marta and Carlos had become interested not only in finding a temporary custodian for José and Igor in the event of deportation, but also in the possibility of having a U.S. citizen adopt the two children. They had also shifted from simply mentioning the idea of *la carta* to me in casual conversation to explicitly asking me to become an adoptive parent. On this afternoon, Marta and Carlos asked if I would consider this possibility and, about an hour into the visit, I recorded the following exchange between us. The transcript begins just after Carlos excuses himself from the conversation because he is going to sleep, exhausted from working all night cleaning a local movie theater.

Example 1:[5]

Sequence A:

1 Ariana: *Pues me alegro verlo Carlos (.) nos vemos en julio*

Well I'm glad to see you Carlos. We'll see each other in July.

2 Marta: [*El o::tro mes*

Next month

3 Carlos: [*Oh::: en julio*! ((laughs))
              Oh in July!

4 Ariana: *Se va volando el* [*tiempo*
              Time flies

5 Carlos: [*Se cuida, se cuida* [*mucho*=
                                  Take care of yourself, take good care

6 Ariana: [*Igua::l* [*mente*
                                            You too

7 Carlos: [=*porque queremos.*
                                                     que siga.
                                                     because we want you
                                                     to continue

8   *alegrándonos. la vida. y dándonos esper*[*anza*
              bringing joy to our lives. and giving us hope.

9 Ariana: [*Igua::lmente*
                                            Same to you

10 Marta: [*Y que lo PIEN*[*ses*
                                            And that you'll think
                                            about it

11 Ariana: [*Ustedes*
                                                           You all

12   *para mi* [*son-*
              for me are

13 Marta: [*con tu esposo PORfavor*↓
                                with your husband please

14 Ariana: OK↓

   This sequence highlights the interactional resources that Marta, Carlos, and
I used to negotiate the tension surrounding *la carta*, a tension heightened by my
impending departure from the field and from Millvalley. Throughout our exchange,
we asserted and adapted our positions about three main topics: the timeline for my
departure, the terms of our relationships with one another, and the proposed adoption.
   As I said good-bye to Carlos, I noted that I would return the following month.
(I had decided to visit the focal families once a month instead of once a week in
this transitional period.) Marta and Carlos emphasized their disapproval of the
time frame by elongating the vowel sound, as in "That's a loooong time!" (lines
2 and 3), and I tried to minimize their concern by responding with the adage
"Time flies" (line 4). As Carlos issued the parting phrase "Take care," he also

named one of the central problems of the departure—understanding that the study was drawing to a close while wanting me to continue being a part of the family's life (lines 7 and 8). Marta identified exactly how I could continue to give the family hope despite the study's ending—by considering the adoption request (line 10) and talking it over with my husband (line 13). Marta's lowered tone conveyed the seriousness of her request, and I honored that by affirming that I would consider their request in a similar tone of voice (line 14). As we continued talking, Carlos attempted to lighten the mood and tenor of our conversation.

Sequence B:

15 Carlos: *NO* [*NO=*

16 Marta: [*NO es una obligación pero es* [*como una plática*
                        No it's not an obligation but it's like a conversation

17 Carlos: [*=fue todo muy pesa:::do y*
                                                       it was all too serious and

18   *obligato:::rio*
                     obligatory

19 Marta: *>No no no no no no no no< no*

20 Ariana: *Yo no.* [*Yo entiendo°. Yo entiendo°.*
                  I don't. I understand. I understand.

21 Marta: [*Yo no me refiero a que- yo quiero hacerlo contigo. Con otras personas* (.)
                           I don't mean that   I want to do it with you. With other people.

22   *QUIEN ACEpte↑=*
                     Whoever accepts.

23 Ariana: Mm-hmm

24 Marta: *=que DIGA↑. Está bien empecemos ese procedimiento* [*legal*
                    who says That's fine let's start the legal process

25 Carlos: [*Para nosotros era más*
                                                                      For us it was more

26   *justo que fuera ustedes*
                     fair that it be you (pl.)

27 Ariana: [*Gracias=*
                  Thank you

28 Marta: [*Sí*

Yes

29 Ariana: [=*es un honor que me lo pregunten. Sí:::: yo hablo con é::::l y to::::-do*

it's an honor that you ask me.   Yes I'll speak to him and everything

30 Carlos: *Sí. Si por casualidad diga su esposo. Uy es muy interesante. [O:::: O::::*

Yes. If by chance your husband says. Oh it's very interesting. Oh Oh

31   *Sería la bendición de Dios.*

It would be a blessing from God.

32 Ariana: Yah

33 Carlos: *Porqué? Porque. Usted? Ya lo empezó a conocer? conocer a los niños? o al niño?*

Why? Because. You? You've begun to know him. know the children. or the child?

34   *Y este-simplemente sería un gran favor. Un gran favor.*

And um it would simply be a huge favor. A huge favor.

As our exchange continued, we tried to reconcile the exigency of Marta and Carlos's request with my inability to respond definitively in the moment. Carlos attempted to change the tone of the conversation; while we all knew that the proposal was not to be taken lightly, he wanted to make it sound easily feasible (just like a big favor, line 34). Marta tried to follow Carlos's lead, but it was hard for her not to express a sense of urgency as she noted that she hoped to find *any*one who would be willing to adopt the children (line 22). Both Carlos and Marta modeled what they hoped that my husband or I would say: either that we would agree to initiate the adoption proceedings, or at the very least find the proposition interesting and be open to further conversation (lines 24 and 30).

The moment when Carlos explained why he hoped that I would agree to sign this version of *la carta* marks the culmination of our conversations about this document (line 26). From his perspective, it was precisely because of my role as ethnographer—participating in the family's everyday life and getting to know the children well—that made me an ideal candidate for becoming an adoptive parent. And yet for me, my identity as ethnographer was defined by my being in the field and was dependent on the fact that I could enter or exit it. This conceptualization of the field would be fundamentally changed by adopting José and Igor, and it was this potentially permanent connection that Marta and Carlos hoped to achieve through adoption. My attempts to express compassion and understanding (line 20) and to reframe the grave request as an honor (line 29) did not offer any resolution to the question of adoption. While I agreed to consider the possibility, I did not furnish either of the responses that Carlos and Marta hoped I would provide.

I felt confused and upset when I left the Utuado-Alvarez home that afternoon—on the one hand I felt that this request upset the delicate balance of intimacy and distance that the family and I had established throughout the course of the study, and on the other hand I believed that this was a legitimate request in could not be ignored. I was moved by the proposal, even though I knew that adopting José and Igor was a tremendous responsibility that I could not assume at the time, but I was troubled to find myself in many ways unprepared for the request. This led me to reflect on how comparatively little my formal education had prepared me to negotiate relationships and responsibilities beyond the traditional confines of the field. While I had engaged the family in a reciprocal exchange of participation and translation during the course of this study, exchanges that strengthened the ties upon which the ethnographic study depended, I expected the intensity of the exchanges to gradually decrease as I prepared to exit the field. I assumed that the detachment and neutrality that I knew was unobtainable (and undesirable) during fieldwork would become more available to me as I stepped out of the field and into the next stage of writing up the results of my study. It was as if I had suddenly confronted all of the dilemmas that constitute Pratt's arrival trope at the moment of exit.

I saw the Utuado-Alvarez family once more before I moved away from Millvalley when I met them at the weekly Spanish-language mass held in a local Catholic church frequented by many members of Millvalley's Latino community. After the mass, I talked with Marta and Carlos; we chatted about my move to New York City and about the family's summer plans. A few weeks before, I had called the central office of the Millvalley Public School District on Marta's behalf to find out if José would receive free transportation to and from the summer school classes that he had been asked to attend; Marta brought me up to speed, letting me know that she had received a letter confirming the school bus route and schedule. Marta began looking around for José and Igor to call them over to give me a hug, but before she could step away I reiterated how thankful I was for all their generosity throughout the last two years. I explained that I had thought more about *la carta* and that, while I was honored to have been considered for that role, I would not be able to make that legal commitment to the family.

I felt that it was impossible to adequately express the complex set of emotions and concerns that I had grappled with as I made my decision. As a result, I simply stated it and did not try to explain the fact that, in the midst of moving, my husband and I didn't feel prepared to take on the responsibility of adoption; that I couldn't reconcile forging this relationship with one focal family and not others (if they were to ask); that there were many other considerations I was wrestling with. Marta and Carlos didn't seem at all surprised in the moment. They wished me well in New York and reminded me to stay in touch. Marta ushered José and Igor over and I said good-bye to them, weaving my way through the congregation, stopping to talk with other families along the way, and then finally exiting the church and returning home. As I left, I felt disappointed—not about my decision, but about my inability to account for it in a way that I felt Marta and Carlos deserved—and I felt the acute insufficiency of just saying good-bye and walking away.

REFLECTING ON *LA CARTA*

While the conversation about *la carta* concluded when I said good-bye to the family that afternoon (I have talked and visited with them since July 2010, but neither they nor I have broached the subject again), the methodological issues raised by my conversations with the Utuado-Alvarez family remain unresolved. Discussions about *la carta* are significant because they call into question the terms of the relationships established by ethnographers and families while highlighting the possibilities and limitations of ethnographic research. Throughout the course of the study, the Utuado-Alvarez family and I had grown very close; they generously opened their homes and hearts to me, and I became both a participant and advocate during our everyday interactions. These exchanges led to the mutual understanding and care upon which humanizing ethnography depends. And yet, during conversations about *la carta*, I confronted the limits of what I was able to do as an individual and of my conceptual vocabulary for managing such issues around exit.

During these discussions, Marta and Carlos acknowledged the deep trust that we had developed throughout the course of the study as well as the emotional content that was inextricable from the particular social phenomena that I was documenting (in this case, talk about migratory status). By proposing that I agree to be named in *la carta*, the parents identified the kinds of social capital that they believed I could leverage to help improve the family's lived experience in the U.S.—privileges associated with my juridical status as a Puerto Rican woman, my class and marital status, and my role as an advocate for them in the educational and social landscape of Millvalley. Meanwhile, I struggled to find a responsible way to relate to the family that sincerely conveyed my solidarity with them while honestly and lovingly expressing my limitations in terms of signing *la carta*.

Looking across the three events that I have described in this essay, we can see that Marta and Carlos developed and discussed two versions of *la carta* that could serve as resourceful strategies to protect their family. By considering the possibilities of either drafting a document that would grant someone temporary custody of their children or initiating a legally binding adoption process that could preserve kinship bonds otherwise threatened by a state that classifies some members as legal U.S. citizens and others as illegal migrants, the family sought to manage the surveillance and threat of deportation that they faced on a daily basis. The version of *la carta* that Marta and Carlos presented me upon exiting was an inversion of the documents that I had asked them to sign upon my arrival—binding contracts approved by my university's Committee for the Protection of Human Subjects (CPHS). In the same way that I mitigated any liability associated with participation in the project at its outset, the parents' proposal was a way of legally foreclosing my typical exit from the field. The appearance and reappearance of *la carta* throughout the course of the fieldwork evinces the importance of this opportunity for the family. It is significant however, that even though *la carta* was referenced multiple times throughout the study, it was not until the very end of the study that they explicitly asked if I would agree to be named in the document.

My goal in recounting this complex of issues is not to offer any concise resolution, but rather to break the silence surrounding the moment of departure in the ethnographic process so that we can begin to raise the urgent questions it raises. Creating the conditions needed to talk about leaving the field is a necessary component of humanizing research because it entails "push[ing] against inequities not only through the findings of research but through the research act itself" (Paris, 2011, p. 140). Scholars working to humanize research have already begun to encourage us to critically rethink the research process and to reexamine particular phases of the ethnographic experience, including participant selection (Paris, 2011), inquiry, and bearing witness (Winn & Ubiles, 2010). Departure is an ethnographic moment that warrants close attention because it foregrounds many of the inequalities inherent in the research process. The most obvious inequities rendered visible in discussions about *la carta* involve the differences between U.S. citizens and noncitizens and the ability to be able to set the terms of engagement with the everyday issues faced by migrant families. If we began to have frank and difficult conversations about leaving the field, we would be better prepared to face these inequities while still present. We would also be able to discover which types of inequalities are generalizable to ethnographic work and which ones might be particular to certain sites (such as the focus on juridical citizenship in my own work).

Initiating this conversation first requires a frank discussion of why this aspect of the process tends to be passed over in silence. Are we afraid to concede failure? Recounting challenging encounters with participants during a study's closure or reporting negative exchanges during exit interviews or member checks would mean relinquishing some of the narrative control of the ethnographer— namely, the power to represent our research in a positive light, smoothing over the tensions that emerge between researcher and researched. Could it be that we are ashamed to account for the ways in which our actions, in or out of the field, contribute to the marginalization of the communities that we study or at least fail to improve the families' circumstances (even though we may hope to advocate for these communities during and after the research)? As Pratt recognized over four decades ago, humanizing research involves challenging the persistent dichotomy between the personal and scientific, or subjective and objective, modes of ethnographic research. Our continued silence around departure gives the researcher the last word in a way that preserves an aura of objectivity.

Calling into question the notion of exiting the field will encourage us to break down the artificial distance between the researcher and researched and force us to examine whether our existing methods honor the humanity that we share with our research participants, colleagues, and students. But what would it mean to bring departure to the forefront of our methodological conversations? What scholarly activities would need revision in order to incorporate these conversations into our research practice? One place to begin would be in the ethnographic training or the dissertation defense required of our graduate students. What if these milestone moments included an explicit discussion of departure? We could consider raising the question of feasibility—currently limited to recruiting participants and carrying out the research—in terms of exiting the field and closing the study. We might begin to conceive of "feasibility" not only in terms of access and implementation but also in relation to those possibilities our research holds for recognizing and strengthening the humanity of those we research as well as ourselves. Would we need to revise our CPHS or Institutional Review Board (IRB) processes for gaining institutional approval for our research? Currently this application focuses on documenting how we will gain admission to a field site, while closing a study entails filling out a one-page form. Working to institutionalize our scholarly concerns about the ethics of departure could lead to more preparation and deliberation in this area. The responsibilities of *la carta* were too much for me to accept as an individual, but that doesn't mean it is obvious that humanizing research shouldn't involve some creative problem solving alongside our participants. For example, what if a multifamily study run through an institution or group of researchers involved a coordinated effort to offer services to mixed-status communities in the event of deportation for a period during or following the study? Debating the merits of—and strategies for—such arrangements would require talking about departure (or complicating the very concept of departure) in advance of and during the course of the ethnographic process.

Another site for investigation could be the publishing process. What if peer viewers routinely raised the question of how the author negotiated the complexity of exit? In conference presentations and peer reviews of my writing, I am often asked to account for how I gained access into a mixed-status community and what measures I take to protect the anonymity of the undocumented family members. These questions are important ones; they are also an indication of ethnographers' continued focus on entry narratives and the particular emphasis placed on anonymity when field sites are geographically proximal and potentially recognizable. As of yet, no one has asked me to consider the politics of maintaining or breaking relations with families with whom I've been involved. No one except for, as we have seen, the families themselves.

Humanizing research requires not relying on outmoded conventions in order to dodge difficult questions. As claims of objectivity and the very nature of the "field" continue to come under scrutiny, we have nevertheless organized ethnographies around tropes of arrival without attending to the complexities of departure.

I was surprised by my own lack of preparedness when a family confronted me with the question of my responsibilities after the formal conclusion of my field-work. I still don't feel I was in a position to sign *la carta*, but I should have at least been in a position to account for my decision in terms that were neither merely personal—implying that the question had no bearing on my research—nor reliant on the traditional defense of scholarly distance. Reorienting research to bring the notion of departure within the domain of scholarly discussion is an important step toward acknowledging that families can and do make claims on researchers that extend beyond fieldwork and demand serious consideration. Perhaps integrating the problem of departure into our scholarship and teaching will involve a confrontation with how "the field" itself is an increasingly shaky construct when a researcher's tax dollars support a militarized border (Massey, 2005) and the researcher's produce is often picked by migrant child laborers (Patel, Hill, Eslocker, & Ross, 2009).

REFLECTIVE QUESTIONS

1. Do you agree that the process of "exiting the field" has been underexamined in educational anthropology? If so, why? If not, how have you as a researcher been trained to negotiate your departure from a research site?

2. What scholarly and pedagogical activities—in addition to those mentioned in the conclusion of the chapter—would need to be changed in order to bring questions of departure into our research practice?

3. How have you articulated the scope and significance of your project to participants, and how have their responses shaped your research? At what moments in the research process have participants expressed their goals and expectations for your relationship?

4. Is the traditional metaphor of the "field"—a site that one can enter and exit—applicable to contemporary research in current conditions of globalization? How can we adapt longstanding anthropological concerns regarding ethics and reciprocity to such conditions?

NOTES

1. Pseudonyms have been assigned to all of the locations, institutions, and people in and around Millvalley.

2. In their 1996 book, *Immigrant America: A Portrait*, Portes and Rumbaut distinguished between *migrants* who crossed the border into the U.S. by land and *immigrants* who entered the U.S. with legal documentation by land, air, or water. The term *migrant* also refers to the temporal and spatial relationships of the individual(s) to the host country—migrants include those with residential impermanence and active cultural frames of reference that cross national borders, while *immigrant* describes those who have permanently

relocated and have begun a process of cultural assimilation (Arzubiaga, Noguerón, & Sullivan, 2009; Lukose, 2007). The Mexican-born family members in this study entered the U.S. without legal permission by crossing the Mexico-U.S. border by land, maintained active relationships with family in both Mexico and the U.S., and had family members or friends who returned to Mexico throughout the course of this study; therefore, I refer to them as migrants or undocumented migrants.

3. This template is an excerpt from a training manual titled *Family Safety Planning* and published by the Washington, DC–based Catholic Legal Immigration Network, Inc. (CLINIC). The manual was used by some of Millvalley's church leaders and community organizers as they worked to educate migrant families on their rights and helped them to plan for an unforeseen detention or deportation. This resource can be found online (http://cliniclegal.org/resources/family-safety-planning-training-manual).

4. The November 2011 report, titled *Shattered Families* and published by the Applied Research Center (Freed Wessler, 2011), examines the connections between policies of immigration enforcement and the placement of children in foster care. The report estimates that approximately 5,100 children of migrants have been placed in the U.S. foster care system upon the deportation of their parents; the number is expected to rise dramatically in the next five years (p. 6).

5. I adhered to the following transcription conventions. It is important to note that "the punctuation marks are *not* used grammatically, but to indicate intonation" (Schegloff, 2007, p. 267).

(.)	"micropause"	CAPS	especially loud talk
.	falling, or final intonation contour	O	talk following was quiet or soft
?	rising intonation	↑↓	sharper intonation rises or falls
::	prolongation of the preceding sound	(( ))	transcriber's description of events
_	stress or emphasis	-	cut off prior word or sound
[	a point of overlap onset	]	the end of a point of overlap

REFERENCES

Arzubiaga, A., Noguerón, S. & Sullivan, A. (2008). The education of children in im/migrant families. *Review of Research in Education, 33*(1), 246–271.

Bhimji, F. (2005). Language socialization with directives in two Mexican immigrant families in South Central Los Angeles. In A. C. Zentella (Ed.), *Building on strength: Language and literacy in Latino families and communities* (pp. 60–76). New York, NY: Teachers College Press.

Bloemraad, I., Korteweg, A., & Yurdakal, G. (2008). Citizenship and immigration: Multiculturalism, assimilation, and challenges to the nation-state. *Annual Review of Sociology, 34* (8), 1–27.

Duranti, A. (1997). Ethnographic methods. In *Linguistic anthropology: A reader* (pp. 84–121). Cambridge, UK: Cambridge University Press.

Eisenhart, M., & Towne, L. (2003). Contestation and change in national policy on "scientifically based" educational research. *Educational Researcher, 32*(7), 31–38.

Fix, M., & Zimmerman, W. (2001). All under one roof: Mixed-status families in an era of reform. *International Migration Review, (35)*2, 397–419.

Freed Wessler, S. (2011, November). *Shattered families: The perilous intersection of immigration enforcement and the child welfare system.* New York, NY: Applied Research Center.

Gonzales, R. G. (2008). Left out but not shut down: Political activism and the undocumented student movement. *Northwestern Journal of Law and Social Policy, 3,* 219–239.

Gupta, A., & Ferguson, J. (Eds.). (1997). *Anthropological locations: Boundaries and grounds of a field science.* Berkeley: University of California Press.

LeCompte, M. D. (1999). Researcher roles. In M. D. LeCompte, J. J. Schensul, M. R. Weeks, & M. Singer (Volume Ed.), *Ethnographer's toolkit: Vol. 6. Researcher roles and research partnerships* (pp. 2–72). Lanham, MD: Altamira Press.

LeCompte, M. D. (2008). Negotiating exit. In L. Given (Series Ed.), *Sage encyclopedia of qualitative research: Vol. 2* (pp. 552–555). Thousand Oaks, CA: SAGE.

Lukose, K. (2007). The difference that diaspora makes: Thinking through the anthropology of immigrant education in the United States. *Anthropology & Education Quarterly, 38*(4), 405–418.

Mangual Figueroa, A. (2011). Citizenship and education in the homework completion routine. *Anthropology & Education Quarterly, 42*(3), 263–280.

Massey, D. S. (2005, June). *Backfire at the border: Why enforcement without legalization cannot stop illegal immigration.* Washington, DC: Center for Trade Policy Studies.

O'Neil, D. (2008). *KINSHIP: An introduction to descent systems and family organization.* Retrieved December 12, 2011, from http://anthro.palomar.edu/kinship/default.htm

Paris, D. (2011). "A friend who understand fully": Notes on humanizing research in a multiethnic youth community. *International Journal of Qualitative Studies in Education, 24*(2), 137–149.

Passel, J. S., & Cohn, D. (2009, April). *A portrait of unauthorized immigrants in the United States.* Washington DC: Pew Hispanic Center.

Patel, A., Hill, A., Eslocker, A., & Ross, B. (2009, October 30). *ABC News investigation: The blueberry children.* Retrieved September 8, 2011, from http://abcnews.go.com/Blotter/young-children-working-blueberry-fields-walmart-severs-ties/story?id=8951044

Portes, A., & Rumbaut, R. (1996). *Immigrant America: A Portrait.* Berkeley: University of California Press.

Pratt, M. L. (1986). Fieldwork in common places. In J. Clifford & G. M. Marcus (Eds.), *Writing culture: The poetics and politics of ethnography* (pp. 27–50). Berkeley: University of California Press.

Schegloff, E. A. (2007). *Sequence organization in interaction: A primer in conversation analysis* (Vol. 1). Cambridge, UK: Cambridge University Press.

Winn, M. T., & Ubiles, J. R. (2010). Worthy witnessing: Collaborative research in urban classrooms. *Studying diversity in teacher education* (pp. 295–308). Lanham, MD: Rowman & Littlefield.

Wortham, S., Murillo, E.G., & Hamann, E. (Eds.). (2002). *Education in the new Latino diaspora: Policy and the politics of identity.* Westport, CT: Ablex.

Doing Double Dutch Methodology

8

Playing With the Practice of Participant Observer

Keisha Green

The good jumpers perform improvised acrobatic feats or complicated body movements as a way of stylizing and individualizing the performance.

—Robin D. G. Kelley (1997)

I n one of my favorite passages about Black popular culture in the United States, Kelley (1997) writes about the unique art of an old childhood game, double dutch, or the intricate sport of jumping between two ropes. Imagine two rope turners standing some distance apart, one facing the other, and twirling two ropes, one per hand, in opposite directions. Skipping in between the ropes is a third participant, the jumper, typically accompanied by music or rhymes chanted by the participants and spectators. Double dutch is frequently portrayed as a street game played among Black girls in urban areas, though Kelley (1997) and Gaunt (2006) write about the institutionalization and, consequently, mainstreaming of double dutch through formalized competitions and championship tournaments. Such a transition, according to Kelley, resulted in "the improvisational character of the game [becoming] sharply circumscribed" (p. 56). Before such restrictions, my earliest memories of playing double dutch involved hot summer days as an adolescent in South Carolina, surrounded by my girl cousins and some rope (or telephone wire if rope was not available). Chanting rhymes like "Teddy bear, teddy bear, turn around. Teddy bear, teddy bear, touch the ground," we rocked back and forth to time our jump into the spinning ropes. We practiced jumping two at a time, sometimes while holding frozen "red"-flavored Kool-Aid in Styrofoam cups. I can recall many times getting entangled in the ropes around my ankles or feeling the sting of a rope slapping my cheek. Once entangled, I would be eliminated, but, as Gaunt (2006) writes, my participation continued as I, from the sidelines, added my own footwork and voice to the musicality of the next double dutch set. Each summer, I got better and less afraid of making mistakes and more confident in expressing my own "black and female" style of jumping (Gaunt, 2006).

Although, in the above epigraph, Kelley is referencing the game of double dutch, his words could as well describe the kind of richness and nuance in skill and technique necessary when navigating qualitative educational research involving urban youth from historically marginalized communities. Though seemingly unrelated, the qualitative research method of participant observation is like playing double dutch. It is inherently complicated and dynamic as the participant observer seeks to at once participate as a "member" of a group and critically observe the ways in which the participants perceive, make meaning of, and reproduce the interactions that define the group over time. Such a performance is, as Kelley notes about the sport, an acrobatic feat that is highly stylized and individualized. The good jumpers (read "researchers") will be skillful and agile enough to improvise and acquire an awareness of rhythm, knowing when and how to enter (Green, 2011; Kelley, 1997; Winn, 2011).

This essay is a reflection of my shifting orientation as an ethnographer during a case study of a youth radio collective in the urban Southeast. In the context of this study, youth enacted critical literacies to produce a radio program focused on important issues in the lives of young people and their communities. I compare my research experience to the sport of double dutch as an attempt to make sense of my fluid roles during the research process. Resisting traditional notions of scientific objectivity, this essay is a meditation on the process and the emergence of a concept that helped me make sense of my research design, questions, methodology, positionality, data collection, and analysis; thereby humanizing the research process. Buying snacks, facilitating workshops, driving a carpool, proofing homework assignments, celebrating "sweet 16" birthday parties, writing letters of recommendation, and attending high school graduations were not moments that I imagined experiencing when designing my first qualitative research project. Now, however, I am convinced that such moments, during which I had to navigate the nuances of my orientation to the research context and work to understand the relevance of such day-to-day activities, are integral to my (re)considerations of what it means to be a participant observer. A Double Dutch Methodology (re)frames these blurred lines of participant observation.

The purpose of this essay is to describe the fortuitous and, ultimately, instructive tensions experienced during the learning-edge moments at which I developed a critical awareness of my need to interrogate what it means to be a participant observer and to be more nuanced in my thinking about the methodological and analytical possibilities that could result from reflecting on the implications of each of my salient identities and roles in the research context. To illustrate such moments, I use examples excerpted from my empirical study field notes taken during the first year of a multiyear ethnographic case study of Youth Voices, a youth radio collective situated in the urban Southeast and comprising Black high school–aged youth. My fieldwork included visits to the weekly Youth Voices meetings, which were held in the office space of a community-based organization and the production studio of a community-based radio station. Both spaces served nondominant communities. The examples from my participant observation field notes taken early in the research study serve as catalytic junctures in my quest for a more authentic method of understanding and documenting the teaching and learning process within marginalized communities.

TOWARD A DOUBLE DUTCH METHODOLOGY

I offer Double Dutch Methodology (DDM) as an alternative way of thinking about qualitative research and as a set of methodological strategies. This essay is my attempt at providing a useful way to think about and practice being a researcher. Essentially, I hope to provide a piece that I would have appreciated reading when I was just starting to conduct ethnographic research with youth of color in an urban context. To that end, I begin by sharing the components of the metaphorical Double Dutch Methodology. The first part of DDM involves "learning the ropes" (Gaunt, 2006, p. 37), or critically exploring researcher positionality. For example, what are the intersecting identities that researchers bring to the research context? And, what are the multiple roles and shifting orientation that a researcher may experience during the research process? The second component of DDM includes "plant[ing] both feet" (Gaunt, 2006, p. 174), or considering the main theoretical standpoints on which DDM or a humanizing qualitative research approach is based. Specifically, what theoretical lens(es), conceptual framework(s), or set of principles informs DDM as a new way of thinking about and doing research? Finally, the third component of DDM entails "keeping time and rhythm," or engaging in participant observation that is complicated, contextually stylized, and improvisational. In particular, during fieldwork, how and when do qualitative researchers, utilizing the method of participant observation, engage as "a participant observer at times, an observer at other times, and a participant at still other times" (Paris, 2011, p. 8)? Moreover, a Double Dutch Methodology is concerned with privileging the everyday interactions, voices, and experiences of the participants. This kind of approach to research invites reflexivity, relevance, and reciprocity, which is transferable to researchers in other disciplines, in particular scholars of color who are struggling with the notion of needing to be "distant" and "neutral" observers in spaces or research contexts that include participants from oppressed or marginalized communities.

Learning the Ropes Before Playing the Field: Exploring My Researcher Positionality

The first component of Double Dutch Methodology involves "learning the ropes" (Gaunt, 2006, p. 37) before playing in the field(work). How much, if any, should my multiple and intersecting identities influence my research trajectory? Should I write myself in or out of the research context? Such questions and other related inquiries are at the center of my exploration of the ways in which *who I am* affects how I might "play" in the field of qualitative research. In other words, as a doctoral student learning the ropes, or learning how to conduct qualitative research, I began to understand that one of the first steps in conceptualizing a research project is the critically important and relevant process of exploring researcher positionality.

Just on the heels of IRB approval, not yet tempered by the wisdom of experience, I sat perched at the edge of my seat intently observing the transactions among a group of southern Black youth and their animated adult facilitator as they prepared to broadcast a 30-minute live public radio program. Pen to paper, scribbling furiously, with the vigor of a novice, I attempted to capture, in great detail, the dialogue, gestures, and activities of this group huddled around a conference table inside the community-based radio station's humble facility. I was, finally, "officially collecting data." Unwittingly and, perhaps, subconsciously, I embodied my new role as an IRB-approved researcher with temporary amnesia of my own personal history and professional experiences as a volunteer in the youth collective space for approximately one year prior to my newest identity. On this rare occasion, I did not participate in the preproduction activities, hold the youngest daughter of one of the founders, co-facilitate the meeting, or offer feedback on a script written by one of the youth. Instead, I sat on the periphery, writing field notes or "collecting data" amid scattered handouts, printed news articles, and assorted snacks.

Soon I noticed the stare of a curious youth participant, Kwame, a Black 16-year-old young man, who leaned over and inquired matter-of-factly, "Are you studying us?" Turning to this young person with a head full of thick locks, I stumbled through a response to the tune of, "Uh, no. I mean yes. Sort of . . . ," despite having engaged in countless informal conversations about his and my life, including his interest in scuba diving, which I found to be surprising given the circumstance of his surroundings. Unusually tongue-tied, I was stunned by my own sudden and uncharacteristic discomfort and managed to conclude my response by mumbling something about my reasons for taking notes, but not without a couple of awkward silences. Unknowingly, Kwame had triggered the core of my insecurities. Although I would later learn that his question came from a genuine desire to simply know what I was doing, his inquiry instructively highlighted the influence of positivist notions of qualitative inquiry that suggest one should adopt a neutral researcher stance, which resulted in my internalizing and placing, albeit briefly, reductive constraints on my role(s) as researcher. Shortly after this pivotal exchange, I began to consider and interrogate assumptions about the appropriate loci of the researcher in the research site, and to question the relationship between such role(s) and research design and analysis.

For example, my dissertation research topic, on which this essay is based, is largely a reflection of an amalgamation of my educational research interests, life experiences, multiple and intersecting identities, personal politics, philosophy of education, and worldview. I pursued doctoral studies in education to engage theory, and to understand more fully the dialectical relationship among such topics as literacy, race, culture, history, and democracy; yet as a Black woman with deep roots in the South and experience working in grassroots organizations and activist circles, I was somewhat conflicted about the notion of being part of a system that has historically (and, some might argue, routinely) marginalized and exploited the communities of which I am a part. However, our practice, and, consequently, my own, was informed by nonwestern or Black nationalist theories that were the driving forces behind critical social movements, including the Zapatista movement in Mexico, the Black power/arts movement in the United States, the Black feminist movement across the globe, and the literacy movement in Brazil. Naturally, as a novice educational researcher, I was concerned about issues related to utilizing a conventional or mechanized approach to ethnography to represent research participants who have often been misrepresented.

Furthermore, my experiences as an activist, teaching artist in community-based organizations, and as a youth development worker in out-of-school spaces, predisposed me to community-based education programs that incorporated popular education tools designed to politicize youth of color. Similarly, my own identity formation, worldview, and philosophy of education were connected to participating in community-based and/or typical middle class African American organizations that were often constitutive of people of color (e.g., the African American Baptist church, the National Association for the Advancement of Colored People, the Urban League, and an all–African American Girl Scout troop). Additionally, my experiences in secondary school were devoid of opportunities to engage the literature, language, and culture specific to my history, yet plentiful of the ways in which schools are largely propagandist apparatuses for mainstream values and dominant discourse practices without critique or agitation. As a result, I was drawn to working with students of color who were engaged in critical literacy learning by participating in activities that were affirming of their communities' histories, relevant to their interests and lives, and immediately useful in improving the social, political, and economic conditions of their communities.

Extending my life and public school experiences is a triangular traverse from points in the Southeast to the Northeast and back again to the Southeast for my doctoral studies and dissertation research. In particular, my Northeast detour introduced me to a national grassroots organization called Blackout Arts Collection (BAC), which is, now, more of an international network of educators, activists, and artists committed to empowering communities of color through the arts, education, and activism. My involvement with BAC was pivotal in shaping my fundamental beliefs about education and research. Additionally, BAC politicized my understanding of critical issues and concepts related to arts and education, popular education, youth-led community activism, and education and incarceration. Through BAC, I had opportunities to complicate dominant narratives of Black student disengagement and underachievement during spoken word poetry, theater, and hip-hop workshops where youth demonstrated their intellectual curiosity and capacity. Further, I had opportunities to work with incarcerated and formerly incarcerated youth and adults, as well as children of incarcerated parents (Green, 2010). Such experiences solidified my desire to be the kind of educational researcher who unapologetically resists temptations to adopt a deficit discourse to frame teaching and learning among communities of color, particularly in Black communities.

Therefore, exploring my researcher positionality shapes how I engage in participant observation. As a child playing double dutch, I used to wait with anticipation to jump in at just the right time to catch the opening in the space between the ropes' rotation. As the two ropes swung, they would blur and become one, and moments later, two again. My memories of double dutch parallel the ways in which I approached my multiple roles in the research context of Youth Voices as observer, documentarian, co-facilitator, mentor, and researcher. Like the turning ropes, my roles are often fluid, with unnoticeable boundaries, and yet at a moment's notice the same roles may be distinctly pronounced, with one role taking precedent over another, perhaps sparked by an opportunity to note a significant occurrence or a need to step up as a workshop facilitator. Now, after intentional exploration, I understand, with greater clarity and certainty, that my layered researcher positionality is shaped by all of my previous life experiences, including alignment with critical social theories that privilege nondominant ways of knowing, and is also the reason why I considered and eventually accepted multiple roles within the research context.

However, during the early stages of my research project, grappling with my researcher identity, I naively vacillated between extremes—that of a community member and volunteer who just happened to be a budding educational researcher at a well-known institution, and that of a clinical observer who just happened to be Black, southern, and interested in young people of color and the ways in which they engage media as a tool for social justice. Such a bifurcated, dichotomous, and one-dimensional way of negotiating the politics of positionality would later prove absurd and unproductive. However, before arriving at such a point of reclamation, I was tentative at best and hypersensitive at worst about my Black research participants' potential perceptions of me as a researcher.

During the exploration phase of my qualitative study, I sat in the office of my academic advisor attempting to describe my participant observations and fieldwork experiences in my research study context up until that point. I explained that I had found myself developing friendships with my research participants, buying snacks, driving youth to their various homes around town, and writing workshop material. I wondered aloud if, in my first foray into ethnography, I had crossed boundaries. Subsequently, I worried that I had already compromised the scientific rigor of my study because of a lack of "neutrality" and "distance." And regarding my own personal limitations, I cautiously considered if I had overcommitted myself, my time, my resources beyond what I could reasonably sustain as a busy doctoral student and novice educational researcher. Yet, how could I, with previous experience as a teacher, as a nonprofit volunteer, with access to private resources, not agree to review homework, drive a youth participant home, or provide university space for workshops? Finally, I blurted out that I felt like I was playing a game of double dutch! Here I was jumping between the lines of traditional educational research methodologies and my own need for a more authentic research approach.

Among the benefits of engaging in this kind of praxis of self-reflexivity, particularly for scholars conducting research in nondominant communities, is the opportunity to critique and disrupt Western research paradigms to create new or, rather, reclaim indigenous pathways to reaching emancipatory educational research goals. While out-of-school literacy scholars do not use the term "double dutch," there are still shared experiences related to conducting research among students of color in urban contexts (Camangian, 2011; Kinloch, 2009; Morrell, 2004, 2007; Paris, 2011; Tucker-Raymond, Rosario-Ramos, & Rosario, 2011; Winn, 2011). Simply put, my presence, attitudes, beliefs, behaviors, and relationship to others in the context of a research study matter. Therefore, how and to what degree does my own positionality shape the research design, planning, data collection, analysis, and distribution of results? What are the advantages and disadvantages of acknowledging researcher positionality? These are a few of the key questions I considered as I reflected on my orientation to the research topic and context.

"Plant Both Feet Before You Start to Alternate [Them]": Theoretical Playing Ground

The second component of Double Dutch Methodology (Gaunt, 2006, p. 174) involves taking time to consider which theoretical constructs are connected to your researcher positionality and, in turn, frame your research questions, design, analysis, and results. In *The Games Black Girls Play*, Gaunt (2006) devotes considerable time in her chapter "Dancing With the Double Dutch Divas" to describing the rhythmical skills of a few dynamic middle-aged Black sisters who had taken up the childhood game in their adult years. After being invited to join the women, Gaunt recalls being reminded by one of the more seasoned players to be sure to jump into the ropes and plant both of her feet before alternating them and advancing to more intricate movements. According to feminist and cultural critic bell hooks, "everything we do in life is rooted in theory" (hooks, 2000, p. 19). Identifying theory may also be an inductive process. In other words, theory may frame the research design, as well as emerge during the process of data collection or analysis. The roots of my methodological stance are planted in several overlapping critical theories, postpositivist constructs, and postmodern principles, which serve to inform my practice. Specifically, my conceptualization of a Double Dutch Methodology is deeply influenced by theories located in the social sciences and humanities, including sociocultural theories of learning, asset-based community development theory, participatory theories, and other critical theories that examine the centrality of race, culture, and gender. Such theories are concerned with emancipatory research conducted ethically and collaboratively with communities in a context where knowledge is made together and used to create change (Cushman, 1998).

For example, most (if not all) doctoral programs in education currently feature a course or, at least, readings related to sociocultural theory. Within the field of education, broadly construed, a sociocultural theory of learning, literacy, and language acquisition and development is built on the notion that all learning is a social process and situated in a particular sociocultural, political, and historical context. We learn in relationship to others. Vygotsky is perhaps one of the most well known theorists to contend that learning is embedded within social events, through participating in activities with other people, objects, texts, and events requiring cognitive and communicative functions. Using the lens of sociocultural theory was a natural framework for understanding the culture of Youth Voices. In particular, the notion that knowledge and skills are to be developed and shared in community was central to the pedagogical strategies of the program facilitators and curricular content central to the weekly workshops and meetings with the youth. One research participant, Niqua, described a typical planning day:

> We get together with the plans [for the upcoming radio broadcast] and once you get that plan then we take action basically. But it's all a process and it's a whole team work[ing] together to get to this process that you trying to get to. And as long as we work together and if anyone else wants to join then that's an even better process . . . 'cause two brains [are] better than one brain. So if anybody . . . [does] what we do and put input in what we doing we get a lot accomplished as far as the show . . . like planning for the show and community action also.

In community, the youth participants learned together. Older youth members of Youth Voices became the youth leaders in the organization, socializing newer (and sometimes younger) members. The adult allies demonstrated Freire's notion of teachers becoming students. Youth were experts in their lived experiences and brought particular knowledge and skills to the Youth Voices context.

As a researcher, such theory and practice informed my own approach to conducting research. Specifically, rather than operating under the assumption that the research process would be a unidirectional transaction or a mechanized experience in which I/the emerging academic was the sole proprietor of best practices regarding educational research theories, literature, and methodology, I welcomed the opportunity to be taught by the research participants—who, after all, had been operating for years under the tutelage of Black radical intellectual and activist history. The Youth Voices context, however, challenged me to interrogate dominant educational research theories and methodologies and validated my inclination to adopt research methods that were community based. As mentioned, my experiences prior to conducting my dissertation research predisposed me to theories beyond the disciplinary boundaries of the field of education. A theory or set of principles that informed my construction of a Double Dutch Methodology stemmed from asset-based community development. Whereas current education research typically pathologizes, patronizes, marginalizes, or essentializes Black communities, parents, youth, and the working-class poor—often deemed uninformed or ill-qualified consultants on the critical issues concerning education policy for the nation—asset-based community development principles prescribe starting with what communities are already doing well.

For example, in my work in and around education and incarceration, communities of color are already engaged in restorative justice and are figuring out ways to help formerly incarcerated individuals reenter society with adequate support structures. Asset-based community theory means starting with and building on the assets already present. Using a sociocultural lens, the Youth Voices research context was replete with evidence that the organization was operating under the assumptions associated with asset-based community development.

To that end, I find it helpful to draw from theories that are asset based rather than reductive. Far too many educational research projects and results are shaped by deficit theory framing Black, Brown, and poor youth as underachieving, underserved, and in need of being saved from themselves. Asset-based theory means focusing on what already exists, what is already happening in the context, builds on what already exists, acknowledges what *is* present. In the research context, the Youth Voices program was getting some things "right" regarding teaching and learning. For example, in the context of Youth Voices, Black youth are engaged and are attending after-school meetings on a voluntary basis. These Black youth, some of whom carry the "troublemaker" or "unmotivated" label in school, are creating projects, working together, and facilitating workshops. For Niqua, the respect afforded the youth explains their active participation:

> Well you can just express yourself . . . not just verbally or physically or however just by knowing and thinking . . . you see somebody who respect you and you respect them. It's all about respect. The way I look at the world . . . a lot of people don't have respect. But when I came here, I seen that most people had respect. I gained more respect. You can tell when somebody don't respect you.

Such community building principles build stronger communities by focusing on their strengths instead of their deficiencies. My goal as a qualitative researcher, then, became trying to understand how this particular community defined themselves; made sense of broad social issues, including power, oppression, and privilege; and addressed access and denial to quality education.

Additional theoretical influences are linked to ongoing readings of postcolonial, critical race, Black feminist, participatory, and activist research theories. A common thread among these theories is a privileging of community-based or indigenous knowledge. As historian of American education, Dr. Vanessa Siddle-Walker, reflects, "The community has a knowledge base that the academy has ignored" (personal communication, October 2009). For example, during my research data collection phase, I accompanied the research participants on a journey to Detroit for the second United States Social Forum. The bus trip included being "schooled" by Nathan, a public intellectual and community organizer with the Youth Voices community. Stepping into the role of teacher, Nathan helped us understand a theory of the African episteme that allows for polyculturalism. He explained his theory of an ecology of knowledge that recognizes the coexistence of other knowledges and ways of being. Thus, on the bus ride to the social forum, Youth Voices participants learned about their role as citizens. Not your typical school field trip; it was, according to an adult ally, "education on wheels." In total, these theoretical constructs helped me make sense of my practice prior to the dissertation research project and my intuitive tendencies during the dissertation research process.

Taken together, each of the theoretical frameworks and experiences serves to "ground" the work. Yet the work is located in a context; therefore, my feet land within a "game" already in motion. I need to understand how and where I stand before *and* while playing. In the context of Youth Voices, as according to Lumumba, one of the adult allies, "working-class and oppressed communities do not have the time or inclination to argue meaningless points." Instead "the goal is to think deeply about pressing issues of the day." Research, then, is a collaborative process to be engaged in by both the researcher and participants; it is emancipatory, or, in other words, used to liberate people and communities, rather than further oppress, marginalize, essentialize, or exploit. In essence, my role as a researcher and the results of my research should forward the goals of the community in which I have been invited to be a part.

Keeping Time and Rhythm: Playing With Participant Observation

> *. . . the jumper, before she / enters the winking, nods in time / as if she has a notion to share, waiting her chance to speak. But she's / anticipating the upbeat / like a bandleader counting off the tune they are about to swing into.*

> —Gregory Pardlo (2001)

The third component of a Double Dutch Methodology entails "keeping time and rhythm," or learning how to negotiate and navigate the act of participant observation. Playing the game of Double Dutch involves "anticipating the upbeat," or knowing when and how to enter the twirling ropes. Sometimes keeping time and rhythm means observing the interactions of others and allowing them to do "their thing" without interruption. From the sidelines, I may play a different, yet important role. For example, my position as a researcher may, at times, keep me at the sidelines or keep me from being at the center of activity. During such moments, I am engaged in "legitimate peripheral participation" (see Lave & Wenger, 1991; Rogoff, 1994)—learning by observing and doing. Furthermore, from the sidelines, as with the game of double dutch, I learn how to utilize my voice: chanting and singing rhymes. According to Walford (2001),

> fieldwork roles in ethnography are not fixed, but gradually change and develop as a result of negotiations between the researcher and those who are the subjects of the

research. The researcher does not simply choose an appropriate role and adhere to it throughout the project; nor is it possible to think in terms of a single role, no matter how dynamic, for a variety of roles must be adopted which will vary with the different individuals with whom the researcher interacts. (p. 62)

As Walford accurately describes, qualitative research is a dynamic process. As a participant observer, I am "jumping" into the phenomenon of something existing, an ongoing slice of reality. The double dutch game is that reality box, the phenomenon that I have decided to put myself in the middle of, and all of a sudden I realize I cannot just stand outside the action.[1] Instead, I am part of the action and have to decide when and how to jump into what at times is a frenzy of activity. Attempting to take notes and stay connected to the participants while "being a researcher" is a moment of real complexity. If qualitative research is reenvisioned as trying to step inside other people's reality boxes in order to understand. or theorize their socially constructed practices, then the process can be intimate, messy, and, at times, unpredictable. Adding to the complexity of keeping time and rhythm is the nuance of my identity as a volunteer prior to assuming and reintroducing myself in a new role as an educational researcher.

According to Paris (2011), writing about the nature of authentic participant observation, "genuine relationships and moments of inspiration are fostered in authentic participation in activities that matter to the participants" (p. 9). Keeping time and rhythm, as a qualitative researcher, means becoming attuned to the tempo and patterns of the research context and participants and implies a willingness to adapt and be flexible, as reality does not adhere to a strict research protocol. In these instances, activist scholars make room for "reciprocal relations" with individuals in the research context (Cushman, 1998), particularly in a community-based organizacontext where resources are usually stretched thin. Providing car rides, helping with homework, and offering meeting space are just a few of the opporavailable for researchers to cultivate trust and enhance the capacity of the research context. In addition to establishing mutual participant-researcher relationships, qualitative researchers have access to tools to aid in the ability to juggle multiple roles and collect rich data. For example, audio recording devices and digital recording programs like GarageBand, as well as camcorders or smaller flip video cameras are useful for capturing communicative activities, workshops, or group talk. Also, to account for the multi-sited and improvisational nature of qualitative research, storing journals and writing utensils in several locations, including your car or personal tote bag, is recommended, as is developing a habit of systematically labeling field notes to document dates, times, and locations. Finally, maintaining a researcher journal to memo (or diagram) reflections, questions, and evolving interpretations of participant perspectives and practices can serve the purpose of producing more robust description of the research context and analyses of research data.

DISMOUNTS AND CONCLUSIONS

As a metaphorical methodological approach, Double Dutch Methodology (DDM) is an alternative way to think about and do qualitative research, specifically participant observation. DDM includes three major components: exploring researcher positionality, establishing theoretical standpoints, and developing an ability to engage in a contextually stylized and improvisational method of participant observation. As I described earlier, the metaphor is not intended to be a literal translation of the research experience, but rather a useful way of conceptualizing the practice of being an educational researcher among youth of color in urban contexts. Essentially, DDM allows space for flexibility, authenticity, and a process for reflexivity. Moving forward, I contend that a Double Dutch Methodology contributes to what we know about the dynamic multidimensional nature of participant observation and problematizes the appropriate loci of the researcher in the research site.

As an emerging literacy scholar, I want to be a socially responsible researcher committed to documenting what Black and Brown children do well across educational contexts to counter the disproportionate abundance of research that overemphasizes the achievement gaps, deficiencies, and lack of student engagement among youth of color. And, as Cushman (1998) posits, "rather than trying to write myself out of the unavoidable hierarchy of discourse in any ethnography," I recognize that I am a part of the story (pp. 21–22). In other words, I am consciously aware of being, as Winn (2011) writes, "between and betwixt" the shifting researcher orientation and the complexity of the research context.

In summary, a Double Dutch Methodology calls into question the usefulness of positivist notions that suggest research is about "what is clear, factual, and open to observation" (Pring, 2004, p. 90). Such a stance renders "meaningless the distinctive ways in which we talk about persons or reduces them to statements about physical or social facts" (p. 94). Qualitative research is about much more than one-dimensional statistics or people. It is an effort to understand and make meaning of situated and complex human actions and experiences through sustained engagement within a particular context. Cushman (1998) elaborates, "without immersion in the community," qualitative educational researchers "would not have . . . access to the private ideologies" of our research participants (p. 25). To that end, Double Dutch Methodology strives to transcend rigid notions of educational research inviting qualitative researchers to jump inside the complex situated realities of research participants equipped with an alternative way to think about and do participant observation toward the goal of humanizing the research process.

REFLECTIVE QUESTIONS

1. Find and review images, photographs, and/or video clips of people playing double dutch. Observe the composition of the activity. Who is doing what? Describe the

motion of the ropes. What are the roles of the participants? Describe the motions and actions of the rope turners and the jumpers as well as of the bystanders, who may watch, chant, sing, or dance. How is one action connected to or dependent on another?

2. Double dutch is associated with a certain amount of physical skill, agility, and rhythm. Additionally, the game is often dynamic, unstructured, and improvised. How do such characteristics of double dutch relate to the practice of participant observation? What types of challenges might you anticipate if you are embodying multiple roles within the context of your research site?

3. Humanizing qualitative research in urban contexts involves a give and take of material resources between the researcher and the research participants. Identify opportunities for reciprocity in your own research context. Research participants have agreed to participate in your research project in exchange for what? What information, skills, or resources might you provide your research participants? In what ways might you, the researcher, and the research participants learn from each other or develop as a result of the experience?

4. The concept of a Double Dutch Methodology is the result of interdisciplinary exploration and curiosity. Name one or two disciplines or theoretical strands that enhance educational qualitative researchers' ability to conceive of alternative and humanizing research methodologies.

NOTE

1. The notion of qualitative research as an act of stepping into an ongoing slice of reality or inside a reality box is based on feedback Dr. Beth Rubin and Dr. Thea Renda Abu El-Haj (both associate professors in social studies education at Rutgers University) share with students in qualitative research methods courses.

REFERENCES

Camangian, P. (2011, March). Making people our policy: Grounding literacy in lives. *Journal of Adolescent and Adult Literacy, 54*(6), 458–460. Retrieved from http://usfca .academia.edu/PatrickCamangian/Papers/1755833/Making_People_Our_Policy_ Grounding_Literacy_in_Lives

Cushman, E. (1998). *The struggle and the tools: Oral and literate strategies in an inner city community.* New York, NY: SUNY Press.

Gaunt, K. (2006). *The games Black girls play: Learning the ropes, from double-dutch to hip hop.* New York: New York University Press.

Green, K. L. (2010). Our lyrics will not be on lockdown: An arts and activist response to the school-to-prison pipeline. *Race, Ethnicity, and Education, 13*(3), 295–312.

Green, K. (2011). *Youth Voices: Youth radio, literacy, and civic engagement.* Unpublished dissertation, Emory University, Atlanta, GA.

hooks, b. (2000). *Feminism is for everybody: Passionate politics.* Cambridge: MA: South End Press.

Kelley, R. D. G. (1997). *Yo' mama's disfunktional! Fighting the culture wars in urban America*. Boston, MA: Beacon Press.

Kinloch, V. (2009). *Harlem on our minds: Place, race, and the literacies of urban youth*. New York, NY: Teachers College Press.

Lave, J., & Wenger, E. (1991). *Situated learning: Legitimate peripheral participation*. New York, NY: Cambridge University Press.

Morrell, E. (2004). *Becoming critical researchers*. New York, NY: Peter Lang.

Morrell, E. (2007). *Critical literacy and urban youth: Pedagogies of access, dissent, and liberation*. New York, NY: Routledge.

Pardlo, G. (2001). *Cave Canem: 2001 anthology*. Brooklyn, NY: Cave Canem Foundation.

Paris, D. (2011). "A friend who understand fully": Notes on humanizing research in a multiethnic youth community. *International Journal of Qualitative Studies in Education, 24*(2), 137–149.

Pring, R. (2004). *Philosophy of educational research*. New York, NY: Continuum International.

Rogoff, B. (1994). Developing understanding of the idea of communities of learners. *Mind, Culture, and Activity, 1,* 209–229.

Tucker-Raymond, E., Rosario-Ramos, E. M., & Rosario, M. L. (2011). Cultural persistence, political resistance, and hope in the community and school-based art of a Puerto Rican diaspora neighborhood. *Equity and Excellence in Education, 44*(2), 270–286.

Walford, G. (2001). *Doing qualitative research: A personal guide to the research process*. London, UK: Continuum International.

Winn, M. (2011). *Girl time: Literacy, justice, and the school-to-prison pipeline*. New York, NY: Teachers College Press.

Revisiting the Keres Study to Envision the Future

Engaging Indigenous Pueblo Youth in Intergenerational Humanizing Research and Praxis

9

Eunice Romero-Little, Christine Sims, and A-dae Romero

This chapter is about *humanizing research* (Paris, 2011) and praxis in gifted education through a methodology that illuminates the Indigenous voices of contemporary Pueblo members while promoting intergenerational transmission of knowledge, understanding, and appreciation among youth, elders, and teachers. It is an ethnographic account[1] of a young Indigenous Pueblo man's struggle to validate, honor, and celebrate his indigeneity in an educational context that *almost* silenced his voice, *almost* constrained his meaningful engagement in learning, and *almost* deprived him of his dignity as a gifted Indigenous individual. To a greater extent, it is a story of emancipation from categorization and labeling as "lesser" or "deficient" vis-à-vis White, middle class, English-speaking norms and a reclaiming of learning *and* teaching and identity through praxis and humanizing research informed by the Keres Study, the study that inspired this chapter. This methodological framework promotes humanizing inquiry and fosters in-depth dialogic interaction, negotiation, and action, leading to "consciousness-raising and the building of relationships of care and dignity for both researchers and participants" (Paris, 2011, pp. 139–140). Ultimately, this humanizing research process prioritizes individual agency and local knowledge in seeking local solutions for social transformation. Using this framework, we take a critical retrospective look at how hegemonic educational policies and practices limit the learning experiences of Indigenous youth. More important, we focus on how this methodology engages them, using an examination of the Keres Study as a means of highlighting their own linguistic and cultural world, and how this ultimately leads to a reclaiming of Indigenous voice, identity, and agency. We end the chapter with a discussion of the significance of and implications for utilizing humanizing methodology, not only as a means of engaging the various parties in respectful and reciprocal research, but also to actively employ the voices, cultural knowledge, and processes that will engage participants in critical thinking and action research. For Indigenous communities, this can have an especially significant impact on sustaining a way of life for future generations of Indigenous people.

A CULTURAL PORTRAIT OF A YOUNG, GIFTED PUEBLO MAN

I first learned of Jim on San Popay Pueblo[2] feast day, but I never met him personally before he entered my resource room as a student. At the time I learned of him, I was teaching special education at a Native American boarding school in the Southwest. The majority of Rio Grande Indian School's 350 seventh- to twelfth-grade students came from the surrounding Pueblo communities of New Mexico. Annually, each of the 19 New Mexican Pueblos (also known as the Rio Grande Pueblos because of their location along the Rio Grande River) has a feast day, a day filled with the synergy of Indigenous and Catholic prayer and celebration. On these vibrant colorful feast days, Native and non-Native visitors are invited to watch "the dances" at the community's plaza, where hundreds of corn dancers of all ages dance throughout the day to the traditional music created by the choir of male singers and a sole drummer. Jim was pointed out to us by his grandfather, Sal. Jim, a tall, slim, attractive young man, gazed to the ground in concentration as he danced with poise and a fine-tuned rhythm at the lead of the line of corn dancers. Like many Pueblo grandparents, Sal had had a special hand in socializing his grandson throughout the developmental continuum, from babyhood to boyhood to manhood, into the cultural intricacies of Pueblo life. When Jim had been an infant, Sal had sung Tewa lullabies and corn dance songs to him. As a special gift, Sal had even composed a buffalo song for his grandson. As soon as Jim could sit quietly on his lap, Sal had taken Jim to the practice house (a community building where social activities and ceremonies took place), where he taught Jim the male cultural traditions and protocols, ranging from greetings to song composition to the everyday and formal prayer and speech required for spiritual and secular leadership. But, most important of all, he taught Jim all of these critical pieces of cultural knowledge in and through the Tewa language. As I listened to Sal describe his grandson, I could sense that he very proud of the budding community leader Jim had become. As I watched Jim dance in deep concentration, not missing one drumbeat, I realized that he was not only a reflection of the compassion, devotion, and hard work of all his various Indigenous socializers, including his Grandfather Sal, but he was a reflection of a gifted Pueblo person. At the time that this ethnographic portrait of Jim was being documented, a Pueblo construct of giftedness was unknown in the field of gifted education (and mainstream society); its founding, however, was emerging from a qualitative research study investigating giftedness among the seven Keresan Pueblo communities of New Mexico.

The Keres Study: Giftedness From a Pueblo Perspective

The Keres Study: Identifying Giftedness Among Keresan Pueblo Indians (Romero, 1994)[3] was conducted from 1990 to 1993, a time when few global studies of giftedness challenged the conventional notion of intelligence as a single entity measured solely by an IQ test, an indispensable mainstream tool for measuring human intellectual ability (and potential), including giftedness.[4]

The Keres Study, named after the seven Keresan[5] Pueblo communities in which the qualitative study took place, strove to understand giftedness from culturally knowledgeable Keres members active in the traditional life of the community. In the first phase of the study, open-ended interviews focused on the notion and nature of giftedness; the identification, description, and representation of and possible Keres terms for giftedness characteristics and/or traits; and the identification of community members who exemplified giftedness from a Keres perspective. These gifted Keresan individuals were interviewed for the second phase of the research; their lived experiences provided further insights into how giftedness was manifested in a cultural context. In all, 22 interviews were conducted and analyzed inter- and intrathematically. In addition to the dimensions of giftedness, findings revealed a number of interrelated elements of a Pueblo construct of giftedness, of which only a few are highlighted here:

- Giftedness is a global human quality encompassed by all individuals.
- The qualities and/or characteristics of giftedness are recognized as such and are not utilized as a basis for distinction or highlighting one above the other.
- The Keres term *chaa'wi ya* refers to a person upon whom unique and special qualities and/or abilities or talents have been bestowed. Such individuals are considered gifted only if they apply these "gifts" in a way that benefits others.
- The qualities and/or characteristics of giftedness are intricately linked with the cultural values and practices of Pueblo society and are represented by four domains:

  1. *A'dzii ayama' guunu*, the humanistic or affective domain, is reflected by individuals who "give from the heart." They give of themselves to others and show compassion and generosity.

  2. *Weeka'dza*, the linguistic domain, is exemplified by individuals with exceptional linguistic abilities. These linguistically gifted people have a notable ability to learn and use the Native language, such as in speech, song, and prayer, to name a few areas.

  3. *Dzii guutuutuni* is the knowledge domain. Someone gifted in this area has abundant cultural knowledge and knows how and when to apply it appropriately.

  4. *Kaam 'asruni* refers to the domain of creativity, associated with fine and gross psychomotor and kinesthetic abilities—for instance, in the case of a potter who creates exquisite ware that requires a combination of fine psychomotor coordination, spatial reasoning, and visualization, or a corn dancer who demonstrates mastery of multimodal forms of learning and exceptional performance.

The Pueblo construct of giftedness is founded on the ontology of Pueblo people and framed by their mother tongues, which have collectively shaped (and continue to shape) their understanding of human spiritual and physical potential and realization. This molding begins very early in the lives of Pueblo children.

Culture, Learning, and Pueblo Giftedness

Despite having been influenced in more recent times by the wider mainstream society, the Rio Grande Pueblos have their own distinctive culture that remains the core of their daily lives today. The Pueblos are collectivist societies that emphasize group solidarity, interdependence, cooperation, and social relationships. In the Pueblo world, collectivist values are manifested in their cultural constructs (such as the construct of giftedness) and in their cultural approaches to socializing their children. It is through the socialization of children that the learning and understanding of the cultural conventions, values, and resources are inculcated. In the lives of Pueblo children, there are frequent occasions for sociolinguistic and cultural learning through the daily informal interactions with adults that occur in the home with the nuclear and extended family. The religious and social life of Pueblo people revolves around a dynamic and complex ceremonial calendar. It is through their active participation in the various religious and communal activities of the community (Suina & Smolkin, 1995) that children begin to formulate their Indigenous identities, to learn and acquire the knowledge and skills needed to function comfortably in the Pueblo world, and to understand their place and responsibilities as community members and, equally important, the intricate network of human relationships. For example, Pueblo children participate in the feast days of their communities as, helpers at home, choir singers, or dancers, as Jim was doing when I first saw him.

By following this dynamic culture framework of socialization and through their engagement with multiple caretaker-teachers (such as Sal, Jim's grandfather), Pueblo children come to acquire their linguistic, sociocultural, and personal identities. Moreover, as the Keres Study revealed, it is within this culture framework that giftedness is nurtured, developed, and manifested. Jim reflected many of the indicators of Pueblo giftedness, such as being exceptional in the mother tongue (as a singer, song composer, and/or orator), keen comprehension of cultural knowledge and traditions and how to appropriately apply them, traditional "performance" (corn dancing), convictions, and contributions to community and to the world at large (see the *A'dzii ayama'guunu* domain above). The day I stood mesmerized by Jim and his incredible corn dance performance, it was clearly evident that he had been bestowed unique gifts (*chaa'wi ya*) and was applying them in ways that benefited others. "This kid is amazing," I thought to myself. Little did I know that my initial perceptions of him would soon be challenged.

CONTESTED INDIGENEITY IN AN EDUCATIONAL CONTEXT

Jim and I crossed paths again soon after that memorable feast day at San Popay, but this time it was in a totally different yet just as unforgettable context —in my high school resource room on the first day of the school year. On this first day of class, five minutes after the bell rang, Jim and two of his buddies swaggered into class. Instantly I recognized Jim, but not having been formally introduced to him I chose to remain anonymous and said nothing about knowing his grand-parents and watching him dance on his community's feast day. "Why are you late?" I asked. Silence and a couple of under-one's-breath laughs filled the room. Rather than force an answer, I chose to teach my six resource room high school students. Unfortunately, I didn't make much progress in teaching that day because everyone except Cindy, the only female in the class, refused to do any work. The daily tardiness and unproductivity of my students continued for the remainder of the week.

The following Monday, frustrated by their lackadaisical attitudes and open resistance to any work, I laid down "the law." I threatened each student with "a write-up," a teacher's last-resort disciplinary action that resulted in unpleasant and boring—according to the students—after-school study hall in a special room reserved just for student infractors. Like the week before, silence and a couple of under-one's-breath laughs filled the room, and I too moved into a silent mode, my typical response when frustrated or angered. Partly frustrated, partly disap-pointed, and partly baffled by their resistance to learning, I knew (maybe naively) that these about-to-enter-the-real-world young adults (juniors and seniors) were very capable of completing their assignments. So after a few minutes of total silence, I humbled myself and spoke to them.

"I know each of you is very capable of doing this work. All of you are very smart. Why are you not interested in learning?" The heavy silence and eye-glanc-ing in the room told me that these young adults sensed that my patience was hanging by a thread.

Breaking the silence, Jim walked up to the blackboard and wrote in large let-ters, "SPED." Without a word, he returned to his seat. He sat there with crossed arms and a sly yet indignant smile. I asked him to explain.

"We're speds. We can't read, write, or learn," Jim replied, his peers nodding in affirmation.

"Do you know why you are in special education?" I asked.

"No."

Their collective reply hit me hard. I now understood why my students, the majority of whom had been in special education since early elementary school, chose not to learn. They were career SPED'ers, and not only had they lost their fascination with learning in the world of school, but they were resisting the stigma that often accompanies special education students. Their resistance was manifested by detachment and resistance to learning. Jim, a "reading-disabled" learner, had been in special education since the second grade. Reports of "negative attitude," "acting out," "refusal to complete assignments," and so on started in the fourth grade, suggesting that his resistance to such a placement began at that time.

At this teachable moment I realized that the Jim who sat in front of me was not the Jim I saw dancing at San Popay. The latter Jim—the authentic Jim— was an exceptionally confident, proud yet humble, culturally knowledgeable, gifted informal leader in the cultural community. Why was this not the case in the school context?

GIFTEDNESS: IN THE EYES OF THE BEHOLDER

Clearly the Pueblo construct of giftedness is quite different from the construct promulgated in gifted education programs in the United States. The latter, founded on Western psychology and an individual-based, competition-oriented paradigm, promotes a monocultural (Euro-American) and monolingual (English) view of giftedness that leaves no room for those besides the mainstream English-speaking learner. This exclusive nature of gifted education leads to limitations, bias, and problems in the policies and practices of schools serving language- and ethnic-minority learners. One of these persistent problems is the identification of these learners. These culturally and linguistically gifted learners (CLGLs) are invisible to the mainstream educator, whose expectations for learning and of learners are based on their own monocultural and monolinguistic background and experiences. Consequently, they are not able to recognize or may devalue the "gifts" that the CLGL brings to the classroom. These students then, in a sense, go undetected or are mistakenly considered slow at learning or suspected of having a learning deficiency or disability and are therefore referred for special education testing—which leads to another prevalent problem in gifted education (and special education in general[6]): the disproportionate representation of CLGLs. In New Mexico, prior to (and after) the Keres Study, these problems were evidenced by a prominence of Native American learners in special education "D-category" programs and an almost nonexistence of them in gifted and talented programs. The term *D-categories* refers to identification areas of special education that denote a deficit orientation, such as learning *dis*abled, speech *de*layed, and behavior *di*sorder. Interestingly, in our preinvestigation of the representation of Native American learners in New Mexico's K–12 public schools, two school districts, one with 90% and the other with 100% Native American students, reported having *no* gifted and talented program because, as one principal reported, "We have no gifted Native Americans students." Yet these schools did have special education classrooms crowded with Native American D-category students. This unbalanced context of gifted education begged us to ask the question that led to the birth of the Keres Study: Where are all the gifted Native American students?

RECLAIMING LEARNING AND THE RIGHT TO LEARN

Cognizant of the ever-present dynamics of power, policy, and practice that contribute to educational inequalities in schools and classrooms and limit the learning potential of CLGLs, and also cognizant of the Pueblo construct of giftedness, I could see through my students' facade, their self-portrayal as incapable learners, and knew the answer to the above question: They were sitting in front of me! As ascertained by the Keres Study, each of them encompassed giftedness; a global human quality, if not already evident, was waiting to be nurtured and activated.

How does one activate someone who has for such a long time been detached from learning and who *by choice* has restricted the curiosity of their mind? I honestly did not know and had no blueprint for reengagement in the love of learning. I did, however, have at hand these culturally gifted students and some powerful tools to help me figure it out. These powerful tools included the Keres Study (research) and our common Pueblo experiences, ways of being, and understandings, all of which are encompassed in the Pueblo construct of giftedness (culture). The process, which took on its own shape, consisted of critical engagement through humanizing research, praxis, and culture; it began with teaching from a Pueblo researcher-teacher foundation and with my students' reclamation of learning that honored their linguistic and cultural worlds, recognized their cultural gifts, and focused on their present realities. The first step was uncovering the mysteries of special education—basically, why they were in a resource room.

The bell interrupted that intense conversation. As the young adults left the room, I promised them that tomorrow I would bring each of their special education folders to class so they could read and discover why they were in special education.

Tomorrow came and so did all my students, but this time they arrived five minutes early. Stacked on each of their desks were their folders, some of them 2 inches thick, indicating the many years certain students had been in special education. I explained the contents and the process of identification and referral. Each of them listened intently while simultaneously skimming through the folders. As they read their folders, they asked questions such as, "What does psy-cho-edu-ca-tion-al mean?" "What is a behavior intervention plan?" "What is limited English proficiency?" Before we knew it the entire class period had swept by, and my students asked to continue reading their files the next day.

The next day all students came early to class again and eagerly continued to *read* their folders and ask questions about their histories and placement in special education. The fourth day, the discussion turned to the determination of ability and cultural biases in assessment, which opened the door for the introduction of the Keres Study. For the remainder of the semester, my students arrived early to class eager to read, discuss, and write about such topics as giftedness from a Pueblo perspective, a perspective that included them as well as others in their own families and community as being culturally gifted; through learning about the life of Ishi, the last survivor of the Yahi tribe, they discussed the importance of upholding Indigenous principles in their contemporary lives. Jim and a couple of other students even started coming to my office to "hang around" to read! Capitalizing on this welcome surprise, I held informal reading lunches twice a week with Ishi's songs playing quietly in the background. The end of the semester came too quickly, but one of the final topics was local and global human rights, with a particular focus on Indigenous human rights, which culminated in the research, planning, and development of various projects in their own communities. Jim planned to start an environmental initiative to protect the eagles on his reservation, while another student wanted to revive farming among his peers in his community. I like to think that each of my students carried out their human rights projects, but I don't honestly know because the semester came to an end and I left teaching to go to graduate school. However, I do know that Jim graduated, and years later I heard that he had been appointed governor of the San Popay Pueblo[7]—one of the youngest ever to receive this honor. This important leadership role required him to capitalize on all his "gifts" to fulfill his responsibility of ensuring peace, social justice, and the continuance of cultural life in San Popay.

RETROSPECTION: GIFTED OR NOT GIFTED?

In New Mexico as well as nationally at the time of the Keres Study, a major concern among educators, policy makers, Native parents, and tribal leaders was the overrepresentation of Native American learners in special education and their underrepresentation in gifted and talented programs. As a culturally engaged member of a Pueblo Indian community as well as a special education teacher in mainstream schools, I found this pattern of misrepresentation in the various schools where I taught. At an elementary public school where I taught special education, many of my Native American students, who apparently had met the state's criteria for being learning disabled and had therefore been placed in my resource room class, were not considered so in their Pueblo Indian communities. Quite the opposite, in fact: In their Pueblo communities they were gifted learners. They were the conscientious thinkers and eager learners, often bilingual speakers of their mother tongues and English, deeply involved in their cultural-spiritual community, and they reflected attributes considered "exceptional" from an Indigenous perspective, such as respect, compassion, and generosity. Some of these special education students were fellow community members who, in their childhood and into adolescence, I had observed on many occasions participating in secular and ceremonial contexts—often as some of the youngest participants and performing notably well.

Later on I became a part-time special education teacher and a part-time in-house educational diagnostician in a Rio Grande Indian school. In the latter role, I administered cognitive, creativity, academic achievement, and psychomotor assessments to Native middle and high school students, testing and evaluating them for possible learning disabilities and speech problems. I found it intriguing that these students, the majority of whom had come from the Rio Grande Pueblos and were very competent and confident in their cultural communities, were performing so poorly in school. As a result of their poor academic progress, they were referred to me for testing. It was through this experience that I came to understand the limitations of the current identification and evaluation process and witness the impact they had on Native American learners' beliefs about their abilities and potential in the school context. However, more concerning to me was how this impact might eventually extend to and reshape the cultural community context.

REVISITING THE KERES STUDY: PERPETUATING INDIGENOUS GIFTEDNESS

This week in my community we have lost 3 elders. It is never easy to lose a loved one and it is definitely not easy to lose an elder with so much history, knowledge, traditions, love, and advice. They were very gifted individuals because of all the knowledge they possessed and they were never shy of sharing any information to community. This is why I feel the idea of Pueblo giftedness is important in our community because it's the way we continue to keep our culture and traditions alive.

—Sicily (Acoma Pueblo, New Mexico), 2012
Revisiting the Keres Study Youth Forum
University of New Mexico

Since the Keres Study, there have been a number of informative research studies from various cultural perspectives across the globe, including perspectives of giftedness among the Mäoris of Atero (New Zealand) (Allan, 2002; Bevan-Brown, 1996), the Diné (Navajo Nation) and Hoopas of northern California in the U.S. (Begay & Maker, 2007; Lara, 2009), and the Ndebele and Shona peoples of Zimbabwe in sub-Saharan Africa (Ngara, 2006; Ngara & Porath, 2007), to name a few. These studies, along with the Keres Study, have shown that the construct of giftedness is "shaped by a group's beliefs, customs, needs, values, concepts, attitudes and language(s) and as these differ between cultural groups then so too will their concepts of giftedness differ" (Bevan-Brown, 2010, p.10). Ahead of its time in 1990, the Keres Study, in addition to addressing the underrepresentation of New Mexico's Indigenous learners in gifted and talented programs (and their overrepresentation in special education learning-disabled programs), revealed a multifaceted cultural construct of giftedness notably different from the mainstream. Moreover, it revealed a Pueblo construct of giftedness represented by an epistemology framed by the mother tongues, systems of thought, and core life values and principles (i.e., "giving back," or reciprocity; compassion; generosity of heart, mind, time, and effort; and so forth) of the Pueblo people, all of which have recently been experiencing tremendous culture and language transitions and loss.

Language endangerment exists worldwide. A UNESCO expert panel, for example, has predicted that of the existing 6,800 languages in the world, 50% to 90% will be extinct by the end of the century. The majority of these lost languages will be Indigenous languages, which is a grave concern to both young and old Indigenous and non-Indigenous peoples because of the loss of the unique epistemological knowledge embedded in them. In New Mexico's Pueblo communities, where oral intellectual traditions continue to serve as a critical link to the native spiritual, governance, and sociocultural domains of daily Pueblo life, addressing Native language and cultural loss is paramount.

For the Pueblo communities, once considered the stronghold of Indigenous culture and language, this has meant facing 21st-century realities, one being that English has permeated and become the language of many Pueblo homes and is the primary and often the only language spoken by its children and youth. A part of this reality, as explained by the young Acoma woman in the excerpt above, is the loss of elders. Elders continue to hold special places in Pueblo societies because they are the speakers of the mother tongue and the keepers and transmitters of knowledge and language. So with each loss of an elder, there is also the loss of irretrievable language and cultural knowledge. Another factor in language loss is the gradual breakdown of intergenerational language transmission and the interruption of the language socialization of children. Both of these processes are the means by which young children acquire their self-identities and cultural identities as well as the cultural and linguistic tools and know-how to function successfully and live harmoniously in the world of the home and community (Romero-Little, 2010). These are also the processes through which cultural constructs such as "giftedness" are shaped and perpetuated.

Another reality of Pueblo peoples today is that schools which were once governmental institutions that served as assimilative tools for eradicating anything that resembled indigeneity are now places that can encourage, support, and teach Indigenous languages and cultural knowledge. A growing body of studies examining successful language renewal initiatives show that the inclusion of the Native language in schools has contributed to this success. These studies also reveal the power of teachers (Native and non-Native) to influence the learning dynamics in the classroom as well as the learning and academic identities of their students (Bevan-Brown, 2010; McCarty, Yamamoto, Watahomigie, & Zepeda, 2001). A close examination of the teachers of Native American learners, however, reveals that the majority are non-Natives who, in many cases, know little about Native children, families, communities, and language(s). A recent national study found, for example, that just 1% of the teachers of Native students are Native American (Stancavage et al., 2006). Moreover, like the average U.S. citizen, many teachers of Native students have little if any credible knowledge and understanding of Native peoples or their cultures, languages, and contemporary realities. This is also the case for many teachers of Pueblo students. Because of these reasons, gifted Indigenous learners are often invisible in classrooms.

In light of the above, we (the authors) are involved in a new initiative[8] that seeks to advance, revitalize, and perpetuate endangered Indigenous knowledge systems and languages by revisiting the Keres Study. In this new project, titled Revisiting the Keres Study, a crucial step in carrying the knowledge forward is reflecting on both the findings and the methodology of past humanizing and praxis-oriented research described in this chapter. The overall aim of this new initiative is to bring together Pueblo youth (high school students), elders, and teachers to reexamine the study through a methodology that illuminates their own voices and transformative agency as contemporary Pueblo people while promoting intergenerational transmission of language, knowledge, understanding, and appreciation among and between themselves. Using the original Keres Study and its findings as a foundation for critical dialogue and reflection, the goal of this Intergenerational Collaborative Methodology (ICM) is to create people consciousness that leads to participants' recommending their own solutions toward extending or perpetuating their own constructs as proposed in the original study. ICM involves a dynamic process of critical dialogue and reflection, both intragenerational (separate elder, youth, and teacher groups) and intergenerational (across generations or a mix of old and younger generations with high school teachers). Given today's realities, including the fact that language changes have taken place since the original study, the Revisiting the Keres Study project seeks to collect candid thoughts on what giftedness means to Pueblo peoples today. For example, considering that language changes have taken place, does language remain one of the key areas of giftedness? What are the views of the youth? What are the elders' and grandparents' views? What are the major differences between youth and elders? This Intergenerational Collaborative Methodology not only serves as an avenue for understanding issues surrounding the disproportionate lack of representation of Native American students in mainstream gifted education, but also, more important, engages participants as co-researchers in critical thinking and collaborative transformative research that seeks creative, innovative, and culturally appropriate and relevant means of (a) reinvigorating and sustaining Indigenous epistemologies, languages, and cultural knowledge for future generations of Pueblo peoples; (b) providing opportunities to create critical conscientiousness and a deep sense of agency and activism among tribal community stakeholders and Pueblo youth, parents, and elders; (c) supporting educators in their work with Pueblo students and communities to create a more equitable education for all learners in a multicultural and democratic society; and (d) expanding our understanding and appreciation of cultural and linguistic diversity worldwide.

Particularly critical for educators, this humanizing, praxis-oriented project aims to increase awareness and understanding of the rich intellectual, sociocultural, and linguistic traditions and systems of thought of Pueblo learners, whether they are identified as gifted or not by schools, and to foster an understanding of the critical role teachers play in encouraging, supporting, and incorporating Native language and culture in their classrooms. By doing so, they in turn ensure that Pueblo learners, like Jim, maintain an irresistible hunger for challenges to the mind and develop confidence and strong cultural and academic identities to help them prepare to engage in shaping their own futures in and outside their communities.

REFLECTIVE QUESTIONS

1. What are some similarities and differences between the mainstream and Indigenous Keres constructs of giftedness?

2. What specific research moves, assumptions, and positionalities in the Keres Study allowed for learning about Keres constructs of giftedness rather than reinforcing mainstream constructs of giftedness?

3. How do learners (Indigenous and/or non-Indigenous) reflect or not reflect their particular "gifts"? Regarding the latter, what are some reasons why a culturally gifted Indigenous learner in your research may not be recognized as "gifted"?

4. How can or do you attend to culturally situated understandings of constructs like giftedness or intelligence in your research? What cultural constructs are important in your research, and how can you come to understand them from the perspectives of the community you are working with?

NOTES

1. Conveyed by co-author Romero-Little.
2. All place and individual names are pseudonyms.
3. The Keres Study was supported by a U.S. Jacob K. Javits Gifted and Talented Students Education Program grant.
4. The exception was Howard Gardner's (1993) multiple intelligences theory, which was making its debut in national and international contexts.
5. Keresan or Keres is spoken by the people of the Acoma, Cochiti, Laguna, San Felipe, Santa Ana, Santo Domingo, and Zia Pueblos of New Mexico.
6. Gifted and talented education is under the umbrella of special education.
7. The Rio Grande Pueblos have a unique theocratic governance system comprised of a traditional and a secular leadership body that share the responsibility of ensuring that the contemporary needs of the Pueblo community are met and that their traditions are protected. In this system, leaders are appointed rather than elected.
8. This research initiative proposes to be carried out in collaboration with the Pueblo Indians of New Mexico, the American Indian Language Policy Research and Teacher Training Center at the University of New Mexico, and Arizona State University's School of Social Transformation and American Indian Studies.

REFERENCES

Allan, B. (2002). *Giftedness in NZ early childhood centres*. Thornton, Wellington, New Zealand: Te Tari Puna Ora o Aotearoa/NZ Childcare Association.

Begay, H., & Maker, C. J. (2007). When geniuses fail: Na-Dene' (Navajo) conception of giftedness in the eyes of the holy deities. In S. N. Phillipson & M. McCann (Eds.), *Conceptions of giftedness: Sociocultural perspectives* (pp. 127–168). Mahwah, NJ: Lawrence Erlbaum.

Bevan-Brown, J. (1996). Special abilities: A Maori perspective. In D. McAlpine & R. Moltzen (Eds.), *Gifted and talented: New Zealand perspectives* (pp. 91–110). Palmerston North, New Zealand: ERDC Press Massey University.

Bevan-Brown, J. M. (2010). Indigenous conceptions in giftedness. In W. Vialle (Ed.), *Giftedness from an Indigenous perspective*. Australian Association for the Education of the Gifted and Talented. Retrieved October 1, 2011, from http://www.aaegt.net.au/DEEWR%20Books/02%20Indig.pdf

Gardner, H. (1993). *Multiple intelligences: The theory in practice*. New York, NY: Basic Books.

Lara, K. D. (2009). *Conceptions of giftedness on the Hoopa Valley Indian reservation*. Unpublished dissertation, Arizona State University College of Education, Tempe, AZ.

McCarty, T. L., Yamamoto, A.Y., Watahomigie, L. J., & Zepeda, O. (2001). Indigenous educators as change agents: Case studies of two language institutes. In L. Hinton & K. Hale (Eds.), *The green book of language revitalization in practice* (pp. 371-383). San Diego, CA: Academic Press.

Ngara, C. (2006). Indigenous conceptions in giftedness in Zimbabwe: A comparison of Shona and Ndebele cultures' conceptions of giftedness. *International Education, 36,* 46–62.

Ngara, C., & Porath, P. (2007). Ndebele culture of Zimbabwe's views of giftedness. *High Ability Studies, 18*(2), 191–208.

Paris, D. (2011). "A friend who understand fully": Notes on humanizing research in a multiethnic youth community. *International Journal of Qualitative Studies in Education, 24*(2), 137–149.

Romero, M. E. (1994). The Keres Study: Identifying giftedness among Keresan Pueblo Indians. *Journal of American Indian Education, 34,* 1–16.

Romero-Little, M. E. (2010). How should young Indigenous children be prepared for learning? A vision of early childhood education for Indigenous children. *Journal of American Indian Education, 49*(1/2), 1–16.

Stancavage, F. B., Mitchell, J. H., Bandeira de Mello, V., Gaertner, F. E., Spain, A. K., & Rahal, M. L. (2006). *National Indian Education Study Part II: The educational experiences of fourth- and eighth-grade American Indian and Alaska Native students*. Washington, DC: U.S. Department of Education, Institute for Education Sciences. Retrieved July 22, 2009, from http://nces.ed.gov/nationsreportcard/pubs/studies/2007454.asp

Suina, J., & Smolkin, L. (1995, Spring). The multicultural words of Pueblo Indian children's celebrations. *Journal of American Indian Education*, pp. 18–27.

PART IV

Revisiting Old Conversations Toward New Approaches in Humanizing Research

Introduction to Part IV

Django Paris

In the first chapter of this section, Kirkland states that the ethnographer "antici-pates and then reimagines the voices of her critics and of her participants in ways that demand a textured transaction between expectations and ethics, representa-tion, responsibility, and respect" (p. 180). Such transactions between anticipation and reimagination, as they map onto and forge new terrain for the ethics of rep-resentation, drive the conversations in the three chapters in this section. The chapters push us in needed new directions through decades-old questions: Why do scholars find qualitative and ethnographic research appropriate to the project of humanization? What methodological and theoretical commitments undergird the work of humanist social scientists? What does or can research do? What should not be researched?

In exploring why he does ethnography, Kirkland tells us that in his study of "the Guys," he "became translator of [his] own witnessings, recording the humble truths of literacy and Black masculinity cast from shadow to light" (p. 184). Such witnessings, Kirkland attests, allowed him to be both near and far, within and without, to see cultural practices in emic ways and, at times, to write about them in etic ways.

Reading Kirkland's piece, I recalled a moment in 2007 when I sat in the back of a high school classroom (see Paris, 2011). Ela, a young Samoan American woman I had been working with for about six months, had thrown her backpack down near me. As I read her inscriptions on the backpack, written in Samoan and African American Language and Hip Hop Nation Language and in various scripts, much about the connections between identity and language and youths' writing on objects and on themselves came into hyperfocus for me. For those who have not yet done extended ethnographic work with youth and communities, I suggest a close reading of Kirkland's piece as a way to think about how to "see the invisible and humanize the marginal" (p. 184).

In the next chapter, Souto-Manning offers a new methodology, which she calls "Critical Narrative Analysis." She traces for us the theoretical and methodological underpinnings of such work and provides a model for understanding how research is undergirded by methodological and theoretic trajectories that stretch across eras. For those interested in doing work that moves beyond the critical (critiquing power) and toward the praxical (taking action to dismantle unequal power relations), Souto-Manning's is a must-read chapter. My encounter with this chapter forced me to do two things: trace and clarify the theoretical and methodological commitments of my own past and present research, and think about the line in my own work between being complacent with critiques of power and taking action to change power relations for participants. I have written elsewhere about the ways my research with youth of color in South Vista did not go far enough to change inequality (Paris, 2011), but Souto-Manning renews such considerations for all of us by asking "Critical for whom?"

In the final chapter of this volume, Tuck and Yang's idea of *refusal* as "attempts to place limits on conquest and the colonization of knowledge by marking what is off limits, what is not up for grabs or discussion, what is sacred, and what can't be known" (p. 225) challenges us to ask ourselves, as researchers in dialogue with our participants, what should and should not be researched?

We are all implicated in their discussion of the *pain narratives* so common in social science. As Tuck and Yang state in Chapter 12, "novice researchers emerge from doctoral programs eager to launch pain-based inquiry projects because they believe that such approaches embody what it means to do social science" (p. 227). And so it was, in many ways, for me as a doctoral student reading reams of research about the failure of Black and Brown youth and the failure of Black and Brown families. In fact, it took nearly two years of reading through my book manuscript (Paris, 2011) with an eye toward resisting romanticization, subjection, and objectification before I finally, in a small way, "refused research" and removed some details about the living and family situation of one of my participants that would have, I decided, perpetuated pain, damage, and deficiency (mostly for my own benefit, not hers). In that case I had to ask, how will this omission change the story I can tell? In what ways do I care about the story and/or the person/community in the story? Most centrally, I had to come to terms with the incredible young friend I had made in my research and to consider how outsiders might (mis)understand her through my writing.

In the end, Tuck and Wang, like Kirkland and Souto-Manning, realize that research in the academy too often "stockpiles examples of injustice, yet will not make explicit a commitment to social justice" (p. 223). Each of these chapters works to change that by seeing research and the academy as a place where scholars can begin to make explicit commitments to social and cultural justice through inquiry and writing.

REFERENCE

Paris, D. (2011). *Language across difference: Ethnicity, communication, and youth identities in changing urban schools*. Cambridge, UK: Cambridge University Press.

Why I Study Culture, and Why It Matters

Humanizing Ethnographies in Social Science Research

David E. Kirkland

I met them, four of the six young men I would study while conducting my dissertation research. There, inside a cold, cluttered classroom in central Michigan, the young men who called themselves the Guys gained my interest. They represented what I thought was the great gulf in literacy studies—the Black male crisis. Initially, I thought that my research would remain there in that cluttered classroom collapsing with broken desks and not enough seats to hold the 35 or so students it enrolled. I was endeavoring to learn about how young Black men read and wrote, and the classroom seemed like the right place to be. I was wrong. The young men that I had decided to study didn't read or write much in the classroom, and what they performed there wasn't indicative of how they practiced literacy at all. To learn about their literacy practices, I had to go beyond the classroom and the cold, sometimes dying data it produced. Their literacies lived across cultural boundaries, stitched into the seams of clothes, folded onto napkins tucked into back pockets, and sometimes scratched on the surfaces of skin, painfully yet beautifully.

The closer I got to locating literacy in their lives, the more I realized that the location of their literacies wasn't in a classroom. How could it be there? And perhaps, it wasn't about studying literacy at all, but about studying literacy in a common culture tied to the activities humans share to make sense of things that are important to them, things that exist within valued, situated settings. I define culture as a fluid space of practices influenced by shared knowledges, values, beliefs, and desires that channel and get channeled through and performed by a cast of human actors. It is a generative place, where people not only find sustenance for existing, but also produce the range of things that occupy, format, and make meaningful that existence. In this place, I would find the Guys reading and writing words and worlds, fashioning meaning within the core of some deep, social, existential place. Here there would be no literacy gulf or Black male crisis. It would be, instead, a place defined by its own unique cultural traits, one where literacy was alive and different from the anatomy of decaying word corpses that lie cold and stiff in most classrooms. This space, both physical and beyond, would be teeming with activity, where six Black males could be seen as victors and less as villains, where they were readers and writers as opposed to passive primitives in opposition to the dowry of enhanced civilization.

In studying them—the Guys—and their practices of literacy, I had to study within their culture. In so doing, I yielded not only to those techniques sensitive to cultural complexities—observation, conversation, excavation, and so on—but also to the wider socio-scientific understandings that ground those techniques: that in whatever we do—from framing problems, such as literacy gulfs and Black male crises, to selecting sites to study, such as a classroom—understanding people matters. In the end, this is what all social science research is about; it's about understanding people in a way that matters.

Thus, this chapter has two broad goals: (1) to defend my research identity, both as a process of critical reflection on the conduct of inquiry in the social sciences and as a way to explain to others why I do what I do and why it is important, and (2) to humanize ethnographies in social science research. The chapter is aimed at colleagues and policy makers hungry for big numbers and silver bullets. To this end, I hope to respond to accusations:

"Your work lacks rigor."

"Small case studies are not scientific and cannot generalize to large populations."

"Ethnography is a farce."

Et cetera.

"YOUR WORK LACKS RIGOR": DEFENDING ETHNOGRAPHIES

Indeed, I take issue with each of these heavy-handed charges. They approach me as strangers, voices foreign to the terrain of ethnography, the ethnographer, and the complex conditions that ethnography and ethnographic methods seek to understand. Ethnography and its methods are among the most comprehensive and rigorous approaches in the constellation of possibilities in the research galaxy. Ask Shirley Brice-Heath or Brian Street, who have been stalwarts of the method, and through it, have brought science closer to the situation of people. There is the voluminous note taking, the countless hours spent in the field, the social intelligence of interaction, the heightened vision of sensitive sight capable of seeing what once seemed invisible, and so on. But these aren't the most rigorous aspects of ethnography. These are, of course, pro forma. Rather, the rigor of ethnography comes in the form of the researcher herself, who always listens to the echoes of possible discontent, who anticipates and then reimagines the voices of her critics and of her participants in ways that demand a textured transaction between expectations and ethics, representation, responsibility, and respect.

In this tradition of morally and intellectually weighted inquiry, small is preferred to large—for large can be cumbersome and eclipsing (it can hide nuance and complexity in ways that do researchers little good). Hence, the goal of ethnography is not to generalize to large populations, nor to provide a cure-all for big or even basic societal problems. Rather, it is to upset this unidirectionality of terse scientific pursuits, offering complementary and sometimes contradictory information complicating the body politic of large "generalizable" findings. It places under a microscope specific parts of the inquired anatomy, which seems large and unknowable. Yet ethnography allows us to see what lives beneath the skin of large, complex, and living things. Ethnography, then, in seeking to generalize beyond the border population, generalizes to theory, rejecting the idea that all people are in some fundamental way the same. It is a science of nuance and complexity, of the local as opposed to the universal, of the culturally specific as opposed to the socially general. It is anything but a farce.

*

I study culture because the study of culture is important to the (r)evolution of human civilization—to prosperity and justice, purpose and improvement. I study culture, and ethnography gives me a way to *see* and *read* it. Of course, ethnography isn't the only lens that one can use to make the cultural matter of human society visible. The intellectual arc of the academic universe is long, and it curves in time, cascading in variegated drifts from one methodological stance to another (Feuer, Towne, & Shavelson, 2002; Jayaratne & Stewart, 1991). However, in the social sciences, this drift is hastened by multiple and sometimes competing disciplines (e.g., history, psychology, sociology, anthropology, linguistics). Each informs, in its own way, knowledge on theory, practice, and policy (Labaree, 2003). Each discipline brings to bear its own sets of questions and approaches for addressing particular lines of inquiry within any given cultural field (Lagemann, 2000; Shulman, 1986, 1997). Each also brings with it a suspicion of the others. This makes the *culture* of social science research a complex and nefarious affair (Gage, 1989).

My point here isn't to pit particular disciplinary traditions against others, for I believe that the transdisciplinary research apparatus of the social sciences is enriched by the fullness of its members, particularly as fault lines blur and intellectual pursuits integrate (cf. Geertz, 1973). While this transdisciplinary cross-pollination of access points allows culture researchers interested in educational issues, for example, to (a) attend to matters at complex and multiple levels and (b) attend to a range of important subjects that cannot be solved through a narrow scope or singular perspective, much has recently been lost in social science research due to the siloing of certain epistemological regimes, chiefly the overemphasis on quantitative methods and measurements and the premature and dangerous academic arrogance resting on their claims to truth.

This quantitative bend has accompanied a fierce assault on the study of culture in social science and the greater interpretive frames needed to understand it (Hesse-Biber & Leavy, 2004). In spite of what we may gain in the social sciences from the interpretive tradition (in this case, ethnography), the current unquestioned trust in numbers has left the ethnographic method in social science research, particularly in education, under assault (hooks, 2004). However, as I reflect on my own ethnographic research, I see two questions emerging in line with the aforementioned dilemma: Why study culture in social science, and why does it matter? To answer these questions, I use data taken from an ethnography of urban youth culture and literacy that I conducted between 2003 and 2006. I frame my reflection around what Willis (2000) terms the *ethnographic imagination*, illustrating how ethnography as opposed to other methods has allowed me to see into the youth culture of a group of African American males. As mentioned earlier, it was here that I found their literacy practices, which I found to be highly sensitive and complex.

DOMINANT SCRIPTS AND NOTES IN THE MARGINS: IMAGINING ETHNOGRAPHICALLY

In his early research on a group of working-class kids who grow up to get working-class jobs, Willis (1977) convincingly illustrates how the ethnographic method bears rich fruit, ripe with theory and replete with seeds of imagination useful for revealing the social puzzle of human interaction and social inequality. Through ethnography, Willis is able to see (and reveal to others) the mechanisms of inequity, a system of inputs and outcomes that gets reproduced at various intersections of stagnant structural conditions and in the fluidity of human agency. While his study of "the lads" stands as a central document in the study of youth culture, Willis's most important contribution to date is perhaps his early articulations of the ethnographic imagination.

For Willis (2000), the ethnographic imagination considers how the researcher must "be there" to grasp meaning in its various forms. Thus, thought and imagination are processes of being present (as opposed to being distant). In being present, the ethnographer is able to collect the intimate products of mind from the proximal locations of situated knowledges, of someone witnessing the world she or he is researching within broader and emergent analytical frames connected to (as opposed to detached from) the site of study. Then, it is within the ethnographic imagination that the cache of cultural knowledge is opened. Here items as elusive as the tangle of domination and subordination, as Willis's work illustrates, are parsed in ways that move beyond how one group determines not only what gets said and heard in public discourses (Scott, 1990, p. 14), but also who controls those discourses. It also illustrates what happens to subordinate groups and how their identities and realities get projected in public spaces in ways that deny the fullness of their humanity (Smitherman & van Dijk, 1988).

It is here, somewhere close to an awareness of power and domination, hope and imagination, where my own work takes shape. Indeed, it involves ethnographic imaginings, as political theorist James Scott (1990) puts it, to reveal discursive and social sites, like literacy, which shape and take shape within "a zone of constant struggle between dominant and subordinate" groups (p. 14). Through ethnography, as opposed to any other method, I have been able to document—much like Willis—how literacy practices (as a particular kind of cultural practice) have, in part, served conflicting public roles for the Guys (see Kirkland, 2006). These roles (i.e., reading and writing) have usually been made acceptable when serving the interests of the social elite and unacceptable when encouraging the perspectives of the socially marginal. However, the purpose of culture—as my ethnographic research illustrates—is not always public to the outsider looking in, and its functions are not altogether conflicting to the insider looking out.

Within the sphere of culture—in this case a particular youth culture influenced by various performances of Black masculinity—items such as literacy emerge as variable, unique to the situations of bounded human experience, where culture is more than the substance of what we do, but also the space in which we think, where our thoughts take shape. To make this case, I cite as an example the literacy practices of the Guys, who performed language and texts in ways that were fundamentally and intimately personal, products of thought and imagination developed sometimes in secret—the written or performed theory that sits behind all doing. From this greater cultural perspective, the Guys' literacy practices can be seen as connecting the richness of their cultural heritages (history and ancestry) to the ascribed complexity of their social circumstances. These practices allowed for the manufacturing of personal narratives and the recasting of personal experiences (which I have talked about in other work; see, e.g., Kirkland, 2009, 2010) that otherwise may have gotten lost in the distances of forgotten memory and the politics of far-reaching oppression. It has been through my ethnographic work that I have learned that, for many young Black men, it is this personal aspect of literacy that is vital for both life and liberty. Within the ethnographic imagination, the deficit theory on Black males and literacy is traded for a profit one, where it is no stretch to envision how literacy affords some Black males agency, or control, over how they are perceived and perceive themselves in relation to a larger society. This has held true in my ethnographic work of studying the culture of literacy among the Guys.

THE ETHNOGRAPHY OF LITERACY AMONG THE GUYS: (PER)FORMING CULTURAL "I"DENTITIES IN TEXTS AND PERSONAL REFLECTIONS ON AUTHORED SELVES

I began my ethnographic work with the Guys in the fall of 2003. Sitting as spectator and willing participant in their lives, I found deeply personal narratives that spoke across the astute aesthetics of the Guys' tattoos and the painful poetics of their raps.

Ethnography gave me vision to see them, to read their world and the narratives written in it. I became translator of my own witnessings, recording the humble truths of literacy and Black masculinity cast from shadow to light. There was no way to ask quantitative questions of my witnessings. No way to anticipate things unknown.

The Guys' narratives were motivated only in part by larger symbolic forces (Smitherman & van Dijk, 1988). As I observed them, it became clearer to me that such forces, or discourses, delved deeply into the corral of consciousnesses—both that of self and of others—and contributed to their shaping as social beings. From an ethnographic perspective, these artifacts of literacy would reveal how the Guys perceived themselves and the multiple and oftentimes tenuous realities (and harmful fictions) that they endured. Discourses in literacy, realized as a complex nexus of distinctive possibilities both read and written in nontraditional ways, rendered the Guys' personal identities visible. While such identities were produced and exercised in thoughts and connected historically to unending streams of meaning, they were volubly voiced and made known through the Guys' human testimonies, which composed a sort of cultural artifact particularly when "written." For me, as an ethnographer, these texts were data.

The data of ethnography is everywhere. I found it on skin where the Guys read and wrote, sometimes using flesh as canvas to comment on the deep things affecting and sometimes afflicting them. Hence, I determined to show ethnographically—blending thick description with theoretical analysis—how the Guys' literacy practices offered them personal reprieve from hijacked identities, formed on the bases of prejudice and dissent. They were not just reading and writing, but actively resisting and rearranging the dominant narrative of Black manhood as a way to carve out a new existence filled with possibility. That is, both literacy and identity for them, while publicly contested, functioned privately in culturally sensitive ways that only the ethnographer could know. In my understanding as an ethnographer of the culture of the Guys, I could see literacy as helping the young men reflect upon personally valued social and cultural narratives and burgeoning ways of being. Further, as I articulate why the study of this aspect of this particular (youth) cultural space and its practices were important to me, I hope that readers will see how ethnography worked to help me see the invisible and humanize the marginal. My larger point in all of this is to say that it has been with the ethnographic eye that I have been able to see, and with the ethnographic pen that I have been able to document how literacy not only influenced major aspects of my participants' social belongings, but also their personal beings. For when they practiced literacy through tattoos, raps, journal entries, comic books, and so forth, the Guys were not only shaping symbols, but they were also shaping themselves with the scalpels of human practice that not all research endeavors are equipped to understand.

For the ethnographer, understanding what people are (as opposed to what they are not) and how people make sense of things (as opposed to how things make sense of them) is essential. Such a focus on the indigeneity of meaning and the self yields a particular understanding of social being and the processes and practices that produce it. In ethnography, we call this insider gaze the *emic* perspective, which is often unfairly put in contrast to the *etic* perspective. By emic, I mean primary data, the account of things within a particular cultural sphere as rendered by the things or individuals within that culture. By contrast, etic has come to describe a source extant from the actual cultural scene described—an observed, assumed to be objective, or outsider view. However, I have taken etic to mean something quite different. I define etic as a translation of the emic into the social (usually academic) vocabularies expressed to bridge the distances of cultural knowledge that exist beyond the borders of membership. The work of the ethnographer, then, deals importantly in both the emic and the etic as ethnographers seek to understand the cultural grammars of a particular people and translate them to a larger public.

My work with Black males and literacy highlights the emic/etic dialogic unit. To translate for others what literacy meant for the young men I studied, I had to understand what it meant to *them*. This was no easy task because, as I found, the practice of literacy is a critical site of identity formation for individuals. The ethnographer who peers into the cultural domain must witness and, at another level, becomes a part of (as opposed to apart from) the relationship between literacy and identity, which ethnographers such as Heath (1983) and others have more clearly understood through what Bakhtin (1979/1993) characterizes as an "act." In this case, the individual who performs an act or deed holds a unique place within the architecture of her or his being (Bakhtin, 1979/1993, pp. 40–41, 53–54). Since the individual holds such an important place in identity formation, and because uniqueness is both given and yet to be achieved, the individual must actualize (or "articulate") her or his own uniqueness (pp. 41–42).

In this way, the individual embodies a distinct view of the world, her or his own sense of meanings, relations, and intentions. From the ethnographic perspective, identity as a result determines and is determined by both cultural and personal formations of things. It is a material production of (and social practice in) a particular time and place shaped within a given cultural field. It has the worldview of the individual it identifies embedded in it, juxtaposed against the multiple worldviews operative in dominant society. In the Bakhtinian (1981) sense, this identity is forged through dialogue (as opposed to contestation) between the self and the society. In this case, dialogue centers on the dynamic relationship between self and society, where self occupies a relative core and, thus, requires society (or the Other) for existence. In Bakhtin's (1986) broad concept of dialogue, all human experience is a complex web of interrelations with other selves. I use this concept of dialogue below as a theory for ethnographic analysis to engage, explain, and (re)present the Guys' literacy practices.

The Ethnographic Process:
Engaging and Explaining the Guys' Literacy Practices

Ethnography is a process of paradox, of being near while being far away, of engaging participants and their situations close enough while still retaining the necessary distance to explain them. It was through this process that I was able to both witness and explain the Guys' being molded by the literacies they practiced as they molded language and other symbolic material as they practiced literacy. To engage and explain their literacy practices, I had to come to understand a kind of alchemy of performance that defined their lives—that they were becoming what they were doing and adjusting what they did as they became. Hence, writing raps, for instance, which helped to establish them as central participants in a larger (hip-hop) community of literate peers, also gave the young men an opportunity to write themselves onto the foreboding tapestry of human experiences. In a conversation with them, the Guys were adamant about the powerful role that writing and reciting raps played in their making:

Shawn: Kirk [referring to me] can't feel my flow.

Kirk: Why can't I feel it?

Shawn: 'Cause you don't hear me. You don't write raps. [This was true.] And you be reading stuff about rap, but that don't make you a rapper. [Smiles]

Keith: You boogie, we 'hood. [Laughs]

The Guys: [Laughs] Aw man.

Kirk: So, I can't get down.

Shawn: You can get down. [Laughs] All I mean is this stuff make us, us. I be writing it for my life. Just like you writing your dissertation for yours, to understand us or something about Black males. I be writing my raps to understand me, to understand what happened to me. I live in my pen and paper. You don't live in it like us.

One of
the Guys: You live in your computer.

The Guys: [Laughs]

Shawn: It don't make you like it make us.

In their verbal play, the Guys effectually constructed me—particularly as they constructed my role as learner and, dialogically, constructed themselves as both like me and importantly unlike me. What was more interesting than the way they were constructing me, however, was the way that they were actively constructing themselves, aligning their being to their acts of literacy, which were more than local. Shawn used the global *us* in describing how acts of literacy work in the factory of identity (e.g., "it makes us"). However, he also commented on the personal (e.g., "I be writing my raps to understand me"). It is this dialogue between the global *us* and the personal *me* that was most important to how I learned to understand what rap meant in the lives of the Guys. At one level, Shawn revealed himself as misunderstood. Writing raps was a practice of discovery/recovery, where he found himself and began to understand essential aspects of life—which, in his words, motivated the things he wrote about.

The conversation continues as other young men chime into the discussion.

Sheldon: I know what he [Shawn] saying. [Directed at me] He saying flow [rap] is a way that we tell about ourself . . .

Jose: [Interrupts, stuttering] Y-Yeah . . . I know when I write [Jose doesn't like to write raps and therefore doesn't write raps often], my stuff come from my heart . . .

Shawn: [Interrupts, serious] And from my life . . . the streets . . . the 'hood . . . all the things that make you, you. You use 'em, and remake yourself . . .

At this point in our conversation, the Guys, while musing over what rap personally meant to them, concurred that the writing of rap served personal and intimate purposes. For Sheldon, writing rap was a global practice, or "way" to "tell about ourself." Adding to Sheldon's understanding of writing raps, Jose contended that the personal tellings privileged in rap were intimate, concerning things that "come from" the "heart"—that, in Shawn's words, "make you, you." Further, there seemed to be agreement among the Guys that the writing of raps was consistent with the authoring of selves. These selves are neither singular nor stable. They simultaneous stretch beyond and reach within the individual. This point was made clearer as the conversation continued.

Derrick: [Laughs] You be giving yourself a verbal makeover.

The Guys: [Laughs]

Derrick: [Serious] You know, you brag and stuff, write and rewrite who you are. That's why rappers, in stuff [fidgeting with a straw], they always talking about who they be . . . this and that. They trying to demonstrate who they are.

Shawn: [Pointing his hand toward Derrick] Sometime you gotta stretch the truth when you doing that because we more than the truth. If you listen to society, all rappers and the Black man are drug dealers, thugs, and basketball players. That's it. That's their truth. We got ours [our truth]. It don't be all lies all the time just like theirs ain't always lies. There is some real to it. But your truth is real to you, too, and the tighter your line [rap?] is, it can be just as real to everybody around you.

Ethnography brings you closer to a situation (a fish in water); it also allows you to, importantly, stand away from it (a curious observer peering into the fish bowl). As ethnographer, I could hear in the conversation above the Guys' complex understanding of authoring. It seemed close to me, close enough for me to under-stand that, for them, authoring was contested and contingent, based upon who had the authority to make truth claims (cf. Foucault, 1975/1995). I could also stand away at some distance from the conversation. Here, I could see that the agency over self that the Guys gained in writing raps was, perhaps, not theirs alone. Rather, the ability to fashion raps that opposed society's other "truths" belonged—in part—to the sociolinguistic traditions to which the Guys belonged. Standing in the distances, I could explain that their linguistic elements were in keeping with important semantic and discursive features of African American Language (AAL). From the distant ethnographic perspective, things like meaning and voice, for me, ceremoniously got played with and complexly performed. Mean-ings were multiplied and inverted (Smitherman, 2000) as living in "the 'hood" or "the streets" became privileged markers of status and being as opposed to deroga-tory ones. Bragging, an AAL mode of discourse, was admittedly practiced, as the Guys both "brag[ged]" and "stretch[ed] the truth" in their "verbal makeover[s]." Even the Guys' discussion of rap was saturated with the richness of AAL. Their verbal play extended into ritual insults (e.g., "You boogie"). As a perceived out-sider, I got signified on as well because I couldn't "feel" Shawn's "flow" due to my "reading stuff about rap," which, to them, didn't make me a rapper.

Clearly operating in AAL, the Guys were mediating their possible selves with existing cultural tools (e.g., rap and AAL) as a way of achieving their desired personal goals of reclaiming their identities. The point, here, was that self-authoring was not divorced from the "landscape of voices" that Dyson (2003) talks about in her study of "the Brothers and Sisters." Like the Brothers and Sisters, the Guys borrowed and revoiced—hence "recontextualized"—symbolic, social, and ideological options from their "landscape of possibilities" (Dyson, 2003). As an ethnographer, I was close enough to hear the young men's voices and far enough away to understand them and their connection to a larger "landscape of possibilities."

The vision of the ethnographic tilts light through the prism of dual perspec-tives, looking within while looking without. This is not the double visionedness explained by DuBois in *Souls of Blackfolk* (1903/1965). Rather, it is the dual vision of a particular scientific process for engaging, examining, and explaining the knowable world. As an ethnographer, I could see within the boundaries of the Guys' cultural space, where the rules for verbal play and performance in rapping and writing raps were not without limits. According to the Guys, where "stretch[ing] the truth" was allowed, stretching the truth too narrowly ran the risk of transgressing boundaries of acceptable verbal play. Closing the distance between the Guys and me, I understood that hyperbole was privileged to under-statement. The following dialogue illustrates this point:

Shawn: . . . you don't lie to make yourself look bad, and you definitely don't lie and don't make your lie look like a lie. [You lie] only about what you can do better than the next man, and, then, you blow it up. Like you say [he begins to flow]—I can put my fist through steel/kill the will of those niggas who be frontin' on me/pulling bills by the mill/gotta breezies sweatin' me . . .

Tony: [Quietly whispers] That's what's up.

Shawn: That's what's me, nigga. [Laughs]

Shawn's acknowledgement that rap stretched the truth seems ironic against his final statement, "That's what's me." This irony can be resolved when we understand Shawn as constructing himself, not as someone who can put his "fist through steel," but as someone capable of authoring complex and exotic metaphors that demonstrate his confidence and strength. Compared to someone who could put a "fist through steel," Shawn believed that he could achieve the extraordinary and, therefore, authored himself as extraordinary: "pulling bills by the mill[ions]" with women "sweatin'" him.

The use of hyperbole as opposed to actual ability was like shouting as opposed to using a normal vocal pitch. I was close enough to hear, yet far enough away to understand this. Like shouting, hyperbolic statements are used to be heard, especially in the midst of dominant ideologies that work to silence urban Black males. Standing away, I connected this particular speech act to the work of Tricia Rose, who in *Black Noise: Rap Music and Black Culture in Contemporary America* (1994) argues that "rap music, more than any other form of black cultural expression, articulates the chasm between black urban lived experience and dominant, 'legitimate' . . . ideologies regarding equal opportunity and racial inequality" (p. 102). It is a place where the voiceless are heard and where the ghetto storytellers can paint authentic urban histories. It is also a place where the invisible is made visible. It is a place where the ethnographer stands and hears, but close up and at a distance. In this place of paradox, we find the ethnographic process—the practice of simultaneously seeing many things at once from close up and from far away. Hence, up close the ethnographer engages the human and the nested world of her belonging, and standing away she explains them.

The Ethics of Ethnography: Representing the Guys' Literacy Practices

Engaging and explaining my participants and their literacy practices is only part of what I do. Another part of my ethnographic work has been to understand how writing on flesh as a cultural practice constitutes literacy. Much of this work deals with the ethics of ethnography, the moral theory that grounds the inquiry and protects people from the jagged possibilities of misrepresentation. Ethnography makes room for people to play a role in how they are represented. This is part of the literacy of self-authoring explained above, where my participants—for example—wrote on flesh in the act of reclaiming their selves. This act involved reclaiming stolen, lost, and sometimes distorted bodies, for throughout history, bodies have been rendered and received. Moreover, Black male bodies have long been the site of struggle and contestation. Bell hooks, in *We Real Cool* (2003), maintains that the Black male body is a place of antimony, given its public presentation of strength lacking dignity. And during chattel slavery, European regimes stole Black bodies and quite literally manipulated them for their own desires, intents, and purposes. In this way, the body has been an important way for me to understand culture, and to represent its consequences. However, it would be careless to discuss the body without first acknowledging the flesh, as the flesh reveals the story of Black bodies, narratives of history and struggle that are represented through embedded wounds and scars.

Spillers (1994) makes this distinction clear, distinguishing between narratives of body and flesh, which she sees as central to understanding captive and liberated subject-positions. For Spillers, before the "body," there is the "flesh," that "zero degree of social conceptualization that does not escape concealment under the brush of" discourse or the reflexes of literacy (p. 457). In the case of Black Americans, if we think of the "flesh" as a primary narrative, we mean its tragic darkness, complicated by its "seared, divided, ripped-apartness" and other types of iconography that reveal the Black body (Spillers, 1994, p. 457). For example, in portraits of African captives, we witness brutal bruises, wounds, and scars that narrate the bondage of Black bodies.

What Spillers terms the "flesh," in other words, is what Shane White and Graham White (1998) discuss as the surface of Black bodies, on which "in freedom, as in slavery . . . the struggle between black and white was often cruelly etched, and on which the record of that struggle may be read" (p. 126). White and White cite, as an example, the story of an ex-captive named Sandie. Sandie mutilated his body and threatened to commit suicide in front of White witnesses who were attempting to return him to bondage after documents attesting to his freedom had been burned in a fire. White and White recount how many years later Sandie, by then a successful farmer who was distinguished for his physical strength, still bore the signs of his struggle for freedom on his body, or, in Spillers's terms, his flesh (1994, pp. 125–126).

In studying the flesh of the Guys, I learned that much of ethnography is about representing what's already represented in our participants' lives, bringing those hidden textualities of human experience to the fore. Representing the Guys' tattoos in my work, for example, helped me ethically to extend their voice. It was their literacy of possibility that spoke for them in ways that I could not. This voice would speak loudly in the many literacy narratives that I would later write about them, as it coined tales that, according to Shawn, "belonged" exclusively to their making. Thus, having tattoos, regardless of their "deeper meanings," afforded the Guys entry into a wider world. Their tattoos marked them and, by association, entered my work both literally and figuratively. In them, the emic and the etic merged, engagement and explanation became one. Moreover, the identities of the Guys were self-authored texts, represented in the texts they etched onto their bodies.

In this way, the tattoos of Derrick and Shawn were of special importance to me because of the explicit linkages the two young men made between their identities and their body texts. As I spent time observing and, indeed, reading these texts, I came to see that this form of representation evinced the will of the Guys to rewrite themselves on a canvas of flesh, even when that flesh was publicly ridiculed. While these texts physically demonstrated the personal dimensions of literacy in their lives, the Guys' tattoos also figuratively demonstrated how the young men used words and flesh to construct themselves through icons and stories that, because of them, became alive (for more on this, please see Kirkland, 2009). Then the question for me as ethnographer wasn't a matter of how I would represent them, but about how they were representing themselves.

While their tattoos represented a range of things, there were of course certain other things they could never represent or that the Guys did not want represented. In this way, my participants used their tattoos to mask their inner vulnerabilities. For Shawn, this use of tattoos offered a way to highlight significant aspects of who he desired to be while quieting those aspects of Black maleness that to him seemed weak and unwanted. By amplifying a particular self in his tattoos, Shawn actively contributed meaning to the complexity and power of his self-authored identity. For example, Jose referred to one of Shawn's tattoos (a black fist enveloped in flames) as "sweet," commenting, "I ain't seen no one else with it. . . . I'm gonna get one just like that, but I gonna put my name in mine." In a similar way, Derrick taunted, "I know it's Shawn. You can tell him by his tattoos. Ain't nobody got ones like he got" (which probably wasn't true). While Shawn's friends could read his desired self in his tattoos, they could never see, like I could, how those texts hid other things about him. Ethically, to me, it seemed wise to allow those narratives of vulnerability that rested under the surface of skin to remain hidden there.

I was there to witness many of the tattoos Shawn acquired in a span of five years (he received his first tattoo at the age of 12). His discussion of one in particular helps to demonstrate the ways in which he used tattoos to represent himself—in this case, his spiritual identity.

Shawn: I got this one [a tattoo saying "Vengeance is Mine thus saith the Lord"] 'cause it remind me [Tu] Pac [Shakur] [who had a tattoo of a cross on his back, which framed the label "Exodus 18:11"].

Such artifacts of literacy bore witness to the young men's lives, occupying a crucial point in ethnography where the emic and the etic meet, where each curves in the direction of a particular, organic truth. This truth is the elected form of the participant, the one that bears her or his voice, and is therefore the most ethical form of representation available. Therefore, the Guys chose their tattoos at times to represent various aspects of themselves. I could see the form using the ethnographic eye, piercing carefully into meaning. The eye for the ethnographer is trained to watch, to bear witness, ever tuned to absorb the cascading voices loosely arranged in the vast sea of cultural phenomena. Then seeing, too, is a matter of ethics, as is knowing how to listen to your participants, privileging their voices in the chaos of cultural noise. In these brisk seas of sound, we find ourselves swimming. And using the ethnographic ear, I could hear the rush of the many waters, voices of my participants exclaiming what literacy is to them—projecting, maintaining, and attempting to understand themselves as they were defined in relation to both their personal and social experiences. In their voices, voices that sometimes spoke through skin, I could hear flesh speaking to me, saying what the young men wanted it to say, encouraging a deeper ethnographic voice to be present in the literacy narratives that would later be written by and about them.

APPROPRIATING RACE IN IDENTITY FORMATION: THEORY IN ETHNOGRAPHY AS A COMPLEX RACIAL LENS

I have described ethnography as a method of cultural explication, wedded to a process and a set of ethical choices that surrender to the participant voice. These elements of humanizing cultural inquiry were essential to me when attempting to understand the Guys' sense of being and their appropriations of race, which in addition to tattoos played an important role in both how they authored themselves and in the literacy practices they used to contribute to their authoring. In understanding the role of race in the young men's self-authoring, it was helpful for me to explain race using Bakhtin's (1984) notion of "carnival." Here again, the practice of cultural study was enhanced by cultural theory to the degree that theory revealed hidden and important spaces in the landscape of the cultural field. From a Bakhtinian perspective, race, like carnival, would be a general sense of the world, a way of life as opposed to a spectacle seen by people. We live in it, and everyone participates because its very idea embraces all people. As a way of being, race is an expression of limits. One is limited to being something and never everything at once. When one becomes a mixture of multiple races, one becomes none of those races at all, but something altogether new and different. In this way, like the Bakhtinian carnival, there is no other life outside of race.

Using cultural theory grounded in ethnography to further understand race, I soon came to see how race not only marked the individual, but also was an invitation to individuals to become a part of a complex unity, a bodily collectivity. In this sense, ethnography for me, in addition to being a process of inquiry and a mode of representation, was a complex racial lens that could be focused through particular theories or angles pointed at particular places in the world. Using Bakhtin, I was able to see race as carnival, where

> the individual body ceases to a certain extent to be itself; it is possible, so to say, to exchange bodies, to be renewed (through change of costume and mask). At the same time the people become aware of their sensual, material bodily unity and community. (Bakhtin, 1984, p. 255)

Other theories also helped me to tune the ethnographic eye in my observance of race. If Bakhtinian theory helped me to define race, critical race theory (CRT), for example, helped me to abandon the idea that authoring at any level was racially innocent. Through the prism of CRT, I came to recognize the affixed normality, hence invisibility, of race in the everyday social and personal expressions of literacy of my participants. For the Guys, race was undeniably an element in the symbolic/personal construction of the self, "negotiated as a social process rather than as a biological determinant" (Greene & Abt-Perkins, 2003, p. 8). In this way, critical race theorists have set forth the premise that race is a permanent feature in one's construction (Bell, 1992). The permanence of race in one's construction means that racial identities influence every aspect of the self, including the literacies one chooses and does not choose to practice—including the ways the ethnographer learns to see. In sum, not only did theory offer me something to see in a vastly crowded ethnographic scene, but through ethnography it also gave me a way of seeing particulars of culture and complex phenomena in such a way that these items gained greater visibility. I present below, as an example, a continued commentary on my ethnography of literacy with the Guys.

While they practiced literacy to reclaim/reinvent their identities, the Guys also practiced literacy to affirm their race. Further, they struggled constantly within themselves to make sense of racial identities that became uniquely and ubiquitously theirs. The body, the flesh, beyond the tattoos etched on it, was a resource, a canvas for expressing the self. The body became both literally and figuratively impossible to sever from the Guys' literate as well as racial identities. Sheldon made this point clearer for me:

> I be reading all the time, but as a Black [male], I can't be reading that stuff they be reading in school, like with my boys. I got a rep[utation] to protect [Laughing] . . . you know it's hard. I still gotta read, though, 'cause I don't want no body to think I'm a dummy. But you gotta keep it on the low 'cause you don't want no body to think you like White [people] either.

Outside of theory, Sheldon's admission of his public and private struggles with race and literacy seemed problematic to me at first because I inaccurately interpreted his comments as suggesting that reading was equivalent to Whiteness. That is, Black males had no inheritance in the practice of reading, as he personally felt obliged to abandon the practice in the presence of peers.

I initially interpreted Sheldon's comments as meaning that reading, beyond not being cool, was also not being Black. After further conversation with him and careful mining of the scholarly literature, I understood that Sheldon was not critiquing reading at all. Rather, his critique had more to do with ways of reading, especially with ways of reading promoted in schools, which according to Heath (1983) also has to do with personal choices and social ways of being. In a similar vein, Ferguson (2000) maintains, "To perform the act [of schooling] too realistically, to appear to adopt whiteness not as a guise but as identity, is seen as an expression of self-hatred and race shame" (p. 213). Extended conversation with Sheldon became crucial. Placed in the context of theory, these conversations helped me to push past my (dominant) misinterpretation. His words were in conversation with hooks (2003), who points out that intelligent Black men "have learned to act as if they know nothing in a world where a smart Black man risks punishment" (p. 33). Publicly rejecting reading was a way for Sheldon to protect himself. Based on what, when, where, and how he read, Sheldon's very construction as a Black male would be questioned, particularly in his cultural scene. Choosing Blackness, Sheldon also chose to be critical of more school-based/ standardized reading practices, which he (and scholars like Heath [1983]) associated with Whiteness. In his case, I needed theory in ethnography to see race and the racial ways that Sheldon was constructing himself as a reader. It was complicated, but above all an artifact of literacy only understood in the contexts of many other voices that gained value in this particular episode.

I had other conversations with the Guys where I needed theory to explicate my racial readings of the episode:

Kirk: What kinds of things do you guys like to read?

Keith: I don't know. I read a lot of stuff, man . . .

Tony: [Interrupting] As a Black man, I gotta read. What you trying to say?

Kirk: [Smiling] I just want to know what you read . . . that's all.

Tony: But you trying to say that Black boys don't read.

Kirk: I'm Black.

Theory in ethnography as a complex racial lens is transitory. And listening to the young men in the above example, I can still see race as it collapses into literacy. Thus, as the Guys viewed themselves as raced—CRT's theory of racial ubiquity—I explained the Guys as constructing views of literacy that were equally raced. Within these views, there were larger tensions at work (e.g., "As a Black man, I gotta read"; "you trying to say that Black boys don't read"). Implied in the example was an internal struggle, which likely stemmed from external messages concerning the negative relationship between Black males and reading. Hence, the external (or "othered") notion of Blackness that society perpetuates was at odds with the internal/personal understanding of Blackness that Jose (and Sheldon before him) had appropriated and chose to perform. That is, if race was carnival, its performance was spectacle, which meant that it would be seen and judged under the gaze of others.

Thus, the clearest way for Jose, for example, to seal off negative connotations of Blackness was through what Bakhtin (1984) calls *parodic*, or a deliberate displacement and subversion of the ideological constraints of the system. In this sense, Jose can be seen as wanting to displace and subvert the ideological system that mystifies and constructs Blackness in the realm of illiteracy. Jose's personal view of race, then, built its own world in place of the official world. His world(view) became a place in which Blackness could both reject the official reading practices of schools and still affirm its own needed/required (e.g., "As a Black man, I gotta read"), valued, and meaningful reading practices.

In some strange way, I became part (or co-author) of Jose's self-authored racial text. This artifact of literacy, the artifact of my participation, is in keeping with Bakhtinian notions of carnival, where even those who seem to be outsiders are members or insiders to the scene, influencing its actions and development. Thus, my role inside Jose's literate narrative was as the dominant Other, which did not sit well with me. Disregarding my own privilege and authority, I was reminded by Jose's statement ("you trying to say Black boys don't read") that my authored self was quite different from theirs though we shared a race.I tried to reason, too, through our shared racial identity that we were not very different. After all, "I'm Black." My insistence on making my Blackness known to them was in concert with Jose's racialized personal discourse (e.g., "As a Black man"). I had, too, appropriated Blackness to construct a self that I personally valued and eagerly wanted the Guys to value also—thus, neither could I escape the ubiquity of race. Instead, I, the ethnographer, became the racial lens, whereby the racial light that shone in my interactions with the young men became visible through the prism of me. Our conversation continued, now, with the focus on me:

Keith & Sheldon:	But you different.
Kirk:	How am I different?
Keith:	I bet you be reading all the time.
Kirk:	I bet you be reading all the time, too. Is something wrong with that?
Shawn:	No. It ain't nothing wrong with reading. I'm saying. It just the stuff people be reading. Like in school, they want us to read this book about some crazy ass White boy who live on a farm [talking about *Of Mice and Men*]. Personally, that ain't gone do me no good.
Kirk:	Why?
Shawn:	Because, I'm Black, and that shit don't apply to me.

Here again, an emphatic enunciation of Blackness is put forth. This time it was Shawn (perhaps the most emphatic of the young men), who reasoned—because he was Black—that *Of Mice and Men* did not apply to him. What was most important was his construction of himself; he did not use being Black as a reason not to read (e.g., "It ain't nothing wrong with reading"). Rather, he argued that structures, like schools, made literacy practices like reading foreign and socially uncomfortable. Given this ethnographic detail, it would be inaccurate to conclude that the Guys rejected reading, for the Guys did not always resist reading per se. From an ethnographic perspective, based on the meanings my participants made of their worlds and the theories explaining their lives that find life in ethnography, the Guys, instead, embraced Blackness, the carnival of race which found little place in their schools.

As our conversation continued, the Guys' embrace of Blackness was made clearer, and theory for me came alive in the ethnographic details of their words. It acted as a complex racial lens, which allowed me to see the tensions of race that marked our interactions in purposeful contradiction. These contradictions revealed the things they did, such as reading, against the things they did not do, such as reading. This contradiction could be explained because texts were raced and gendered by them but never in a totalizing manner. From my ethnographic vantage point, the racial construct of literacy alive in their interactions with books sanctioned acceptable norms of reading and writing, particularly when one chooses Blackness as a social characteristic—where one can be both reader and nonreader simultaneously. Explaining the difference between the reading he didn't do in school and the reading he did at home, Shawn said, "It's okay to read stuff that make you Black." To be Black (and male) meant to read things acceptable within that discursive franchise of race, where race is performance much like carnival. It further meant to reject texts that did not find value within the given discourse community of flailing interpersonal expressions of self. Our conversation continued:

Kirk: Derrick, you are smiling, but haven't said anything.

Jose: [With an X-Men comic book in his hand] I know I read.

Derrick: That's the point. We all read. [Laughing] At least I hope we all read. None of us want to be call a dummy 'cause we can't read. I know I be reading stuff all the time, stuff like magazines, the newspaper . . .

Kirk: [Interrupting] What part of the newspaper?

Derrick: [Smiles] The sports section.

Kirk: Do you read any other stuff?

Derrick: Yeah. Comics and horoscope.

Shawn: I be reading stuff like that too, stuff that interesting, like about those dudes that got shot at 7-Eleven. I think I knew one of them. He use to go to my school.

Jose: I read Black magazines too.

The Guys: Oh yeah . . . yeah . . . me too.

Jose: Like *Vibe*, *Source*.

Tony: I be on *King*.

Jose: They [I'm not sure who he is talking about] don't get it. This the stuff that makes us, us. It's what we interested in. So we do be reading, but y'all don't call the stuff we be reading, reading.

Kirk: I do.

Here, the Guys revealed a litany of texts that they engaged in their personal lives. As their social worlds connected, their personal choices in reading intersected. Being was ever instilled in their reading selections (e.g., "I read Black magazines" . . . "me too"). It was being Black (or at least "acting" it) that became an affirmed choice, an identifier, for the Guys. But how did this being Black look? How was it performed? More important, was it even possible to be Black? And better yet, how was it helpful? Indeed, an important part of the ethnographic ethic is ongoing interrogation of things, constant questioning of self and surroundings in the process of gaining understanding. Then there is complexity always alive in what the ethnographer perceives. Her perception yields questions more than it does insights. Hence, as one puts theory into ethnography, one also gets theory out.

From my ethnographic vantage point, I could begin to see what wasn't there by perceiving the complexities that were. The young men were not illiterate, but in what ways were they literate? Race was painting the world that they lived in, influencing how they read and wrote. But what was race to them, and in what ways did it shift between my conversation with and observation of them? The young men appropriated race in their identity formation, performed it in their literacy practices. How did they change its surface and unsettle its core? These questions depend much on theory in ethnography as a complex racial lens, yet there responses depend on pushing theory toward more just ends. Through the ethnographic experience, the lens of theory is bent, adjusted, or recalibrated to see the world more acutely. And the more acute our sight, the more humane are our visions.

CONCLUSION

In this chapter, I have attempted to explain ethnography as a humanizing approach to social science research in that its processes of inquiry, explanation, and representation are grounded in the cultural artifacts located in human reality and curve toward the visceral will housed in our participants' voices. Indeed, the work is polymorphous and always in conversation with and through the many voices that exist within and upon the communities and peoples we seek to better know. In this way, ethnography gets us closer to the borders of cultural understanding more so than any other approach to inquiry. Thus, I study culture ethnographically as a way to humanize my research in youth culture, particularly among Black males. My hope is that the illustrations that I have provided here demonstrate the importance of ethnography in bearing witness to culturally complex phenomenon in a quest for pointed accuracy in our generative quest to understand things unknown and in our attempt to better theorize the not yet well explained. Such bearing witness remains particularly important in understanding and theorizing the experiences of Black people, males in particular, as our interpretations of Black people continue to be often divorced from the cultural contexts in which we exist, and therefore continue to bear deficit, racist imprints. In this way, I study culture for them and for us, not just to understand complex cultural practices but to change things.

Therefore, studying culture, and studying it well, is important because our research on culture has real consequences for real people. I take again, for example, the Guys, whose culture of literacy offered life. It helped to construct those personal narratives of self, which commented on their commitments and curiosities about their particular existences. It also mediated their realities and spoke to how they saw themselves specifically in a narrow personal world and globally in relation to larger social landscapes. Then, in ethnography, literacy products like tattoos, raps, magazines, and newspaper articles about sports and violence become more visible, more complete. These items, given over to the humanizing cadence of ethnographic concern, begin to bear witness to the Guys' social innovations, involved competitions, and personal struggles, whose distinct and ever-evolving patterns, structures, and meanings shaped the idiom of—in this case—contemporary Black masculine cultures, and by association, Black males like the Guys more generally. Of course, these items resist quantification, for they emerge from the space of everyday life, twisted and rearranged frequently in protean shapes with bold new meaning.

As I reflect back on the humanity I found in ethnography, I can still remember the Guys constantly striving for subjectivity (i.e., self-identity, a sense of themselves, and their individual possibilities for acting/enacting), while society was at work reproducing itself and its versions of valued literate practices. As an ethnographer, I saw these scenes of the cultural apparatus that play tableau on the page come alive. It became apparent, somewhere in the cycle of my own ethnographic imaginings amid observation, participation, conversation, and so on, that literacy artifacts such as the body were no longer an objective arena. They were the subject of great tension, though acted upon by self and other, by individual and society.

In keeping marginal certain acts of literacy, research approaches that stare at the dead corpse of the word, that deny the complexity of culture and its many moving elements, risk reproducing the self-other dichotomy that lies at the heart of most social fragmentations (e.g., racism, nationalism). While literacy for the Guys facilitated the entry of knowledge and information that had previously been suppressed or hidden in the public domain, I could only know this element of literacy through ethnography. It could be seen as personal transgression measured against the Guys' ability to tell their stories and write (about) themselves—a literacy we must always see. Hence, ethnography as a stance to studying culture is important if we are, in fact, to hold to the moral standard of humanizing research, shedding interpretive light upon the darknesses of misunderstanding, which hides the particular truths of our experienced realities beneath the shades of simplicity.

REFLECTIVE QUESTIONS

1. How does one define culture in humanizing research, and how might broader, bolder, and more generative definings of culture situate cultural research in ways that disrupt static hierarchies of and frames for knowing?

2. How might ethnography be seen as a culturally sustaining (Paris, 2012) research methodology and defend against positivist ideologies that regard certain research practices as lacking rigor and/or validity?

3. What is the rigor in ethnography? How might this rigor differ from and complicate normalized notions of rigor (i.e., empiricism)?

4. What role(s) might human imagination play in humanizing research, and how might this imagination be calibrated to seek out inquiry-based logics that yield more just findings?

5. What are some of the roles of theory in ethnography, and how might theory be useful for helping ethnographers see particular phenomena more precisely?

REFERENCES

Bakhtin, M. M. (1981). Discourse in the novel. In M. Holquist (Ed.), *The dialogic imagination: Four essays* (pp. 257–422). Austin: University of Texas Press.

Bakhtin, M. M. (1984). *Problems of Dostoevsky's poetics* (C. Emerson, Ed., Trans.). Minneapolis: University of Minnesota Press.

Bakhtin, M. M. (1986). The problem of speech genres. In C. Emerson & M. Holquist (Eds.) and V. W. McGee (Trans.), *"Speech Genres," and other late essays* (pp. 60–102). Austin: University of Texas Press.

Bakhtin, M. M. (1993). *Toward a philosophy of the act* (V. Liapunov, Ed.; M. Holquist, Trans.). Austin: University of Texas Press. (Original work published 1979)

Bell, D. (1992). *Faces at the bottom of the well: The permanence of racism.* New York, NY: Basic Books.

Dubois, W. E. B. (1965). *The souls of blackfolk.* New York, NY: Avon Books. (Original work published 1903)

Dyson, A. H. (2003). *The brothers and sisters learn to write: Popular literacies in childhood and school cultures.* New York, NY: Teachers College Press.

Ferguson, A. (2000). *Bad boys: Public schools in the making of Black masculinity.* Ann Arbor: University of Michigan Press.

Feuer, M. J., Towne, L., & Shavelson, R. J. (2002). Scientific culture and educational research. *Educational Researcher, 31*(8), 4–14.

Foucault, M. (1995). *Discipline and punish: The birth of the prison.* New York, NY: Vintage Books. (Original work published 1975)

Gage, N. L. (1989). The paradigm wars and their aftermath: A "historical" sketch of research on teaching since 1989. *Teachers College Record, 91*(2), 135–150.

Geertz, C. (1973). *The interpretation of cultures.* New York, NY: Basic Books.

Greene, S., & Abt-Perkins, D. (Eds.). (2003). *Making race visible: Literacy research for racial understanding.* New York, NY: Teachers College Press.

Heath, S. B. (1983). *Ways with words.* New York, NY: Cambridge University Press.

Hesse-Biber, S., & Leavy, P. (2004). *The practice of qualitative research.* Thousand Oaks, CA: SAGE.

hooks, b. (2003). *We real cool: Black men and masculinity.* New York, NY: Routledge.

hooks, b. (2004). Culture to culture: Ethnography and cultural studies as critical intervention. In S. Hesse-Biber & P. Leavy (Eds.), *Approaches to qualitative research.* New York, NY: Oxford University Press.

Jayaratne, T. E., & Stewart, A. J. (1991). Quantitative and qualitative methods in the social sciences: Current feminist issues and practical strategies. In M. Fonow & J. Cook (Eds.), *Beyond methodology: Feminist scholarship as lived research* (pp. 85–106). Bloomington: Indiana University Press.

Kirkland, D. E. (2006). *The boys in the hood: Exploring literacy in the lives of six urban adolescent black males.* Doctoral dissertation, Michigan State University, East Lansing, MI.

Kirkland, D. (2009). The skin we ink: Tattoos, literacy, and a new English education. *English Education, 41*(4), 375–395.

Kirkland, D. (2010). English(es) in urban contexts: Politics, pluralism, and possibilities. *English Education, 42*(3), 293–306.

Labaree, D. F. (2003). The peculiar problems of preparing educational researchers. *Educational Researcher, 32*(4), 13–22.

Lagemann, E. C. (2000). *An elusive science: The troubling history of education research.* Chicago, IL: University of Chicago Press.

Paris, D. (2012). Culturally sustaining pedagogy: A needed change in stance, terminology, and practice. *Educational Researcher, 41*(3), 93–97.

Rose, T. (1994). *Black noise: Rap music and Black culture in contemporary America.* Middletown, CT: Wesleyan University Press.

Scott, J. (1990). *Domination and the arts of resistance: Hidden transcripts.* New Haven, CT: Yale University Press.

Shulman, L. S. (1986). Paradigms and research programs in the study of teaching: A contemporary perspective. In M. C. Wittrock (Ed.), *Handbook of research on teaching* (3rd ed., pp. 3–36). New York, NY: Macmillan.

Shulman, L. S. (1997). *Complementary methods for research in education.* Washington, DC: American Educational Research Association.

Smitherman, G. (2000). *Talkin that talk: Language, culture and education in African America.* NY: Taylor & Francis.

Smitherman, G., & van Dijk, T. A. (1988). *Discourse and discrimination.* Detroit, MI: Wayne State University Press

Spillers, H. (1994). Mama's baby, papa's maybe: An American grammar book. In A. Mitchell (Ed.), *Within the circle: An anthology of African American literary criticism from the Harlem Renaissance to the present* (pp. 454–481). Durham, NC: Duke University Press.

White, S., & White, G. (1998). *Stylin': African American expressive culture from its beginning to the zoot suit.* Ithaca, NY: Cornell University Press.

Willis, P. (1977). *Learning to labour: How working class kids get working class jobs.* Farnborough, UK: Saxon House.

Willis, P. (2000). *The ethnographic imagination.* Cambridge, UK: Polity.

Critical for Whom?

Theoretical and Methodological Dilemmas in Critical Approaches to Language Research

Mariana Souto-Manning

11

This chapter addresses the question "Critical for whom?" as it investigates theoretical and methodological dilemmas associated with critical approaches to language research. In doing so, it takes on the challenge of formulating an analytical approach to research and praxis that can accommodate both the power of the discursive social field as well as the moral impulse to take a stand—bringing critical discourse analysis and conversational narrative analysis together to establish Critical Narrative Analysis (Souto-Manning, 2007, 2010a).

CRITICAL FOR WHOM? CHALLENGING ETHNOCENTRIC RESEARCH PRACTICES

In humanizing research, language researchers must ask the question "Critical for whom?" as we seek to take a critical stance. Not doing so would be equivalent to colonizing participants—or, at the very least, to ethnocentrically imposing our own understandings, assumptions, and experiences upon them. Ethnocentrism is the "view of things in which one's own group is the center of everything, and all others are scaled and rated in reference to it" (Sumner, 1906, p. 12). In deeming research critical, it is thus important to look closely and listen carefully in order to understand the perspectives and experiences of participants in their own terms rather than superimposing our own perspectives of what is problematic and needs to be transformed. After all,

> [t]o impose a value judgment from one's own community on the cultural practices of another—without understanding how those practices make sense in that community—is ethnocentric. Ethnocentrism involves making judgments that another cultural community's ways are immoral, unwise, or inappropriate based on one's own cultural background. (Rogoff, 2003, p. 15)

So, when researchers do not seek to understand what participants are trying to say and pursue, we act ethnocentrically. Instead of standing for democracy and freedom, we become colonizers imposing our own understandings and critiques onto other people's lives (even if unknowingly). As we seek to humanize research, we need to move away from such ethnocentric positionings: from thinking that our own practices—as an organization, as a person—are positioned as better than others' practices.

Theoretically, critical researchers need to carefully consider the central place of the physical person and of material conditions (Archer, 2000, 2003). This means recognizing not only how the system in place (e.g., government, institution) colonizes this lifeworld (Habermas, 1987)—the everyday stories people tell—but also how these everyday stories can appropriate the system with regard to specific situations and concerns affecting individuals (e.g., minimum wage or the rigid implementation of educational standards).

Methodologically, one means critical researchers studying language have to understand the relationship between the system and the ways individuals narratively make sense of their lives (lifeworlds) is the analysis of conversational narratives. Conversational narratives are a complex weave of individuals' unique concerns and recycled institutional discourses. Through conversational narratives, individuals can commence questioning their realities and problem solving, a critical process. Critical Narrative Analysis (CNA) combines the two research methodologies of critical discourse and narrative analyses in such a way that they can each productively inform the other. Not only analyzing narratives critically in the lifeworld, but also simultaneously deconstructing the different discourses present in these narratives, "allows researchers to deal with real-world issues and develop critical meta-awareness with participants (Freire, 1970), demystifying the social constructions of specific realities within particular contexts, challenging commonly accepted definitions of critical, and reframing social interactions as places for norms to be challenged and changed" (Souto-Manning, in press).

In terms of praxis—the wedding of reflection and action to foster positive social change—this chapter offers immediate lifeworld implications. One way of envisioning this sort of praxis is an engagement in liberatory pedagogical practices which start from the very issues affecting the lives of participants (Souto-Manning, 2010b), in which individuals engage in problematizing what is (the status quo) from an agentive position and seek to change it in their own situations, in their own lifeworlds, while considering the constraints imposed by institutional and systemic structures. Students in such a pedagogical space engage simultaneously with the word (language) and the world (social practices and contexts). One example of such a praxis is the reinvention of Freirean pedagogy—starting from generative themes, which are then problematized dialogically and lead to action (Souto-Manning, 2010b; in press).

The development of this critical meta-awareness (which Freire, 1970, referred to as "*conscientização*") allows any individual "to engage in social action to solve problems and address issues they identify in their own narratives" (Souto-Manning, in press) and lives. So, it is not up to researchers to "save" participants from occurrences in their own lives—which would imply a cultural deprivation perspective (Goodwin, Cheruvu, & Genishi, 2008) and function against the very premise of critical research. "This meta-awareness allows any individual to have a relationship of appropriation (as opposed to colonization) with language (Chouliaraki & Fairclough, 1999)" (Souto-Manning, in press). Such meta-awareness leads to individual research participants' applying "critical analysis to identify, problematize, take a stand, and engage in social action to change their own respective situations" (Souto-Manning, in press). It moves away from assuming that researchers have enough knowledge to determine what is critical based solely on larger institutional, systemic, and media discourses. Critical meta-awareness embraces humility—recognizing that no one knows it all, yet no one is ignorant of everything (Freire, 1998)—thus empowering humanity in research and beyond. In the second part of this chapter clarity, I will anchor my discussion of theoretical and methodological dilemmas in my analysis of dropping-out-of-school narratives of three Brazilian women (cf. Souto-Manning, 2005).

THE STUDY OF LANGUAGE IN USE

Discourse analysis—or the study of language in use—is concerned with the constructive effects of discourse by closely and thoroughly investigating texts. Discourse analysis is interdisciplinary, wedding the fields of linguistics, sociology, and anthropology. As a result, it brings linguistics and the social sciences together for a more complete research method. It is more than method. Discourse analysis is also an orientation to the nature of language and how it relates to societal issues. Wood and Kroger (2000) asserted that discourse analysis is a "related collection of approaches to discourse . . . that entail[s] not only practices of data collection and analysis, but also a set of metatheoretical and theoretical assumptions and a body of research claims and studies" (p. x).

When the analysis of discourses originated—half a century ago in the field of linguistics—it sought to study language structures above sentence levels (Schiffrin, 1994). Today, discourse analysis is increasingly considered and applied as a tool in the social sciences as it attempts to explore the construction of socially created ideas and things in the world as well as their maintenance over time. Discourse is thus an inherent and inseparable part of the social world, of the broader social context.

For example, in studying globalization, "discourse analysis is interested in how the concept of globalization came about—why it has a particular meaning today" (Wood & Kroger, 2000, p. 8). Researchers may learn how other discourses formed the globalization discourse, then relate the globalization texts to a broader context to show how it portrays a particular point of view. Specific questions that can be asked from a critical discourse analytic perspective include, "How do more powerful groups control discourse? . . . How does such discourse control mind and action of (less) powerful groups, and what are the social consequences of such control, such as social inequality?" (van Dijk, 2001, p. 355). Thus, employing a critical perspective to discourse analysis (to the study of language in use) is a way to change what is and to fashion more equitable futures; yet some dilemmas—theoretical and methodological—need to be considered by critical language researchers.

THEORETICAL DILEMMAS

The contexts in which individuals live shape their moral compasses—their ideas of what is right or wrong, of what is desirable or not, of what is equitable or not. Their narratives—the ways they make sense of their experiences—are thus framed by such situated moralities. To engage in truly critical research, researchers must take such moral compasses into consideration—not simply assuming our own orientations, but understanding them according to the experiences and perspectives of the individuals our research affects. Therefore, in seeking to humanize research, we encounter a theoretical dilemma. This is especially the case in critical studies of language use, in critical discourse analysis. A few years ago, together with colleagues, I wrote,

> We need a theoretical and a practical way of understanding how moral sources are generated and what they do for all individuals (not just the intellectual in the field of critical discourse studies). We must admit that a purely deconstructionist or structuralist theory (or any combination of the two) is incompatible theoretically with the idea that we could have a social agenda grounded on value. The challenge, then, is to formulate a social theory leading to research and praxis that can accommodate both the power of the discursive social field and the moral impulse to take a stand. (Rymes, Souto-Manning, & Brown, 2005, p. 196)

The challenge remains.

Theoretically, critical language researchers need to position the experiences of individual participants (the physical person) front and center while recognizing that these experiences are framed by larger systemic contexts and institutional discourses. Understanding the person-centered nature of what is deemed problematic and oppressive needs to become a more central concern of critical language researchers. In conducting research from a critical perspective, it is essential that researchers understand what it means to take a stand—and whose stand we are taking. It is important to gain an understanding of how participants make sense of their lives—and moralities. One can only do so by listening closely to the narratives they tell. After all, according to Bruner (1987), "there is no such thing psychologically as 'life itself.' At the very least, it is a selective achievement of memory recall; beyond that, recounting one's life is an interpretive feat" (p. 13).

Bruner (1990) proposed that narrative is one of the most widely used ways of organizing human experience. "Telling stories is the most universal means human beings have for conveying to others who we are, what we believe, how we feel, what we value, and how we see the world" (Rymes, 2001, p. 163). It is through narrative that experiences are permeated with meaning and ordered. Narrative is "an organizing principle by which people organize their experience in, knowledge about, and transactions with the social world" (Bruner, 1990, p. 35).

However, narratives are influenced by larger events, by mass media and systemic injunctions that are a focus of "much theorizing and research, [so] taking up value-laden stances needs to be centered in an understanding of the lived experience of these forms of discourse" (Rymes et al., 2005, p. 197). While such stances influence the narratives and everyday lives of individuals, they do not dictate what happens. Thus, theoretically, the challenge for critical language researchers is to seek to understand the effects of mass media and expert systems through their instantiation in the lifeworld, at the personal level, in everyday narratives participants tell. This means recognizing not only how particular systems colonize the experiences of everyday people (what critical researchers typically seek to ascertain), but also how everyday experiences and narratives can appropriate (and even recast) the system in many different ways that are determined by individual and collective concerns (Habermas, 1987; Rymes et al., 2005).

METHODOLOGICAL DILEMMAS

In conducting research, one way for critical language researchers to access and understand the relationship between system and lifeworld is the simultaneous analysis of conversational narratives and institutional discourses, considering the ways in which conversational narratives bring together individuals' unique concerns while intertextually employing institutional discourses. Through stories, individuals make sense of their realities, come to question issues affecting their lives, and start problem solving. And narrators potentially engage in action (at personal and/or social realms) as a result of identifying the social construction of their situations and the presence of institutional discourse recycled within their narratives.

Thus, to reach a more humane and full understanding of participants' situations while addressing the methodological dilemma and dispelling the myth that institutional discourses (the system) affect individual lives (lifeworlds) only in specific and unidirectional ways, critical researchers studying language can employ critical discourse analysis and narrative analysis to productively inform each other. Analyzing narratives in the lifeworld—the everyday stories individuals tell—and deconstructing the different discourses present in these narratives allow critical language "researchers to deal with real-world issues and develop critical meta-awareness (Freire, 1970), demystifying the social construction of reality . . . [making] social interaction a place for norms to be challenged and changed"

(Souto-Manning, in press), and bringing the individually situated deliberations and the person into focus within a context of critical discourse analysis.

Addressing this methodological dilemma, "I question the micro-macro separation in discourse analysis" (Souto-Manning, in press) and propose that the mostly macroanalytic perspective (critical discourse analysis, or CDA) informs the predominantly microanalytic perspective (analysis of personal/conversational narratives) and vice versa. Thus, I bring together two discourse analytic perspectives—narrative analysis and critical discourse analysis—and explore here how one informs the other. I specifically examine the focus of CDA on institutional discourses, question the definition of power discourses, and suggest the intertextual recycling of institutional discourses in personal narratives and the adoption of personal narratives in institutional discourses. By no means do I exhaust here the ways in which these two perspectives inform one another; nevertheless, I suggest that this can be a mutually beneficial union (Souto-Manning, 2007, 2010a, in press).

CRITICAL NARRATIVE ANALYSIS

In the combination of these two analytic approaches—critical discourse and narrative analyses—I explore the "link between macro-level power inequities and micro-level interactional positioning" (Rymes, 2003, p. 122). "Wedding CDA with narrative analysis results in methodological affordances and comes closer to its aim of dealing with real-world issues and promoting positive changes in society" (Souto-Manning, in press).

Critical discourse analysis focuses on institutional discourses. As such, it has been criticized for its "high level of abstractness. . . It claims to examine the relationship among language, power, and social structures" (Souto-Manning, in press). But how do we know if institutional discourses are really powerful? How do we know when they are influencing people's lives if not by analyzing the conversational narratives resulting from everyday storytelling? We can start answering these questions through the analysis of conversational narratives and simultaneous verification of recycled institutional discourse intertextually woven into their very fabric. As individuals, we incorporate pieces of institutional discourses into our own narratives. By uncritically recycling these pieces and therefore buying into the ideologies they convey, we become subjected to language colonization (Chouliaraki & Fairclough, 1999).

I propose that we analyze conversational narratives, a more concrete form of discourse—more concrete because it is closer to a person's experiences and is temporally organized (Ochs & Capps, 2001; Souto-Manning, in press). In analyzing conversational narratives and deconstructing the different discourses present in a particular narrative, we can deal with real-world issues and develop critical meta-awareness (Freire, 1970) in demystifying the social constructions of reality, working to change how interactions work, making a place for them to be challenged

and changed (Souto-Manning, in press). "[W]hen the listener perceives and understands the meaning (the language meaning) of speech, he simultaneously takes an
active responsive attitude towards it" (Bakhtin, 1986, p. 68). "The critical meta-awareness of how institutional discourses are recycled in conversational narratives can then
allow narrators to understand the social construction of the realities in which they
live" (Souto-Manning, in press). This also invites language researchers to gain further
insights and to understand that there are indeed multiple understandings of a certain
issue—and that not taking this into consideration may result in the language
researcher taking the role of language colonizer (Chouliaraki & Fairclough, 1999).

It is through conversational narratives, through storytelling, that narrators commence questioning their realities and problem solve. Finally, narrators will
engage in social action as a result of identifying the social construction of their
situations in the presence of institutional discourse recycled within their narratives (intertextually; Kristeva, 1986). Such a critical cycle is present in culture
circles (Freire, 1959). A culture circle is

> a group of individuals involved in learning . . . [and] in the political analysis of their
> immediate reality and national interests. In culture circles, reading demands more
> than decodification of linguistic symbols. It is viewed as political "reading" of the
> world. (Giroux, 1985, p. viii)

The process encompasses the experiences of participants, considering multiple
perspectives valid while moving toward critically transforming realities which
are not a priori, predetermined realities. It proposes that authority can be dialec-
tically negotiated (Freire, 1970). Culture circles illustrate critical discourse analysis in action informed by conversational narratives, leading to social action and
change (Souto-Manning, 2010b). An example of this is forthcoming.

Critical discourse analysis views institutional discourses as colonizing. It
assumes that institutional discourses have the power to transform social relations. But by assuming such, it positions participants—everyday people—as
unable, as merely subjects of institutional actions. My premise is that narrative
analysis and CDA can productively inform one another. "Narrative analysis
without CDA can remain at an uncritical level. . . [I]f we look only at macro
level power discourse without looking at narrative construction at the level of
conversation, we don't know if it . . . really is a power discourse. . . [A] discourse is powerful when it is recycled in stories everyday people tell" (Souto-
Manning, in press). While there is a call "for a joint and balanced focus on
social issues as well as linguistic (textual) analysis in discourse studies, much
is needed to unveil the complex ways in which language and the social world
are intertwined" (Souto-Manning, in press). There is no such tendency to analyze discourse at both the personal and the institutional level simultaneously. I
argue that narrative analysis can be a resource to assess the power of a discourse emanating from institutions in place.

CNA IN ACTION

In this section, I employ Critical Narrative Analysis to make sense of how three Brazilian women—Josi, Neide, and Elena (pseudonyms)—shaped their dropping-out-of-school narratives. On a societal level, I explore their recycling of institutional narratives as they told their stories. On a more situated level, I examine how they portrayed themselves regarding agency. I look at two displays of agency: grammatical agency and framing agency. Grammatical agency is agency portrayed linguistically by the use of subject plus active verb. When one portrays oneself as an actor in the sentence (subject) as opposed to a passive recipient of the action (object), grammatical agency is displayed. When a person is the object of a sentence, such as in "My teacher gave me bad grades" instead of the possible construction "I got bad grades," grammatical agency is mitigated. Framing agency is the narrator's character alignment with normative and situated morals. Even though a person may be responsible for a certain action, he or she shapes it in such a way as to portray himself or herself as a person orienting to morality. For example, when we explore Josi's dropping-out narrative, you will see she employed framing agency as she shaped her narrative so as to draw empathy from the listener and to portray herself in terms of goodness. Instead of saying, "I dropped out of school," she listed many actions by other people that led her to leave school. She ended her narrative with, "So I couldn't. I wanted to go but I couldn't." Josi, therefore, displayed framing agency (framing herself in a positive light) while displaying no grammatical agency. You will read other examples of agency (both grammatical and framing) being mitigated and displayed as we analyze the narratives of these three women.

Josi worked full time in a landfill going through trash bags looking for recyclable items to sell to the city recycling facility. Her day started very early. She was the single mother of two elementary school boys. She had dropped out of school after second grade and hadn't returned until 2003, when she was 24 years old. She lived with her two sons.

Neide was the proud mother of an adoptive daughter. A 34-year-old woman, she lived with her husband and daughter. She lived in the same city as Josi. She had dropped out of school after third grade. Her husband had also dropped out of school as a child.

Elena was 33 at the time I interviewed her. She had grown up in the rural area of Pernambuco, Brazil. She had two children in primary school—a boy and a girl. She worked as a domestic worker in the state's largest city. She had been married to a man who had been employed as a security guard for nearly 10 years. She worked from 8 a.m. to 5 p.m. As you will read in her narrative, she had attended fourth grade two times before dropping out of school.

In choosing the tellings analyzed below, I selected narrative episodes from three interviews that display how the narrators had portrayed themselves in dropping out of school as children. I decided to employ Critical Narrative Analysis to look at their narrative construction in terms of moral stance and in terms of grammatical agency in their narratives. Moral stance is determined in terms of linguistic positioning of narrator in the story and elicitation of feelings of empathy.

Geography or Gender? Josi's Dropping-Out Narrative

Mariana: Until what grade [did you go to school as a child]?

Josi: Until the third grade, and then I wasn't given an opportunity to study anymore. My parents moved to a farm to work there . . . and there was no school there. My brothers could ride the horse to the city to go to school, but my father didn't let me. I asked to go. My father said that women [and girls] wore skirts and didn't ride horses and he said that women [and girls] who went away from home without their father and mother became badly spoken of. So I couldn't go. I wanted to go but I couldn't.

Josi's narrative depicts the socially reproduced role of women. As is often the case worldwide, Josi, as a girl, dropped out of school during the elementary years. In her specific case, geographical limitations were cited as she recounted her parents' move to a farm, another situation beyond her control, thereby placing her far from schools. In the following sentence, however, gender was unveiled as the major issue, as her brothers were allowed to go to school, but she wasn't. The explanation for such rested on situated morals couched in traditional patriarchal ideas of what a woman is supposed to be and how she is to behave. In Josi's narrative, women were constructed as subjugated by societal norms and expectations, orienting to morals, not becoming "badly spoken of." She constructed herself as an object of someone else's actions—her father's. She constructed her father as the subject, playing a major role in her dropping out of school.

For example, in "My father didn't let me [go to school]," the pronoun *me* is an object of someone else's actions. She constructed herself as someone who could not do anything but be a victim of others' actions. By starting her narrative with "I wasn't given an opportunity to study," Josi was constructing herself as passive and grammatically mitigating her agency—her ability to change her situation, her life story. When Josi said that she "wasn't given an opportunity to study anymore," she portrayed her situation with orientation to a moral stance. Education was portrayed as an "opportunity," but she was not given that opportunity. Therefore, she portrayed this person who did not give her the opportunity to study anymore as the person responsible for her dropping out of school. She ended her narrative with "I wanted to go but I couldn't," which portrayed her inability to go to school.

In saying "My father said that women wore skirts and didn't ride horses," Josi oriented to external norms, which were not questioned but accepted in absolute and deterministic terms. She constructed her narrative to show that because she was a woman (something she had no control over), she could not ride horses, and therefore, she could not go to school. Riding a horse would position her against the definition of goodness. She, therefore, didn't ride a horse, dropped out of school, and oriented to societal morals. Finally, she portrayed herself as wanting to go to school, but not able to ("I couldn't"), again framing herself positively and orienting her narrative in terms of morals. This is a common description as perceived by the women in this community, and as strengthened by the analysis of other transcripts.

Even today, about two decades following the incident Josi narrated above, the perception of the role of women as creatures of the domestic realm still remains, as portrayed by her narrative of people's perceptions when she went back to school. When I asked about people's reactions to her reentrance to school as an adult, she responded by constructing the narrative as follows: "Oh, people criticized a lot. One of my [male] neighbors said, 'Ah, because a married woman shouldn't leave the children at home for her husband to take care just to go and study.'" There are societal expectations and norms in place for girls and women locally, in northeastern Brazil, and also globally. This structure in place tends to maintain the status quo of subordinated and exploited women whose agencies are greatly limited.

Retention and Dropping Out: Neide's Narrative

In constructing her dropping-out narrative (below), Neide portrayed herself as a victim of other people's actions, decisions, and perceptions:

Mariana: Have you repeated the year anytime?

Neide: I was one time in second grade. I liked going to school. My father and my mother let me go, but then when I was held back it was different. I didn't want to go back to school. That was not a good year for me. All my friends were in third grade. My mother said girls helped at home. It was better to learn how to take care of the house than to go to school. The last year I went to school my teacher gave me bad grades and . . . then my father said I should stop going to school. He said to help my mother. She needed help. Then I didn't go anymore.

The narrative started by portraying Neide as an active subject of her actions and enjoying school when she was in second grade. Dropping out of school was attributed to being held back by someone else (not the narrator), indicated by "I was held back" as opposed to "I repeated the year." Her use of "I was," a passive construction, further strengthened her stance of being an object of someone else's actions. She constructed her story in a linear narrative, in a progression of events. She further supported her stance as object of others' actions by saying "my teacher gave me bad grades," using *me* as object and portraying herself as victim of her teacher's actions. She portrayed herself as incapable of doing anything that would change the course of her dropping-out story. Much different from "I got bad grades," for example, she portrayed herself as someone good who aligned with the situated morals in her community. The dropping-out action followed her father's plea for help and her teacher giving her bad grades—she did not portray herself as having grammatical agency in either situation. The teacher gave her bad grades, and thus she again portrayed herself as a victim of what happened.

The combination of statements such as, "My father said I should stop going to school. He said to help my mother. She needed help," created a rapport with me (the listener), an orientation to morals. She constructed her narrative in a way that anyone in her place would be prone to do as she did, acting the same way. This passage clearly illustrates how structure acts on and curtails agency. This narrative, in accord with others these women told, oriented to societal assumptions of the traditional patriarchal systemic discourse. So, while these women displayed framing agency within their narratives, orienting to such institutional discourses, they did not change or challenge social conditions. This institutional discourse was taken at face value and colonized these women's narrative tellings and their lives.

In the passage above, Neide's logic of helping her mother because she needed help used the widely accepted practice of girls being apprenticed into household chores instead of furthering their formal schooling—as was the case with Josi, explored earlier in the chapter, and as observed worldwide (Souto-Manning, 2005). Neide recycled widely used institutional discourses in her narrative. Respect and obedience for elders is a discourse typically used in the Catholic Church, and Catholicism is Brazil's official religion. Broadly accepted patriarchal discourses of girls helping at home and being excluded from formal schooling were also forefronted in the above telling.

Neide did not cast herself as responsible for dropping out, but emphasized that she could do nothing to prevent it—she was held back, she was given bad grades, and her father advised her to drop out because her mother needed help. She oriented her story not to her own agency, but to what a good girl in her situation had to do. Who would challenge a father's plea to help one's mother? The narrator in this case used framing agency to locate herself as a good person, whose actions aligned with an assumed definition of moral goodness, while portraying herself as an object of societal positioning and not as a subject capable of deciding her own future and enacting change at either a personal or a systemic level.

Elena's Story: Until Fourth Grade

Elena: I went to school until the fourth grade. When I finished fourth grade my teacher wanted me to go to Vitória [a bigger town/city] to the fifth grade. I cried much, but my mother didn't let me. Girls didn't go to Vitória. Only boys, really. Then, my teacher let me repeat the fourth grade two times. I could do nothing, nothing really. My brothers went to the fifth grade and I couldn't. Can you imagine? I had to help her at home. My mother taught me how to cook and do all this stuff. The men of the house all left early in the morning. My mother and I stayed cooking, washing, ironing . . .

In the beginning of her narrative, Elena placed herself as an active subject of an agentive verb in "*I went* to school . . ." However, some tension was portrayed in Elena's narrative as she said that her teacher wanted her to move ahead and go to school in another city, but her mother didn't let her. At this point, Elena started positioning herself as an object of others' actions. Her action of crying created an affective stance, in which she sought to secure an empathetic listener ("Can you imagine?"). She displayed framing agency (for me, the listener), but through a mitigated grammatical agency—portraying herself as an object, as a victim of other people's actions. She was not the agent in wanting to continue her education—her teacher was the one who wanted her to go to the city of Vitória. By saying "my mother didn't let me," Elena was conveying a sense of inability, portraying herself as an object of her mother's actions. What was unsaid here is that Elena's mother also did not have an opportunity to go to school. She married and started taking care of her own house. Being a member of that community, Elena's mother started aligning her actions with the gendered morals of the community—that is, girls stay at home and are apprenticed into domestic work while boys go to school.

In social interactions such as the one retold here by Elena, the role of conflict is paramount. These conflicts were routinely represented in narratives through language and portray the interconnectedness of the personal and the institutional level. In terms of grammatical agency, Elena portrayed herself as having none—all she could do was cry. Her narrative represents a conflict that demonstrates the patriarchal-sponsored beliefs of boys' independence and girls' dependence. Boys could travel alone; girls could not. To ensure this, these values are couched in societal values. Elena portrayed herself as someone good, who liked going to school, and even who stayed in school for as long as she was allowed—"my teacher let me repeat the fourth grade two times." While aligning with the morals in place and portraying herself in a positive light, Elena still portrayed her teacher as the agent and herself as the object of her teacher's actions. She followed this sentence with a complete flaunt of inability, by saying "I could do nothing, nothing really." She framed herself agentively while indicating her complete mitigation of grammatical agency by repeating the word *nothing* followed by the intensifier *really*.

Aligned with the dimensions of narrative telling (Ochs & Capps, 2001), Elena's tale is highly tellable—and she sought to secure the audience's attention by placing a question which is two pronged: "Can you imagine?" First, the question confirmed that the listener was engaged and paying attention to her story. Second and most importantly the narrator sought to create common ground in terms of moral stance and critique the practice in place at the time of the narrative. "Can you imagine?" was therefore not only interactional, but value laden. It referred to her, in the present, questioning such gender imageries.

She went on to tell that she had no choice but to help her mother at home. That's when the last piece of her dropping-out narrative came in. While her brothers continued their formal schooling, aligning with the other narratives analyzed above and those here represented, Elena was apprenticed into housework by her mother. She again conveyed herself as the object of the action—she was being apprenticed by her mother. At the very end of this narrative episode, Elena contrasted again the activities of the members of her family segregated by gender: "The men of the house all left early in the morning. My mother and I stayed cooking, washing, ironing . . ." Here Elena's story ended with the traditional patriarchal practice of men as advancing academically, becoming breadwinners, and women dropping out of school, becoming caretakers. Elena's narrative, therefore, oriented to a broader traditional institutional discourse that has been propagated throughout the ages. Elena used narrative to locate herself as a good person, as a member of the community in which she grew up, and as someone whose actions aligned with situated morals.

Across Narratives

Each of the narratives above oriented to the situated moral values of the communities in which these women lived at the time these events took place—to the institutional discourse regarding gender roles that were in place. This is made explicit above, as I analyze each of these women's stories, as well as by the fact that by and large, girls didn't go to school, and they were apprenticed into housework. All of these women dropped out of school as children after the second, third, or fourth grade (Neide, Josi, and Elena, respectively). Moral stance was clearly conveyed in each telling.

In all three narratives above, the narrators portrayed themselves in terms of moral goodness—as defined within normative patriarchal morality. They all dropped out of school as children, but none of them constructed a dropping-out narrative in which they portrayed themselves as agents of that change. Their stories place the agency with some other character or concatenation of events and societal perceptions (e.g., Josi portrayed herself as not challenging the *societal* rule that women didn't ride horses, which resulted in her dropping out of school). Their stories oriented to a normative morality that positioned the tellers as unable to remain in school. Institutional discourses and societal beliefs clearly influenced their narrative constructions.

While the actions and episodes the women narrated may reflect a particular and situated framing agency, their orientation to goodness as situated within a particular moral framework is portrayed in their narratives. The content of their stories as well as the way the women told their stories indicate the moral stance of the women narrators. These women made sense of their own lives by narratively aligning their actions with what was morally defined as good. To recall, "social roles, social identity and moral agency are reconstituted collaboratively through narrative and in turn construct narrative" (Rymes, 1995, p. 497); therefore, it is important to remember the role of narrative in making sense of or stabilizing chaotic lives. The women's narratives were meaning making sites in which they made sense of their previous experiences and negotiated more hopeful futures. Through the ways each of them positioned themselves in their dropping-out narratives and in later returning-to-school narratives (not portrayed here), these women negotiated agentive shifts, coming to construct themselves as able and ready to return to school. Stories or narratives, after all, account for past and present experiences and anticipate future ones. In what follows I will illustrate the use of culture circles as a means of supporting and further propelling such praxis with Josi and other participants.

PRAXICALLY HUMANIZING RESEARCH

As we critical language researchers seek to praxically humanize research, our research findings must reveal immediate lifeworld implications. We need a reconstructivist orientation (Luke, 2004 Rymes, Souto-Manning, & Brown, 2005); One way of envisioning this sort of reconstructive orientation to praxis is through Freirean culture circles (Souto-Manning, 2010b), in which individuals engage simultaneously with words and worlds. Freire (1970) proposed the development of a critical meta-awareness, which allows individuals to engage in social action to solve problems and address issues they identify in their own narratives. This meta-awareness allows them to have a relationship of appropriation with language (Chouliaraki & Fairclough, 1999) and to use critical discourse analysis to identify, problematize, take a stand. Culture circles are pedagogical spaces in which participants engage in social action to change their situations. This approach emphasizes that our research is about people, who can read, write, and make sense of their own worlds, instead of living in the world that someone else is making sense of on their behalf.

A Culture Circle in Action[1]

On a Monday evening in June, as darkness began to settle and the heat gave some signs of weakening, women and men, from late teens to early 70s, started entering the room in which they routinely met for their culture circle in Northeastern Brazil. Some of them came right from work, which could be noted by their clothes and hands dusted with soil, signaling their agricultural employment. Some of them talked about the work on the tomato farms in the region, as many of them were engaged in this kind of work. Others looked tired, as if ready to go to bed. It was almost 7 o'clock. The facilitator was there, but she could hardly be identified apart from the participants as she sat and talked with some of them. There wasn't an official start routine. Conversations about everyday themes and issues that started small developed to a point in which they involved all, as everyone engaged in dialogue and problem solving—two inherent parts of the culture circles.

From the beginning, daily work was clearly the topic of the night. Whether in the tomato fields or in someone's kitchen, they all kept hard work schedules; many led double journeys, double lives, working harshly inside as well as outside their homes. As culture circle participants started talking about their work, money and salary emerged naturally as the conversation topic, as a theme to which they could all relate. Josi expressed her frustration by saying,

> It doesn't matter how much I work, I am always owing something to someone; I am always late with my bills. I live with fear. Fear that one day I will get home and not have enough money to pay the rent, or to give food to my children.

Participants, men and women, nodded. Another woman, Solange, asked Josi, "But don't you make a minimum [wage] salary?"

Josi answered affirmatively.

"What does that mean?" asked Sandra, the facilitator.

Solange immediately answered, "That means she should have enough to live."

They continued in the following dialogue:

Josi: I work hard, but the salary is not enough. I don't know what I am doing wrong=

José: =Wrong?

Josi: Yes, because I work, earn a minimum [wage] salary, but it's never enough to pay the bills and put food on the table.

Solange: But the minimum [wage] salary is enough. Isn't it? ((Looks around, seeking approval))

Miriam: I don't have enough money for all my bills either. Do you have=

Solange: =What? Enough money?

Josefa: Yes=

Solange: =No. I am not the owner of my own house. I pay rent every month. I can't buy everything that my family needs. Some days all we eat is [manioc] flour. A handful of flour to fill the belly. We don't have meat on the table. ((Many nod, showing agreement and empathy))

The group started talking about minimum wage and how most of them could identify with Josi's situation. They all made minimum wage salaries, which, according to governmental definition, should allow for a decent living, but they arrived at the conclusion that it didn't, at least in their experiences. They worked hard, but the minimum wage established by federal law was what most of them earned. Some earned even less. After arriving at the understanding that the minimum wage salary wasn't allowing most of them to lead a decent life—to have food on the table and to pay utility bills and housing expenses—they started problematizing the definition of a minimum wage salary (the generative theme) dialogically.

José: So who decided how much is enough?

Marina: I don't know. It wasn't me.

((Laughter))

Solange: Who was it?

((Side talk as they try to figure out who sets the minimum wage salary))

Sandra: The government is who approves the minimum [wage] salary=

Josi   =That's not fair. They don't earn a minimum salary. I just saw Lula [the Brazilian president] in a big car on a store's television. I can't buy a car like that. I can't even pay to go to work by bus. I go walking.

Miriam: Me too.

Solange: Who earns a minimum [wage] salary?

((Most raise their hands))

Solange: Who earns less than a minimum [wage] salary?

((Four women raise their hands))

José: Do you work the entire day?

Laurinda: I work=

Neto: =the entire week?

((Women who earn less than the minimum wage nod))

Laurinda: Who earns more than the minimum [wage] salary?

((Five of the eight men in the room raise their hands))

Sandra: What do you perceive?

Luís: That we earn more than they [do].

Solange: Men earn more money=

Neto: =but it's not enough to live.

The women and men in the culture circle realized that economic injustice was a reality, but there was also gender discrimination in terms of salaries. The gender issue erupted through the problematizing of salaries as a theme of discussion. Even though the minimum wage salary was clearly not enough to lead a decent life in the experience of this culture circle's participants, the women had a clear disadvantage as they made less money than the men, even if they worked at the same place and performed the same kind of job, as was the case with two circle participants, Neto and Miriam.

After much discussion, dialogue, and reflection on the issue of economic and gender-based discrimination and injustice, culture circle participants decided to calculate what would be a livable minimum wage (enough to pay for utilities, food, clothing, transportation, and rent). The Brazilian minimum wage law was established during the 1940s; specific wages have been revisited and adjusted over the years. According to Neumark, Cunningham, and Siga (2006), such a dialogue was highly significant, as studies reporting research on the effects of minimum wages in Brazil are sparse. Families earning minimum wage and below are many, but due to the informal job sector and self-employment, exact percentages are hard to calculate. Nevertheless, this percentage is higher than the reported 52.4% of families living below the poverty line in the metropolitan area of Recife, Pernambuco (Neumark et al., 2006). Minimum wage–earning Brazilians spend between 57% and 64% of their wages on food (Pereira, 2005). After adding up monthly rent, utilities, transportation to and from work, clothing, and food (not restricted to manioc flour and water) for a family of three, this culture circle found that they would need around three minimum wage salaries to survive (adequate food, shelter, clothing, and transportation).

Circle participants concluded that day's session by charting two plans for action—one on the personal and one on the societal level. On the personal level, they were going to further their studies so as to be better qualified for better-paying jobs. Both men and women also decided to ask their employers why the women were making less money than men for the same jobs. Bridging the personal and the institutional realms, they were determined to initiate a dialogue with their employers about the importance of equal pay across genders for the same kind of work. Finally, on the institutional level, they decided to write a letter to their government representative that read, "Three salaries is what allows [us] to live. [We] have to study very much." Their letter ended by calling for action on the institutional level. The participants' nonuniform lettering and limited traditional literacy skills did not stop them from taking action, from attempting to promote change.

The teacher-facilitator, Sandra, in the meeting reported above, took advantage of certain moments to further the participants' queries and inquiries; she provided information but did not necessarily dictate what went on in the circles. Nor did she take the stance of teacher as the holder of knowledge.

Participants were acquiring tools to articulate problems and coming up with possible solutions to their personal challenges through dialogue and problem solving. They didn't necessarily find solutions to each problem, but worked toward breaking monologically oppressive discourses by exploring multiple issues through dialogue and considering alternative perspectives. They became aware of some of the issues that constructed their institutional identities. As some of the participants narrated, a number of them were starting to reconstruct themselves as they explored the implementation of discursively constructed solutions in their lives and engaged in change enacted on the personal level. Such personal actions can contribute to social change over time.

As active contributors in the culture circle, participants constantly engaged in the analysis of their own narratives. They considered multiple perspectives (both personal and institutional) and became researchers of their own situations as they analyzed narratives of livable wages, work ethics and skills, and being good mothers, for example. In the case analyzed above, of the minimum wage conversational narrative, circle participants found that the minimum wage as defined by the government was not a livable wage for a family of three, thereby dispelling the common institutional discourse affirming the adequacy of one minimum wage salary to provide for the basic needs of a family. Together, they subsequently planned two courses of action, one in the personal realm and another in the societal sphere. The societal plan was to make politicians in office aware of the disparity and of the need to approve a minimum wage that equaled a living wage. In the personal realm, they realized that by further developing academic skills such as literacy and problem solving, they would be better prepared to secure a higher-paying job, therefore addressing the situated issue. This exemplifies a first step toward engaging in the concrete critical research that CNA can accomplish.

The implications of such a practice are both empirical (as explored above) and theoretical, as it influences the field of discourse analysis in very real ways.

> As Luke argued, we need a reconstructivist orientation—but it needs to be built within the lifeworld of those we are studying, based on an understanding of their unique agency, not exclusively our own. This is consistent with an empowering agenda centered in theory and research that is always tied to praxis—an engaged praxis that accounts for the deliberative capacity of all individuals. . . . One way of envisioning this sort of praxis is a neo-Freirean engagement in circles of literacy(ies)—in which individuals engage simultaneously with the word and the world. (Rymes et al., 2005, p. 197)

While the theoretical discussion of institutional discourses that often takes place in the field of CDA is important, if we are to engage in productive social change, we must start by listening to and analyzing the stories people tell, and help them to engage in Critical Narrative Analysis themselves. CNA fosters critically meta-aware individuals who are able to create distance from a story and understand how it is being constructed . CNA fosters metalinguistic skills that provide insights into the power of language to mislead and/or deceive. Such meta-awareness is an important life skill that involves listening critically and considering life's challenges from multiple perspectives.

IMPLICATIONS: CRITICAL NARRATIVE ANALYSIS AS PRAXIS

Through culture circles, participants engage in analyzing a process whereby narrative tellings are shaped and come into existence. They come to recognize that personal events and institutional discourses blend together in narrative tellings. Without being aware of the distinct ingredients of this mix, narrators perceive the wedding of these two to be personal beliefs shaped according to their own ideas. Instead, institutional discourse infiltrates their narratives without being questioned. Adopting institutional discourses as one's own set of beliefs and espousing them in one's narratives may lead to passive acceptance of one's own location in society.

With the very intention of separating these perceived personal beliefs into two constituents (albeit only analytically), culture circles invite participants to engage in problem posing. The process seeks to investigate which parts of the narrative tellings are portraying institutional discourses, which parts are constructed to fit normative morals, and which parts are geared at understanding what transpired (personal events). Dialogue is of paramount importance as participants break the seemingly monological narration of events. In culture circles, participants seek to recognize the infiltration of institutional discourse into personal narrative and challenge its absolute voice. They come to view any institutional discourse as one understanding of an issue, an understanding that might actually be curtailing their agency and trapping them in a cycle of low income and poor working conditions, for example.

Culture circles encourage the problematization of participants' individual and collective situations. Communities cannot preserve their unique social identities and worldviews if they are not aware of them. Promoting social justice, therefore, often starts at the cultural awareness level or with conscientization efforts (Freire, 1970; Marsiglia, 2003). By fostering the appropriation of discourse, the understanding of discourses as framed in a particular way, culture circles seek to counter the all-too-common colonization—the maintenance of oppressive social structures. Culture circles seek to promote dialogue aimed at deconstructing narrative tellings.

Dialogically problematizing and deconstructing everyday narratives into their basic components and identifying the institutional discourses infiltrating their narratives, participants come to question information that has previously been conceived as universal truth, as fact. Culture circles thus provide participants with tools to engage in Critical Narrative Analysis of their own situations, thereby giving them tools to enact agency on situated levels. Culture circles evolve from deconstruction to constructivism. From this perspective, language is not representational, or even relevantly systematic, and therefore it is potentially colonizing. Even the structural, grammatical regularities of language are infinitely manipulated so that their ability to represent is reduced to mere play at best, or ideological confusion at worst. The role of circles and the process it fosters, then, is to uncover this ideological component—so that people will not be taken in by it. The constructivist, building her or his own resistant analysis, rises from the deconstructed ashes generated by the process of problem posing and dialogue.

In the circles, analyzing narratives in the lifeworld (Habermas, 1987) and deconstructing the different discourses present in these narratives allow circle participants to deal with real-world issues and develop critical meta-awareness (Freire, 1970), demystifying the social construction of reality, making social interaction a place for norms to be challenged and changed, and bringing the individually situated deliberations and the person into focus within the context of Critical Narrative Analysis (Souto-Manning, in press). In terms of praxis, beyond incorporating a focus on narrative in our own investigative and communicative practices, culture circles have immediate implications, built within the lifeworld of respective participants and based on an understanding of their unique agency—both individual and collective (Souto-Manning, in press). This is consistent with an empowering agenda centered in theory and research that is always tied to praxis.

SO WHAT? REVISING THEORETICAL AND METHODOLOGICAL DILEMMAS

It is important to understand that if we are serious about promoting equity, about critiquing oppressive conditions, critical language research cannot take a stand on its own, distinct from the lifeworlds of those it claims to help. In addressing such dilemmas, critical language researchers must resist asserting an a priori moral stance for humanity and envision the role of critical discourse studies as one of inquiry into the unique personal commitments of individuals situated within and subject to complex social discourses. Ultimately, rather than taking a stand, critical discourse studies inform theory and research and, ultimately, praxis, based on developing understandings of the uniquely situated commitments of individuals.

Finally, critical language researchers interested in humanizing approaches must understand that while the theoretical discussion of institutional discourses that often takes place in the field of CDA is important, we must start by listening to and analyzing the stories people tell every day if we are to engage in social change.

REFLECTIVE QUESTIONS

1. Souto-Manning asks the question, "Critical for whom?" How might this question be important to the research you are considering, designing, or conducting?

2. What are some of the theoretical and methodological dilemmas in your critical approach to research? How do you plan to address them?

3. Souto-Manning writes, "In deeming research critical, it is thus important to look closely and listen carefully in order to understand the perspectives and experiences of participants in their own terms rather than superimposing our own perspectives of what is problematic and needs to be transformed." What are the methodological and theoretical safeguards you employ in order not to superimpose your own perspective onto participants?

4. What does it mean to engage in critical language research? What are the challenges and possibilities entailed by taking such a stance? What are the ways in which Critical Narrative Analysis can help you engage in language research that is critical to both researcher and participants?

5. In your proposed or existing research, how can or do you accommodate both the power of the discursive social field and the moral impulse to take a stand?

NOTE

1. An earlier version of this section was previously published in *Freire, Teaching, and Learning: Culture Circles Across Contexts* (Souto-Manning, 2010b).

2. These interviews were conducted in Portuguese (Souto-Manning's first language). While she strives to capture both the meaning and form of the narratives conveyed by the women who participated in the study, there may be some limitations due to the double translation (Behar 2003) of interviews - from oral to written and from Portuguese to English.

REFERENCES

Archer, M. (2000). *Being human: The problem of agency.* Cambridge, UK: Cambridge University Press.

Archer, M. (2003). *Structure, agency and the internal conversation.* Cambridge, UK: Cambridge University Press.

Bakhtin, M. (1986). *Speech genres and other late essays.* Austin: University of Texas Press.

Behar, R. (2003). *Translated woman: Crossing the border with Esperanza's story* (Tenth Anniversary Edition). Boston, MA: Beacon Press.

Bruner, J. (1987). Life as narrative. *Social Research, 54*(1), 11–32.

Bruner, J. (1990). *Acts of meaning.* Cambridge, MA: Harvard University Press.

Chouliaraki, L., & Fairclough, N. (1999). *Discourse in late modernity.* Edinburgh, UK: Edinburgh University Press.

Freire, P. (1959). *Educação e atualidade brasileira.* Unpublished doctoral dissertation, Universidade de Recife, Recife, Brazil.

Freire, P. (1970). *Pedagogy of the oppressed.* New York, NY: Continuum.

Freire, P. (1998). *Teachers as cultural workers: Letters to those who dare teach.* Boulder, CO: Westview Press.

Giroux, H. (1985). Introduction. In P. Freire, *The politics of education: Culture, power, and liberation.* Westport, CT: Bergin & Garvin.

Goodwin, A. L., Cheruvu, R., & Genishi, C. (2008). Responding to multiple diversities in early childhood education: How far have we come? In C. Genishi & A. L. Goodwin (Eds.), *Diversities in early childhood: Rethinking and doing.* New York, NY: Routledge.

Habermas, J. (1987). *The theory of communicative action: Vol. 2. Lifeworld and system: A critique of functionalist reason.* London, UK: Heinemann.

Kristeva, J. (1986). *Desire in language: A semiotic approach to literature and art.* New York, NY: Columbia University Press.

Luke, A. (2004). Notes on the future of critical discourse studies. *Critical Discourse Studies, 1*(1), 149–152.

Marsiglia, F. F. (2003). Culturally grounded approaches to social justice through social work with groups. In Association for the Advancement of Social Work With Groups (Ed.), *Social work with groups: Social justice through personal, community, and societal change.* Binghamton, NY: Haworth Press.

Neumark, D., Cunningham, W., & Siga, L. (2006). The effects of the minimum wage in Brazil on the distribution of family incomes: 1996–2001. *Journal of Development Economics, 80*(1), 136–159.

Ochs, E., & Capps, L. (2001). *Living narrative: Creating lives in everyday storytelling.* Cambridge, MA: Harvard University Press.

Pereira, L. (2005, July 5). *Brazilian worker spends 57% of minimum wage on food.* Retrieved May 30, 2007, from http://www.brazzilmag.com/content/view/3072/49/

Rogoff, B. (2003). *The cultural nature of human development.* New York, NY: Oxford University Press.

Rymes, B. (1995). The construction of moral agency in the narratives of high-school drop-outs. *Discourse and Society, 6*(4), 495–516.

Rymes, B. (2001). *Conversational borderlands: Language and identity in an alternative urban high school.* New York, NY: Teachers College Press.

Rymes, B. (2003). Relating the word to world: Indexicality during literacy events. In S. Wortham & B. Rymes (Eds.), *Linguistic anthropology of education.* Westport, CT: Praeger.

Rymes, B., Souto-Manning, M., & Brown, C. (2005). Being "critical" as taking a stand: One of the central dilemmas of CDA. *Journal of Critical Discourse Studies, 2*(2), 195–198.

Schiffrin, D. (1994). *Approaches to discourse analysis.* New York, NY: Wiley-Blackwell.

Souto-Manning, M. (2005). *Critical narrative analysis of Brazilian women's schooling discourses: Negotiating agency and identity through participation in culture circles.* Unpublished doctoral dissertation, University of Georgia, Athens, GA.

Souto-Manning, M. (2007). Education for democracy: The text and context of Freirean culture circles in Brazil. In D. Stevick & B. Levinson (Eds.), *Reimagining civic education: How diverse nations and cultures form democratic citizens* (pp. 121–146). Lanham, MD: Rowman & Littlefield.

Souto-Manning, M. (2010a). Critical narrative analysis of classroom discourse: Culture circles as a framework for empowerment and social action. In L. Jennings, P. Jewett, T. T. Laman, M. Souto-Manning, & J. L. Wilson (Eds.), *Sites of possibility: Critical dialogue across educational settings.* Cresskill, NJ: Hampton Press.

Souto-Manning, M. (2010b). *Freire, teaching, and learning: Culture circles across contexts.* New York, NY: Peter Lang.

Souto-Manning, M. (in press). Critical narrative analysis: The interplay of critical discourse and narrative analyses. *International Journal of Qualitative Studies in Education.*

Sumner, W. G. (1906). *Folkways: A study of the sociological importance of usages, manners, customs, mores, and morals.* New York, NY: Ginn.

van Dijk, T. (2001). Multidisciplinary CDA: A plea for diversity. In R. Wodak & M. Meyer (Eds.), *Methods of critical discourse analysis.* London, UK: SAGE.

Wood, L., & Kroger, R. (2000). *Doing discourse analysis: Methods for studying action in talk and text.* Thousand Oaks, CA: SAGE.

R-Words: Refusing Research

12

Eve Tuck and K. Wayne Yang

This is not a story to pass on.

—Toni Morrison (1987, p. 275)*

I knew that there were limits to what
I could ask—and then what I could say.

—Audra Simpson (2007, p. 73)

We're telling all of you, but we're not telling anyone else.

—Fred Moten and Stefano Harney (2010, p. 5)

Research is a dirty word among many Native communities (Tuhiwai Smith, 1999), and arguably, also among ghettoized (Kelley, 1997), Orientalized (Said, 1978), and other communities of overstudied Others. The ethical standards of the academic industrial complex are a recent development, and like so many post–civil rights reforms, do not always do enough to ensure that social science research is deeply ethical, meaningful, or useful for the individual or community being researched. Social science often works to collect stories of pain and humiliation in the lives of those being researched for commodification. However, these same stories of pain and humiliation are part of the collective wisdom that often informs the writings of researchers who attempt to position their intellectual work as decolonization. Indeed, to refute the crime, we may need to name it. How do we learn from and respect the wisdom and desires in the stories that we (over)hear, while refusing to portray/betray them to the spectacle of the settler colonial gaze? How do we develop an ethics for research that differentiates between power—which deserves a denuding, indeed petrifying scrutiny—and people? At the same time, as fraught as research is in its complicity with power, it is one of the last places for legitimated inquiry. It is at least still a space that proclaims to care about curiosity. In this essay, we theorize refusal not just as a "no," but as a type of investigation into "what you need to know and what I refuse to write in" (Simpson, 2007, p. 72). Therefore, we present a refusal to do research, or a refusal within research, as a way of thinking about humanizing researchers.

We have organized this chapter into four portions. In the first three sections, we lay out three axioms of social science research. Following the work of Eve Kosofsky Sedgwick (1990), we use the exposition of these axioms to articulate otherwise implicit, methodological, definitional, self-evident groundings (p. 12) of our arguments and observations of refusal. The axioms are (I) The subaltern can speak, but is only invited to speak her/our pain; (II) there are some forms of knowledge that the academy doesn't deserve; and (III) research may not be the intervention that is needed. We realize that these axioms may not appear self-evident to everyone, yet asserting them as apparent allows us to proceed toward the often unquestioned limits of research. Indeed, "in dealing with an open-secret structure, it's only by being shameless about risking the obvious that we happen into the vicinity of the transformative" (Sedgwick, 1990, p. 22). In the fourth section of the chapter, we theorize refusal in earnest, exploring ideas that are still forming.

Our thinking and writing in this essay is informed by our readings of postcolonial literatures and critical literatures on settler colonialism. We locate much of our analysis inside/in relation to the discourse of settler colonialism, the particular shape of colonial domination in the United States and elsewhere, including Canada, New Zealand, and Australia. Settler colonialism can be differentiated from what one might call exogenous colonialism in that the colonizers arrive at a place ("discovering" it) and make it a permanent home (claiming it). The permanence of settler colonialism makes it a structure, not just an event (Wolfe, 1999). The settler colonial nation-state is dependent on destroying and erasing Indigenous inhabitants in order to clear them from valuable land. The settler colonial structure also requires the enslavement and labor of bodies that have been stolen from their homelands and transported in order to labor the land stolen from Indigenous people. Settler colonialism refers to a triad relationship, between the White settler (who is valued for his leadership and innovative mind), the disappeared Indigenous peoples (whose land is valued, so they and their claims to it must be extinguished), and the chattel slaves (whose bodies are valuable but ownable, abusable, and murderable). We believe that this triad is the basis of the formation of Whiteness in settler colonial nation-states, and that the interplay of erasure, bodies, land, and violence is characteristic of the permanence of settler colonial structures.

Under coloniality, Descartes' formulation, *cognito ergo sum* ("I think, therefore I am") transforms into *ego conquiro* ("I conquer, therefore I am"; Dussel, 1985; Maldonado-Torres, 2007; Ndlvou-Gatsheni, 2011). Nelson Maldonado-Torres (2009) expounds on this relationship of the conqueror's sense-of-self to his knowledge-of-others ("I know her, therefore I am me"). Knowledge of self/Others became the philosophical justification for the acquisition of bodies and territories, and the rule over them. Thus the right to conquer is intimately connected to the right to know ("I know, therefore I conquer, therefore I am"). Maldonado-Torres (2009) explains that for Levi Strauss, the self/Other knowledge paradigm is the methodological rule for the birth of ethnology as a science (pp. 3–4).

Settler colonial knowledge is premised on frontiers; conquest, then, is an exercise of the felt entitlement to transgress these limits. Refusal, and stances of refusal in research, are attempts to place limits on conquest and the colonization of knowledge by marking what is off limits, what is not up for grabs or discussion, what is sacred, and what can't be known.

> To speak of limits in such a way makes some liberal thinkers uncomfortable, and may, to them, seem dangerous. When access to information, to knowledge, to the intellectual commons is controlled by the people who generate that information [participants in a research study], it can be seen as a violation of shared standards of justice and truth. (Simpson, 2007, p. 74)

By forwarding a framework of refusal within (and to) research in this chapter, we are not simply prescribing limits to social science research. We are making visible invisibilized limits, containments, and seizures that research already stakes out.

One major colonial task of social science research that has emerged is to pose as voicebox, ventriloquist, interpreter of subaltern voice. Gayatri Spivak's important monograph, *Can the Subaltern Speak?* (2010), is a foundational text in postcolonial studies, prompting a variety of scholarly responses, spin-offs, and counterquestions, including *does* the subaltern speak? Can the colonizer/settler *listen*? Can the subaltern *be heard*? Can the subaltern *act*? In our view, Spivak's question in the monograph, said more transparently, is *can the subaltern speak in/ to the academy?* Our reading of the essay prompts our own duet of questions, which we move in and out of in this essay: *What does the academy do? What does social science research do?* Though one might approach these questions empirically, we emphasize the usefulness of engaging these questions pedagogically; that is, posing the question not just to determine the answer, but because the rich conversations that will lead to an answer are meaningful. The question—What does or can research do?—is not a cynical question, but one that tries to understand more about research as a human activity. The question is similar to questions we might ask of other human activities, such as, why do we work? Why do we dance? Why do we do ceremony? At first, the responses might be very pragmatic, but they give way to more philosophical reflections.

Returning to Spivak's question, in *Can the Subaltern Speak?* Spivak casts Foucault and Deleuze as "hegemonic radicals" (2010, p. 23) who

> unwittingly align themselves with bourgeois sociologists who fill the place of ideology with a continuistic "unconscious" or a parasubjective "culture." . . . In the name of desire, they tacitly reintroduce the undivided subject into the discourse of power . . . (pp. 26–27)

Observing Foucault and Deleuze's almost romantic admiration for the "reality" of the factory, the school, the barracks, the prison, the police station, and their insistence that the masses know these (more) real realities perfectly well, far better than intellectuals, and "certainly say it very well," (Deleuze, as cited in Spivak, 2010, p. 27), Spivak delivers this analysis: "The ventriloquism of the speaking subaltern is the left intellectual's stock-in-trade" (2010, p. 27). Spivak critiques the position of the intellectual who is invested in the ventriloquism of the speaking subaltern for the banality of what serves as evidence of such "speech," and for the ways in which intellectuals take opportunity to conflate the work and struggle of the subaltern with the work of the intellectual, which only serves to make more significant/authentic their own work (p. 29). All of it is part of a scheme of self-aggrandizing.

Rosalind Morris, reading Spivak, criticizes nostalgia in the academy that "bears a secret valorization and hypostatization of subalternity as an identity—to be recalled, renarrated, reclaimed, and revalidated" (2010, p. 8).

> Subalternity is less an identity than what we might call a predicament, but this is true in a very odd sense. For, in Spivak's definition, it is the structured place from which the capacity to access power is radically obstructed. To the extent than anyone escapes the muting of subalternity, she ceases being a subaltern. Spivak says this is to be desired. And who could disagree? There is neither authenticity nor virtue in the position of the oppressed. There is simply (or not so simply) oppression. Even so, we are moved to wonder, in this context, what burden this places on the memory work in the aftermath of education. What kind of representation becomes available to the one who, having partially escaped the silence of subalternity, is nonetheless possessed by the consciousness of having been obstructed, contained, or simply misread for so much of her life? (Morris, 2010, p. 8)

We take this burden of speaking in/to the academy, while being misrecognized as the speaking subaltern or being required to ventriloquate for the subaltern, as a starting dilemma for the work of representation for decolonizing researchers. It is our sense that there is much value in working to subvert and avert the carrying out of social science research under assumptions of subalternity and authenticity, and to refuse to be a purveyor of voices constructed as such.

This is the place from which we begin this essay, inside the knowledge that in the same ways that we can observe that the colonizer is constituted by the production of the Other, and Whiteness is constituted by the production of Blackness (Fanon, 1968; Said, 1978), the work of research and the researcher are constituted by the production and representation of the subaltern subject. Further, as we explore in Axiom I, representation of the subject who has "partially escaped the silence of subalternity" (Morris, 2010, p. 8) takes the shape of a pain narrative.

AXIOM I: THE SUBALTERN CAN SPEAK, BUT IS ONLY INVITED TO SPEAK HER/OUR PAIN

Elsewhere, Eve (Tuck, 2009, 2010) has argued that educational research and much of social science research has been concerned with documenting damage, or empirically substantiating the oppression and pain of Native communities, urban communities, and other disenfranchised communities. Damage-centered researchers may operate, even benevolently, within a theory of change in which harm must be recorded or proven in order to convince an outside adjudicator that reparations are deserved. These reparations presumably take the form of additional resources, settlements, affirmative actions, and other material, political, and sovereign adjustments. Eve has described this theory of change[1] as both colonial and flawed, because it relies upon Western notions of power as scarce and concentrated, and because it requires disenfranchised communities to position themselves as both singularly defective and powerless to make change (2010). Finally, Eve has observed that "won" reparations rarely become reality, and that in many cases, communities are left with a narrative that tells them that they are broken.

Similarly, at the center of the analysis in this chapter is a concern with the fixation social science research has exhibited in eliciting pain stories from communities that are not White, not wealthy, and not straight. Academe's demonstrated fascination with telling and retelling narratives of pain is troubling, both for its voyeurism and for its consumptive implacability. Imagining "itself to be a voice, and in some disciplinary iterations, *the* voice of the colonised" (Simpson, 2007, p. 67, emphasis in the original) is not just a rare historical occurrence in anthropology and related fields. We observe that much of the work of the academy is to reproduce stories of oppression in its own voice. At first, this may read as an intolerant condemnation of the academy, one that refuses to forgive past blunders and see how things have changed in recent decades. However, it is our view that while many individual scholars have chosen to pursue other lines of inquiry than the pain narratives typical of their disciplines, novice researchers emerge from doctoral programs eager to launch pain-based inquiry projects because they believe that such approaches embody what it means to do social science. The collection of pain narratives and the theories of change that champion the value of such narratives are so prevalent in the social sciences that one might surmise that they are indeed what the academy is about.

In her examination of the symbolic violence of the academy, bell hooks (1990) portrays the core message from the academy to those on the margins as thus:

> No need to hear your voice when I can talk about you better than you can speak about yourself. No need to hear your voice. Only tell me about your pain. I want to know your story. And then I will tell it back to you in a new way. Tell it back to you in such a way that it has become mine, my own. Re-writing you I write myself anew. I am still author, authority. I am still colonizer the speaking subject and you are now at the center of my talk. (p. 343)

Hooks's words resonate with our observation of how much of social science research is concerned with providing recognition to the presumed voiceless, a recognition that is enamored with knowing through pain. Further, this passage describes the ways in which the researcher's voice is constituted by, legitimated by, animated by the voices on the margins. The researcher-self is made anew by telling back the story of the marginalized/subaltern subject. Hooks works to untangle the almost imperceptible differences between forces that silence and forces that seemingly liberate by inviting those on the margins to speak, to tell their stories. Yet the forces that invite those on the margins to speak also say, "Do not speak in a voice of resistance. Only speak from that space in the margin that is a sign of deprivation, a wound, an unfulfilled longing. Only speak your pain" (hooks, 1990, p. 343).

The costs of a politics of recognition that is rooted in naming pain have been critiqued by recent decolonizing and feminist scholars (Hartman, 1997, 2007; Tuck, 2009). In *Scenes of Subjection*, Sadiya Hartman (1997) discusses how recognizing the personhood of slaves enhanced the power of the Southern slave-owning class. Supplicating narratives of former slaves were deployed effectively by abolitionists, mainly White, well-to-do, Northern women, to generate portraits of abuse that ergo recognize slaves as human (Hartman, 2007). In response, new laws afforded minimal standards of existence, "making personhood coterminous with injury" (Hartman, 1997, p. 93), while simultaneously authorizing necessary violence to suppress slave agency. The slave emerges as a legal person only when seen as criminal or "a violated body in need of limited forms of protection" (p. 55). Recognition "humanizes" the slave, but is predicated upon her or his abjection. *You are in pain, therefore you are.* "[T]he recognition of humanity require[s] the event of excessive violence, cruelty beyond the limits of the socially tolerable, in order to acknowledge and protect the slave's person" (p. 55). Furthermore, Hartman describes how slave-as-victim as human accordingly establishes slave-as-agent as criminal. Applying Hartman's analysis, we note how the agency of Margaret Garner or Nat Turner can only be viewed as outsider violence that humane society must reject while simultaneously upholding the legitimated violence of the state to punish such outsider violence. Hartman asks, "Is it possible that such recognition effectively forecloses agency as the object of punishment . . . Or is this limited conferral of humanity merely a reinscription of subjugation and pained existence?" (p. 55).

As numerous scholars have denoted, many social science disciplines emerged from the need to provide justifications for social hierarchies undergirded by White supremacy and manifest destiny (see also Gould, 1981; Selden, 1999; Tuck & Guishard, forthcoming). Wolfe (1999) has explored how the contoured logic of settler colonialism (p. 5) can be mapped onto the microactivities of anthropology; Guthrie (1976) traces the roots of psychology to the need to "scientifically" prove the supremacy of the White mind. The origins of many social science disciplines in maintaining logics of domination, while sometimes addressed in graduate schools, are regularly thought to be just errant or inauspicious beginnings—much like the ways in which the genocide of Indigenous peoples that afforded the founding of the Unites States has been reduced to an unfortunate byproduct of the birthing of a new and great nation. Such amnesia is required in settler colonial societies, argues Lorenzo Veracini, because settler colonialism is "characterized by a persistent drive to supersede the conditions of its operation," (2011, p. 3); that is, to make itself invisible, natural, without origin (and without end), and inevitable. Social science disciplines have inherited the persistent drive to supersede the conditions of their operations from settler colonial logic, and it is this drive, a kind of unquestioning push forward, and not the origins of the disciplines that we attend to now.

We are struck by the pervasive silence on questions regarding the contemporary rationale(s) for social science research. Though a variety of ethical and procedural protocols require researchers to compose statements regarding the objectives or purposes of a particular project, such protocols do not prompt reflection upon the underlying beliefs about knowledge and change that too often go unexplored or unacknowledged. The rationale for conducting social science research that collects pain narratives seems to be self-evident for many scholars, but when looked at more closely, the rationales may be unconsidered, and somewhat flimsy. Like a maritime archaeological site, such rationales might be best examined *in situ*, for fear of deterioration if extracted. Why do researchers collect pain narratives? Why does the academy want them?

An initial and partial answer is because settler colonial ideology believes that, in fiction author Sherril Jaffe's words, "scars make your body more interesting," (1996, p. 58). Jaffe's work of short, short of fiction bearing that sentiment as title captures the exquisite crossing of wounds and curiosity and pleasure. Settler colonial ideology, constituted by its conscription of others, holds the wounded body as more engrossing than the body that is not wounded (though the person with a wounded body does not politically or materially benefit for being more engrossing). In settler colonial logic, pain is more compelling than privilege, scars more enthralling than the body unmarked by experience. In settler colonial ideology, pain is evidence of authenticity, of the verifiability of a lived life. Academe, formed and informed by settler colonial ideology, has developed the same palate for pain. Emerging and established social science researchers set out to document the problems faced by communities, and often in doing so, recirculate common tropes of dysfunction, abuse, and neglect.

Scholars of qualitative research Alecia Youngblood Jackson and Lisa Mazzei (2009) have critically excavated the privileging of voice in qualitative research, because voice is championed as "true and real," and "almost a mirror of the soul, the essence of self," (p. 1). The authors interpret the drive to "make voices heard and understood, bringing meaning and self to consciousness and creating transcendental, universal truths" as gestures that reveal the primacy of voice in conventional qualitative research (p. 1). We contend that much of what counts as voice and makes voice count is pain. In an example drawn from outside of social science research, in Wayne's work as a writing instructor with Southeast Asian refugee students, he learned from them that much of the writing they were encouraged to do followed a rarefied narrative pattern of refugee-as-victim. As it were, youth and young adults learn these narratives in schools, in which time and again refugee-victim stories are solicited by well-intentioned ESL teachers who argue that such narratives are poetic, powerful, and represent the "authentic voice" of the student. Similarly, Robin Kelley (1997), speaking about the Black experience in Harlem in the 1960s, describes White liberal teachers as "foot soldiers in the new ethnographic army" (p. 20), soliciting stories from their students about pain in their lives and unwittingly reducing their students to "cardboard typologies who fit neatly into their own definition of the 'underclass'" (p. 17). Such examples of teachers' solicitations of youth narratives of pain confirm the deep relationship between writing or talking about wounds, and perceptions of authenticity of voice.

Craig Gingrich-Philbrook (2005) articulates a related critique of autoethnography, positioning himself as a "narrator who appreciates autoethnography, at least as compared to its positivist alternatives, but one who simultaneously distrusts autoethnography's pursuit of legitimacy in the form of the patriarch's blessing and family values" (p. 298). Gingrich-Philbrook locates his concern in what autoethnography/ers are willing to do to secure academic legitimacy (p. 300): "My fears come down to the consequences of how badly autoethnography wants Daddy's approval" (p. 310). By this Gingrich-Philbrook means that much of autoethnography has fixated on "attempting to justify the presence of the self in writing to the patriarchal council of self-satisfied social scientists" (p. 311). Though Gingrich-Philbrook does not go into detail about how precisely the "presence of the self" is justified via the performativity of subjugated knowledges (what we are calling pain narratives), he insists that autoethnography is distracted by trying to satisfy Daddy's penchant for accounts of oppression.

> In my own autobiographical performance projects, I identify this chiasmatic shift in the possibility that all those performances I did about getting bashed only provided knowledge of subjugation, serving almost as an advertisement for power: "Don't let this happen to you. Stay in the closet." In large part motivated by Elizabeth Bell's writings about performance and pleasure, I decided to write more about the gratifications of same-sex relationships, to depict intimacy and desire, the kinds of subjugated knowledges we don't get to see on the after school specials and movies of the week that parade queer bruises and broken bones but shy away from the queer kiss. (p. 312)

Participatory action research and other research approaches that involve participants in constructing the design and collection of voice (as data) are not immune to the fetish for pain narratives. It is a misconception that by simply building participation into a project—by increasing the number of people who collaborate in collecting data—ethical issues of representation, voice, consumption, and voyeurism are resolved. There are countless examples of research in which community or youth participants have made their own stories of loss and pain the objects of their inquiry (see also Tuck & Guishard, forthcoming).

Alongside analyses of pain and damage-centered research, Eve (Tuck 2009, 2010) has theorized desire-based research as not the antonym but rather the antidote for damage-focused narratives. Pain narratives are always incomplete. They bemoan the food deserts, but forget to see the food innovations; they lament the concrete jungles and miss the roses and the tobacco from concrete. Desire-centered research does not deny the experience of tragedy, trauma, and pain, but positions the knowing derived from such experiences as wise. This is not about seeing the bright side of hard times, or even believing that everything happens for a reason. Utilizing a desire-based framework is about working inside a more complex and dynamic understanding of what one, or a community, comes to know in (a) lived life.

Logics of pain focus on events, sometimes hiding structure, always adhering to a teleological trajectory of pain, brokenness, repair, or irreparability—from unbroken, to broken, and then to unbroken again. Logics of pain require time to be organized as linear and rigid, in which the pained body (or community or people) is set back or delayed on some kind of path of humanization, and now must catch up (but never can) to the settler/unpained/abled body (or community or people or society or philosophy or knowledge system). In this way, the logics of pain has superseded the now outmoded racism of an explicit racial hierarchy with a much more politically tolerable racism of a developmental hierarchy.[2] Under a developmental hierarchy, in which some were undeterred by pain and oppression, and others were waylaid by their victimry and subalternity, damage-centered research reifies a settler temporality and helps suppress other understandings of time.

Desire-based frameworks, by contrast, look to the past and the future to situate analyses.

> Desire is about longing, about a present that is enriched by both the past and the future; it is integral to our humanness. It is not only the painful elements of social and psychic realities, but also the textured acumen and hope. (Tuck, 2010, p. 644)

In this way, desire is time-warping. The logics of desire is asynchronous just as it is distemporal, living in the gaps between the ticking machinery of disciplinary institutions.

To be clear, again, we are not making an argument against the existence of pain, or for the erasure of memory, experience, and wisdom that comes with suffering. Rather, we see the collecting of narratives of pain by social scientists to already be a double erasure, whereby pain is documented in order to be erased, often by eradicating the communities that are supposedly injured and supplanting them with hopeful stories of progress into a better, Whiter, world. Vizenor talks about such "the consumer notion of a 'hopeful book,'" and we would add hopeful or feel-good research, as "a denial of tragic wisdom" bent on imagining "a social science paradise of tribal victims" (1993, p. 14). Desire interrupts this metanarrative of damaged communities and White progress.

AXIOM II: THERE ARE SOME FORMS
OF KNOWLEDGE THAT THE ACADEMY DOESN'T DESERVE

Across academic disciplines, examples of ethical misconduct in human research are abundant. Rebecca Skloot's (2010) account of the experiences of Henrietta Lacks and her children, after cells from Ms. Lacks's cervix were harvested after her death in 1951, without consent, and reproduced in laboratories by the millions, if not billions, portrays the ways in which families can be haunted by decisions made by researchers, long after the facts. More recently, the Havasupai tribe, who live in the Grand Canyon, won a settlement from Arizona State University because of the deceptive practices of a biomedical researcher, Therese Markow (Harmon, 2010). Dr. Markow had permission from the tribe to collect blood samples to study diabetes, but did not have permission to use the samples in the numerous other genetic studies on schizophrenia and on the geographic origins of the tribe that she conducted with her students. Years after the samples had been drawn, members of the tribe learned that their blood had been used to test a variety of theories and conditions—some of which contradicted their own generational knowledge regarding sovereign claims to land. The samples, kept in a freezer on campus, became the stuff upon which researchers earned tenure and promotion, and their doctoral degrees. More than two dozen publications were based on the samples (Harmon, 2010).

Though one might read these cases as instances of misconduct with which only those in the biomedical or biological sciences must be concerned, it is important to point out that the misuse of human cells, blood, or tissue is not only about the handling of such materials, but also about the ways in which those materials are used to construct particular stories and narratives about an individual, family, tribe, or community. The misconduct is in the fabrication, telling, and retelling of stories. Academe is very much about the generation and swapping of stories, and there are some stories that the academy has not yet proven itself responsible enough to hear. We are writing about a particular form of loquaciousness of the academy, one that thrives on specific representations of power and oppression, and rarefied portrayals of dysfunction and pain.

One might ask what is meant by the academy, and by the academy being undeserving or unworthy of some stories or forms of knowledge. For some, the academy refers to institutions of research and higher education, and the individuals that inhabit them. For others, the term applies to the relationships between institutions of research and higher education, the nation-state, private and governmental funders, and all involved individuals. When we invoke the academy, or academe, we are invoking a community of practice that is focused upon the propagation and promulgation of (settler colonial) knowledge. Thus, when we say that there are some forms of knowledge that the academy does not deserve, it is because we have observed the academy as a community of practice that, *as a whole*:

- Stockpiles examples of injustice, yet will not make explicit a commitment to social justice
- Produces knowledge shaped by the imperatives of the nation-state, while claiming neutrality and universality in knowledge production
- Accumulates intellectual and financial capital, while informants give a part of themselves away
- Absorbs or repudiates competing knowledge systems, while claiming limitless horizons

Like the previous axiom's question—Why collect narratives of pain?—we ask nonrhetorically, what knowledges does the academy deserve? Beyond narratives of pain, there may be language, experiences, and wisdoms better left alone by social science.

Paula Gunn Allen (1998) notes that for many Indigenous peoples, "a person is expected to know no more than is necessary, sufficient and congruent with their spiritual and social place" (p. 56). To apply this idea to the production of social science research, we might think of this as a differentiation between what is made public and what is kept sacred. Not everything, or even most things, uncovered in a research process need to be reported in academic journals or settings. Contrasting Indigenous relationships to knowledge with settler relationships to knowledge, Gunn Allen remarks,

> In the white world, information is to be saved and analyzed at all costs. It is not seen as residing in the minds and molecules of human beings, but as—dare I say it?—transcendent. Civilization and its attendant virtues of freedom and primacy depend on the accessibility of millions of megabytes of data; no matter that the data has lost its meaning by virtue of loss of its human context . . . the white world has a different set of values [from the Indigenous world], one which requires learning all and telling all in the interests of knowledge, objectivity, and freedom. This ethos and its obverse—a nearly neurotic distress in the presence of secrets and mystery—underlie much of modern American culture (p. 59)

As social science researchers, there are stories that are entrusted to us, stories that are told to us because research is a human activity, and we make meaningful relationships with participants in our work. At times we come to individuals and communities with promises of proper procedure and confidentiality-anonymity in hand, and are told, "Oh, we're not worried about that; we trust you!" Or, "You don't need to tell us all that; we know you will do the right thing by us." Doing social science research is intimate work, worked that is strained by a tension between informants' expectations that something useful or helpful will come from the divulging of (deep) secrets, and the academy's voracious hunger for the secrets.

This is not just a question of getting permission to tell a story through a signature on an IRB-approved participant consent form. Permission is an individualizing discourse—it situates collective wisdom as individual property to be signed away. Tissue samples, blood draws, and cheek swabs are not only our own; the

DNA contained in them is shared by our relatives, our ancestors, our future generations (most evident when blood samples are misused as bounty for biopiracy). This is equally true of stories. Furthermore, power is protected by such a collapse of ethics into litigation-proof relationships between individual and research institution. Power, which deserves the most careful scrutiny, will never sign such a permission slip.[3]

There are also stories that we overhear, because when our research is going well, we are really in peoples' lives. Though it is tempting, and though it would be easy to do so, these stories are not simply y/ours to take. In our work, we come across stories, vignettes, moments, turns of phrase, pauses, that would humiliate participants to share, or are too sensationalist to publish. Novice researchers in doctoral and master's programs are often encouraged to do research on what or who is most available to them. People who are underrepresented in the academy by social location—race or ethnicity, indigeneity, class, gender, sexuality, or ability—frequently experience a pressure to become the n/Native informant, and might begin to suspect that some members of the academy perceive them as a route of easy access to communities that have so far largely eluded researchers. Doctoral programs, dissertations, and the master's thesis process tacitly encourage novice researchers to reach for low-hanging fruit. These are stories and data that require little effort—and what we know from years and years of academic colonialism is that it is easy to do research on people in pain. That kind of voyeurism practically writes itself. "Just get the dissertation or thesis finished," novice researchers are told. The theorem of low-hanging fruit stands for pretenured faculty too: "Just publish, just produce; research in the way you want to after tenure, later." This is how the academy reproduces its own irrepressible irresponsibility.

Adding to the complexity, many of us also bring to our work in the academy our family and community legacies of having been researched. As the researched, we carry stories from grandmothers' laps and breaths, from below deck, from on the run, from inside closets, from exclaves. We carry the proof of oppression on our backs, under our fingernails; and we carry the proof of our *survivance* (Vizenor, 2008) in our photo boxes, our calluses, our wombs, our dreams. These stories, too, are not always ours to give away, though they are sometimes the very us of us.

It needs to be said that we are not arguing for silence. Stories are meant to be passed along appropriately, especially among loved ones, but not all of them as social science research. Although such knowledge is often a source of wisdom that informs the perspectives in our writing, we do not intend to share them as social science research. It is enough that we know them.

Kahnawake scholar Audra Simpson asks the following questions of her own ethnographic work with members of her nation: "Can I do this and still come home; what am I revealing here and why? Where will this get us? Who benefits from this and why?" (2007, p. 78). These questions force researchers to contend with the strategies of producing legitimated knowledge based on the colonization of knowledge.

Indigenous and non-Indigenous scholars of Native education have queried the dangers of appropriation of Native knowledge by mainstream research and pedagogical institutions (e.g., Castagno & Brayboy, 2008; Lomawaima & McCarty, 2006; Richardson, 2011). Lomawaima and McCarty (2006) describe the "safety zone" as ways in which Indigenous knowledges are included into even overtly anti-Indian spaces such as boarding schools designed to assimilate Native children. Indigenous knowledge is made harmless to settler colonial pedagogies by relegating it to the safety zone of the margins. Troy Richardson extends this analysis by discussing "inclusion as enclosure" (2011, p. 332), the encircling of Native education as part of a well-intentioned multiculturalist agenda. Such gestures, he contends, reduce the Indigenous curriculum to a supplement to a standard curriculum.

Moreover, some narratives die a little when contained within the metanarrative of social science. Richardson (2011) theorizes Gerald Vizenor's concept of trickster knowledge and the play of shadows to articulate a "shadow curriculum" that exceeds the material objects of reference—where much meaning is made in silence surrounding the words, where memories are not simply reflections of a referent experience but dynamic in themselves. "The shadow is the silence that inherits the words; shadows are the motions that mean the silence" (Vizenor, 1993, p.7). Extending Richardson's analysis of Vizenor's work, beneath the intent gaze of the social scientific lens, shadow stories lose their silences, their play of meaning. The stories extracted from the shadows by social science research frequently become relics of cultural anthropological descriptions of "tradition" and difference from occidental cultures. Vizenor observes these to be the "denials of tribal wisdom in the literature of dominance, and the morass of social science theories" (Vizenor, 1993, p. 8).

Said another way, the academy as an apparatus of settler colonial knowledge already domesticates, denies, and dominates other forms of knowledge. It too refuses. It sets limits, but disguises itself as limitless. Frederic Jameson (1981) writes, "[H]istory is what hurts. It is what refuses desire and sets inexorable limits to individual as well as collective praxis" (p. 102).

For Jameson, history is a master narrative of inevitability, the logic of teleos and totality: All events are interconnected and all lead toward the same horizon of progress. The relentlessness of the master narrative is what hurts people who find themselves on the outside or the underside of that narrative. History as master narrative appropriates the voices, stories, and histories of all Others, thus limiting their representational possibilities, their expression as epistemological paradigms in themselves. Academic knowledge is particular and privileged, yet disguises itself as universal and common; it is settler colonial; it already refuses desire; it sets limits to potentially dangerous Other knowledges; it does so through erasure, but importantly also through *inclusion*, and its own imperceptibility.

Jameson's observation also positions desire as a counterlogic to the history that hurts. Desire invites the ghosts that history wants exorcised, and compels us to imagine the possible in what was written as impossible; desire is haunted. Read this way, desire expands personal as well as collective praxis.

AXIOM III: RESEARCH MAY NOT
BE THE INTERVENTION THAT IS NEEDED

As social science researchers, we are trained to believe that research is useful (even if only vaguely useful) and that it can compel needed change (even if the theory of change is somewhat fuzzy, or flawed). Indeed, the hidden theory of change in the metanarrative of social science research is that research itself leads to change. This is the hidden curriculum of social science: that the researched need change and that social science will compel it. As such, when we see something that needs attention, resources, critique, or intercession, our initial inclination may be to conduct research on it. We generally do research to meet an unmet need. Yet there are far more instances than are commonly realized in which research is not the most useful or appropriate intervention. They include situations in which:

- The researcher already has a very clear sense of what she wants her research to say or do
- The research is constructed to convince a group of people of something that they are completely closed to hearing
- The research is meant to legitimize community knowledge that is already deeply recognized
- The researcher would like to say something that has already been said, but this time in the voices of youth, community, elders, and so on
- There is too much at stake for a research process to reveal findings that counter a researcher or community's position on an issue

In these instances, research is reduced to a performance of inquiry in order to acquire legitimacy. This is when research is the most cynical about inquiry, and the most conceited about its own efficacy. In cases in which an intervention is needed, there are many other ways of developing and communicating ideas, including billboards, blogs, bumper stickers, letters, compelling spokespersons, flash mobs, YouTube videos, curricula, open houses, community talking tours, postcards, and the many forms of art.[4]

Many scholars may feel motivated to reimagine such activities as research, presumably in order to expand the umbrella of legitimacy to include more media, or modes of communication. There is an assumption that relabeling some forms of knowledge as research helps to increase the use or influence of those forms of knowledge. Thus we often hear that performance can be research, poetry can be autoethnography, my grandmother's wisdom is a form of research, and so forth. In a critique of autoethnography's appropriation of art, Gingrich-Philbrook describes this domestication of knowledge by social science research as an "epistemological assimilation game" (2005, p. 302) by which the academy "seduces us with its Good Labkeeping Seal of Approval" (p. 306). Indeed, if one were to map a hierarchy of human ways of knowing, research would appear at the top. We contend that although research is a space of inquiry and although it does traffic in cultural capital, there are forms of knowledge better off without the scientific stamp of model citizen knowledge. This is not to say that multimedia and other modes of communication have no place in the academy, but that the label *research* need not be the only descriptor deemed legitimate or valuable.

Research is just one form of knowing, but in the Western academy, it eclipses all others. In this way, the relationship of research to other human ways of knowing resembles a colonizing formation, acquiring, claiming, absorbing, consuming. In the current neoliberal moment, there are few spaces that remain dedicated to human curiosity and human inquiry aside from research. This component of research is valuable, and worth sustaining, yet we must simultaneously protect and nurture other nonresearch spaces/approaches for curiosity and inquiry. Calling everything research doesn't help to ensure that there are multiple opportunities to be curious, or to make meaning in life. We aren't advising anyone to insert artificial or insurmountable barriers between research and other forms of human inquiry, or to think of research and art as impermeable or discrete—just to attend to the productive tensions between genres/ epistemologies, to gather the benefits of what might be a dialogical relationship between research and art.

Indeed, there are many instances in which research may not be the best sociopolitical intervention, and it might not even be the best theoretical intervention. Theory works deliciously differently in the social sciences and in art. Consider works such as Toni Morrison's *Beloved* (1987), Joy Harjo's (2003) No, and Ken Gonzalez-Day's (n.d.) *Erased Lynching* series (discussed later in this chapter). Each of these works actively theorizes the remnants of domination, the shadows of terrible dances and grief songs (see Harjo, 2003, pp. 95–96). Engaging literature and art as theory—especially decolonial literature and art—intervenes upon modes of theorizing in the social sciences, setting limits to social science research and also making those limits permeable to other forms of inquiry. The relationship between research and art can be one of epistemological respect and reciprocity rather than epistemological assimilation or colonization.

THEORIZING REFUSAL

Here is a strange and bitter crop.

—Abel Meeropol, New York City
public school teacher
and lyricist of the 1939
Billie Holiday song *Strange Fruit**

In this final section, our task is to engage in a more tentative, more shifting and information discussion of refusal—indeed, a theorizing of refusal as an operationalization of the three axioms we have already presented. Far from axiomatic, this discussion is more speculative and less sure-footed. Here we will consider this question: Without a wholesale dismissal of social science research, how do we understand the researcher's and researched's relationships to knowledge circulated and recirculated by the academy? Our discussion relies heavily upon a rich and dynamic 2007 article by Kahnawake scholar Audra Simpson, titled "On Ethnographic Refusal: Indigeneity, 'Voice,' and Colonial Citizenship." We engage a close discussion and description of Simpson's work in order to begin to piece together a methodology around refusal, not as a simple or extremist or prohibitive stance, but as a generative orientation. In part, we are trying to help readers think through what there is instead of pain for social science research to look at, and also to provide some ways of theorizing the political and sovereign advantages of ascribing limits to settler colonial social science research. It is our conviction that once social science research is understood as settler colonial knowledge, nothing less and nothing more, it then makes sense why limits must be placed on it. If social science research is not understood as such, then talk of limits reads as a violation of the universal benefits of knowledge production, and perhaps of humanity itself. There is no rulebook, no set of step-by-step directions to follow for refusal. It means stepping to the side of the march of the academic industrial complex, taking stock of its recruiting of conscript knowledges, and formulating ways to do things differently. Refusal, taken seriously, is about humanizing the researcher.

Simpson's (2007) article is in many ways a director's-cut commentary on her ethnography on Mohawk nationhood and citizenship, and is a layered example of refusal centered in the Kahnawake Nation, within which she herself is a member. Simpson opens her article with a critique of the need to know as deeply connected to a need to conquer, a need to govern. In light of this, how Canada "knows" who is and isn't Indigenous is imbricated with law. The Indian Act,

> a specific body of law that recognises Indians in a wardship status in Canada, created the categories of person and rights that served to sever Indian women from their communities upon marriage to white men. It did the reverse to Indian men—white women gained Indian status upon their marriage into an Indian community. (p. 75)

In 1984, Bill C-31 amended the act to add Indian women and their descendants back into the federal registry of Indians in Canada, leaving it up to individual nations to determine whether to reinstate them in their local registries. The politics of membership generated a series of massive predicaments for people who had assimilated versions of the law for the past 150 years and found ways to resist it all the same. Kahnawake's own blood quantum membership code, developed in defiance of Canadian regulations for political recognition, was "contested and defended by, it seemed, everyone within the community and sometimes all at once" (p. 73). The question of who is and isn't Mohawk is not only politically contentious but one that is implicated within the very logic of settler colonial knowledge. Instead of surfacing the personal predicaments of "cousins and friends and enemies that comprise my version of Kahnawake" (p. 74), Simpson turns her ethnography toward the ways in which Kahnawake participants incorporated, dismissed, thwarted, and traversed notions of membership, especially via constructions of citizenship that intentionally drew upon logics found outside settler colonialism.

There are three concurrent dimensions of refusal in Simpson's analysis—in Simpson's words, her ethnography "pivoted upon refusal(s)" (p. 73). The first dimension is engaged by the interviewee, who refuses to disclose further details: "I don't know what you know, or what others know . . . no-one seems to know." The second dimension is enacted by Simpson herself, who refuses to write on the personal pain and internal politics of citizenship.

> "No one seems to know" was laced through much of my informant's discussion of C-31, and of his own predicament—which I knew he spoke of indirectly, because I knew his predicament. And I also knew everyone knew, because everyone knows everyone's "predicament." This was the collective "limit"—that of knowledge and thus who we could or would not claim. So it was very interesting to me that he would tell me that "he did not know" and "no one seems to know"—to me these utterances meant, "I know you know, and you know that I know I know . . . so let's just not get into this." Or, "let's just not say." So I did not say, and so I did not "get into it" with him, and I won't get into it with my readers. What I am quiet about is his predicament and my predicament and the actual stuff (the math, the clans, the mess, the misrecognitions, the confusion and the clarity)—the calculus of our predicaments. (p. 77)

The interviewee performs refusal by speaking in pointedly chosen phrases to indicate a shared/common knowledge, but also an unwillingness to say more, to demarcate the limits of what might be made public, or explicit. The second dimension of refusal is in the researcher's (Simpson's) accounting of the exchange, in which she installs limits on the intelligibility of what was at work, what was said and not said, for her readers. Simpson tells us, "In listening and shutting off the tape recorder, in situating each subject within their own shifting historical context of the present, these refusals speak volumes, because they tell us when to stop," (p. 78). In short, researcher and researched refuse to fulfill the ethnographic want for a speaking subaltern.

Both of these refusals reflect and constitute a third dimension—a more general anticoloniality and insistence of sovereignty by the Kahnawake Nation—and for many, a refusal to engage the logic of settler colonialism at all.

For the purposes of our discussion, the most important insight to draw from Simpson's article is her emphasis that refusals are not subtractive, but are theoretically generative (p. 78), expansive. Refusal is not just a "no," but a redirection to ideas otherwise unacknowledged or unquestioned. Unlike a settler colonial configuration of knowledge that is petulantly exasperated and resentful of limits, a methodology of refusal regards limits on knowledge as productive, as indeed a good thing.

To explore how refusal and the installation of limits on settler colonial knowledge might be productive, we make a brief detour to the *Erased Lynching* series (2002–2011) by Los Angeles–based artist Ken Gonzales-Day (see Figure 12.1). Gonzales-Day researched lynching in California and the Southwest and found that the majority of lynch victims were Latinos, American Indians, and Asians. Like lynchings in the South, lynchings in California were events of public spectacle, often attended by hundreds, sometimes thousands of festive onlookers. At the lynchings, professional photographers took hours to set up portable studios similar to those used at carnivals; they sold their images frequently as postcards, mementos of public torture and execution to be circulated by U.S. post throughout the nation and the world. Lynching, we must be reminded, was extralegal, yet nearly always required the complicity of law enforcement—either by marshals or sheriffs in the act itself, or by judges and courts in not bothering to prosecute the lynch mob afterward. The photographs immortalize the murder beyond the time and place of the lynching, and in their proliferation, expand a single murder to the general murderability of the non-White body. In this respect, the image of the hanged, mutilated body itself serves a critical function in the maintenance of White supremacy and the spread of racial terror beyond the lynching. The spectacle of the lynching is the medium of terror.

Figure 12.1   The wonder gaze (St. James Park)

Source: Photo from *The Wonder Gaze (St. James Park), Erased Lynching Series*, by Ken Gonzales-Day.

Gonzales-Day's *Erased Lynching* series reintroduces the photographs of lynching to a contemporary audience, with one critical intervention: The ropes and the lynch victim have been removed from the images. Per Gonzales-Day's website (n.d.), the series enacted a conceptual gesture intended to direct the viewer's attention, not upon the lifeless body of lynch victim, but upon the mechanisms of lynching themselves: the crowd, the spectacle, the photographer, and even consider the impact of flash photography upon this dismal past. The perpetrators, if present, remain fully visible, jeering, laughing, or pulling at the air in a deadly pantomime. As such, this series strives to make the invisible visible.

The *Erased Lynching* series yields another context in which we might consider what a social scientist's refusal stance might comprise. Though indeed centering on the erasure of the former object, refusal need not be thought of as a subtractive methodology. Refusal prompts analysis of the festive spectators regularly backgrounded in favor of wounded bodies, strange fruit, interesting scars. Refusal shifts the gaze from the violated body to the violating instruments—in this case, the lynch mob, which does not disappear when the lynching is over, but continues to live, accumulating land and wealth through the extermination and subordination of the Other. Thus, refusal helps move us from thinking of violence as an event and toward an analysis of it as a structure.

Gonzales-Day might have decided to reproduce and redistribute the images as postcards, which, by way of showing up in mundane spaces, might have effectively inspired reflection on the spectacle of violence and media of terror. However, in removing the body and the ropes, he installed limits on what the audience can access, and redirected our gaze to the bodies of those who were there to see a murder take place, and to the empty space beneath the branches. Gonzales-Day introduced a new representational territory, one that refuses to play by the rules of the settler colonial gaze, and one that refuses to satisfy the morbid curiosity derived from settler colonialism's preoccupation with pain.

Refusals are needed for narratives and images arising in social science research that rehumiliate when circulated, but also when, in Simpson's words, "the representation would bite all of us and compromise the representational territory that we have gained for ourselves in the past 100 years" (p. 78). As researcher-narrator, Simpson tells us, "I reached my own limit when the data would not contribute to our sovereignty or complicate the deeply simplified, atrophied representations of Iroquois and other Indigenous peoples that they have been mired within anthropologically" (p. 78). Here Simpson makes clear the ways in which research is not the intervention that is needed—that is, the interventions of furthering sovereignty or countering misrepresentations of Native people as anthropological objects.

Considering *Erased Lynchings* dialogically with *On Ethnographic Refusal*, we can see how refusal is not a prohibition but a generative form. First, refusal turns the gaze back upon power, specifically the colonial modalities of knowing persons as bodies to be differentially counted, violated, saved, and put to work. It makes transparent the metanarrative of knowledge production—its spectatorship for pain and its preoccupation for documenting and ruling over racial difference. Thus, refusal to be made meaningful first and foremost is grounded in a critique of settler colonialism, its construction of Whiteness, and its regimes of representation. Second, refusal generates, expands, champions representational territories that colonial knowledge endeavors to settle, enclose, domesticate. Simpson complicates the portrayals of Iroquois, without resorting to reportrayals of anthropological Indians. Gonzales-Day portrays the violations without reportraying the victimizations. Third, refusal is a critical intervention into research and its circular self-defining ethics. The ethical justification for research is defensive and self-encircling—its apparent self-criticism serves to expand its own rights to know, and to defend its violations in the name of "good science." Refusal challenges the individualizing discourse of IRB consent and "good science" by highlighting the problems of collective harm, of representational harm, and of knowledge colonization. Fourth, refusal itself could be developed into both method and theory. Simpson presents refusal on the part of the researcher as a type of calculus ethnography. Gonzales-Day deploys refusal as a mode of representation. Simpson theorizes refusal by the Kahnawake Nation as anticolonial, and rooted in the desire for possibilities outside of colonial logics, not as a reactive stance. This final point about refusal connects our conversation back to desire as a counterlogic to settler colonial knowledge.

Desire is compellingly depicted in Simpson's description of a moment in an interview, in which the alternative logics about a "feeling citizenship" are referenced. The interviewee states,

> Citizenship is, as I said, you live there, you grew up there, that is the life that you know—that is who you are. Membership is more of a legislative enactment designed to keep people from obtaining the various benefits that Aboriginals can receive. (p. 76)

Simpson describes this counterlogic as "the logic of the present," one that is witnessed, lived, suffered through, and enjoyed (p. 76). Out of the predicaments, it innovates "tolerance and exceptions and affections" (p. 76). Simpson writes (regarding the Indian Act, or blood quantum), "'Feeling citizenships' . . . are structured in the present space of intra-community recognition, affection and care, outside of the logics of colonial and imperial rule" (p. 76).

Simpson's logic of the present dovetails with our discussion on the logics of desire. Collectively, Kahnawake refusals decenter damage narratives; they unsettle the settler colonial logics of blood and rights; they center desire.

By theorizing through desire, Simpson thus theorizes *with* and *as* Kahnawake Mohawk. It is important to point out that Simpson does not deploy her tribal identity as a badge of authentic voice, but rather highlights the ethical predicaments that result from speaking as oneself, as simultaneously part of a collective with internal disputes, vis-à-vis negotiations of various settler colonial logics. Simpson thoughtfully differentiates between the Native researcher *philosophically* as a kind of privileged position of authenticity, and the Native researcher *realistically* as one who is beholden to multiple ethical considerations. What is tricky about this position is not only theorizing *with*, rather than theorizing *about*, but also theorizing *as*. To theorize *with* and *as* at the same time is a difficult yet fecund positionality—one that rubs against the ethnographic limit at the outset. Theorizing with (and in some of our cases, as) repositions Indigenous people and otherwise researched Others as intellectual subjects rather than anthropological subjects. Thus desire is an "epistemological shift," not just a methodological shift (Tuck, 2009, p. 419).

CULMINATION

At this juncture, we don't intend to offer a general framework for refusal, because all refusal is particular, meaning refusal is always grounded in historical analysis and present conditions. Any discussion of Simpson's article would need to attend to the significance of real and representational sovereignty in her analysis and theorizing of refusal. The particularities of Kahnawake sovereignty throb at the center of each of the three dimensions of refusal described above. We caution readers against expropriating Indigenous notions of sovereignty into other contexts, or metaphorizing sovereignty in a way that permits one to forget that struggles to have sovereignty recognized are very real and very lived. Yet from Simpson's example, we are able to see ways in which a researcher might make transparent the coloniality of academic knowledge in order to find its ethical limits, expand the limits of sovereign knowledge, and expand decolonial representational territories. This is in addition to questions her work helpfully raises about who the researcher is, who the researched are, and how the historical/representational context for research matters.

One way to think about refusal is how desire can be a framework, mode, and space for refusal. As a framework, desire is a counterlogic to the logics of settler colonialism. Rooted in possibilities gone but not foreclosed, "the *not yet*, and at times, the *not anymore*" (Tuck, 2010, p. 417), desire refuses the master narrative that colonization was inevitable and has a monopoly on the future. By refusing the teleos of colonial future, desire expands possible futures. As a mode of refusal, desire is a "no" and a "yes."

Another way to think about refusal is to consider using strategies of social science research to further expose the complicity of social science disciplines and research in the project of settler colonialism. There is much need to employ social science to turn back upon itself as settler colonial knowledge, as opposed to universal, liberal, or neutral knowledge without horizon. This form of refusal might include bringing attention to the mechanisms of knowledge legitimation, like the Good Labkeeping Seal of Approval (discussed under Axiom III); contesting appropriation, like the collection of pain narratives; and publicly renouncing the diminishing of Indigenous or local narratives with blood narratives in the name of science, such as in the Havasupai case discussed under Axiom II.

As long as the objects of research are presumably damaged communities in need of intervention, the metanarrative of social science research remains unchallenged: which is that research at worst is simply an expansion of common knowledge (and therefore harmless), and that research at best is problem solving (and therefore beneficial). This metanarrative justifies a host of interventions into communities, and treats communities as frontiers to civilize, *regardless of the specific conclusions of individual research projects.* Consider, for example, well-intended research on achievement gaps that fuels NCLB and testing; the documentation of youth violence that provides the rationales for gang injunctions and the expansion of the prison industrial complex; the documentation of diabetes as justification for unauthorized genomic studies and the expansion of anti-Indigenous theories. Instead, by making the settler colonial metanarrative the object of social science research, researchers may bring to a halt or at least slow down the machinery that allows knowledge to facilitate interdictions on Indigenous and Black life. Thus, this form of refusal might also involve tracking the relationships between social science research and expansions of state and corporate violence against communities. Social science researchers might design their work to call attention to or interrogate power, rather than allowing their work to serve as yet another advertisement for power. Further, this form of refusal might aim to leverage the resources of the academy to expand the representational territories fought for by communities working to thwart settler colonialism.

We close this chapter with much left unsaid. This is both because there is so much to say, and also because, as we have noted, all refusal is particular. Refusal understands the wisdom in a story, as well as the wisdom in not passing that story on. Refusal in research makes way for other r-words—for resistance, reclaiming, recovery, reciprocity, repatriation, regeneration. Though understandings of refusal are still emergent, though so much is still coming into view, we want to consolidate a summary of take-away points for our readers. A parting gift, of sorts, as each of us takes our leave to map our next steps as researchers, as community members, within and without academe. We think of this list as a tear-away sheet, something to cut out and carry in your pocket, sew into a prayer flag, or paste into your field notebooks.

What can be said about refusal in social science research?

- Refusal can be a generative stance for humanized researchers.
- Refusal is not just a "no."
- Refusal must be situated in a critical understanding of settler colonialism and its regimes of representation (i.e., the disappearance of Indigenous people, the enslavability and murderability of Black people, the right to make interdictions on Othered lives).
- Refusal makes space for desire and other representational territories, such as making the spectator the spectacle, and turning settler colonial knowledge back on itself.
- Refusal is multidimensional, in dynamic relationship between communities who refuse, the researched who refuse, and the researcher who refuses—or who do not.

- Social science knowledge is settler colonial knowledge. It also refuses (refuses the agency, personhood, and theories of the researched), and it also set limits (limits the epistemologies of the colonized/colonizable/to-be-colonized) and hides its own refusals and limits in order to appear limitless.
- Thus, refusal makes visible the processes of settler colonial knowledge. Refusal, by its very existence and exercise, sets limits on settler colonial knowledge.
- Similarly, refusal denudes power (and power-knowledge) without becoming an advertisement for power.
- Refusal problematizes hidden or implicit theories of change.
- Most efficacious might be the refusal by the researcher, how she determines the limits on what she can ask or what she will write. This refusal might take the form of turning off the tape recorder; not disclosing what was on the tape even if it was recorded; hearing a story and choosing to listen and learn from it rather than report it; resisting the draw to traffic theories that cast communities as in need of salvation.

REFLECTIVE QUESTIONS

1. The authors ask the question, "How do we learn from and respect the wisdom and desires in the stories that we (over)hear, while refusing to portray/betray them to the spectacle of the settler colonial gaze?" How might this question be important to the research you are considering, designing, or conducting?

2. In which ways is the stance of refusal in social science research "more than just a 'no'"? The authors provide several examples of refusal by writers and authors, such as Audra Simpson and Ken Gonzalez-Day. Can you think of other examples of refusal? What do these refusals accomplish? How might the stance of refusal be necessary in your research?

3. The authors assert that "the collection of pain narratives and the theories of change that champion the value of such narratives are so prevalent in the social sciences that one might surmise that they are indeed what the academy is about." Do you agree with this assertion? Why or why not?

4. The authors ask readers to consider whether there are some forms of knowledge that the academy doesn't deserve. What is your reaction to this notion? Why do you think you have this reaction?

NOTES

1. Another impetus for much of social science research is to document best practices, or effective models, presumably to learn what works in order to transfer onto other spaces, or to scale up. We also question the underlying theory of change in this social science research trope. Is there such a thing as a universal best practice? Can context-specific practices be successfully scaled up? We are not so fast to be sure.

2. This works in much the same way that settler colonialism always seeks to supersede itself, to make itself natural and undetectable (Veracini, 2011).

3. In their forthcoming chapter, Eve Tuck and Monique Guishard critique the collapsing of ethics to IRB individual-institutional protections, and present an ethical framework of decolonial participatory action research.

4. Upon reading this list, one might complain that these are low-status activities in the academy, activities that, alone, will not lead to tenure or promotion. We do not see tenure or promotion alone as compelling enough reasons to conduct research.

REFERENCES

Castagno, A., & Brayboy, B. (2008). Culturally responsive schooling for Indigenous youth: A review of the literature. *Review of Educational Research, 78*(4), 941–993.

Dussel, E. D. (1985). *Philosophy of liberation.* Maryknoll, NY: Orbis Books.

Fanon, F. (1968). *The wretched of the earth.* New York, NY: Grove Press.

Gingrich-Philbrook, C. (2005). Autoethnography's family values: Easy access to compulsory experiences. *Text and Performance Quarterly, 25*(4), 297–314.

Gonzales-Day, K. (n.d.). *Erased Lynching* series [Webpage photographs and postcards]. Retrieved August 17, 2011, from http://www.kengonzalesday.com/projects/erased lynching/

Gould, S. J. (1981). *The mismeasure of man.* New York, NY: W. W. Norton.

Gunn Allen, P. (1998). Problems in teaching Leslie Marmon Silko's Ceremony. In D. A. Mihesuah (Ed.), *Natives and academics: Researching and writing about American Indians* (pp. 55–64). Lincoln: University of Nebraska Press.

Guthrie, R. (1976). *Even the rat was white: A historical view of psychology.* New York, NY: Harper & Row.

Harjo, J. (2003). "No." Reprinted in S. Hamill (Ed.), *Poets against the war* (pp. 95–96). New York, NY: Thunder's Mouth Press/Nation Books.

Harmon, A. (2010, April 21). *Indian tribe wins fight to limit research of its DNA.* Retrieved from http://www.nytimes.com/2010/04/22/us/22dna.html

Hartman, S. V. (1997). *Scenes of subjection: Terror, slavery, and self-making in nineteenth-century America.* New York, NY: Oxford University Press.

Hartman, S. V. (2007). *Lose your mother: A journey along the Atlantic slave route.* New York, NY: Farrar, Straus and Giroux.

hooks, b. (1990). Marginality as a site of resistance. In R. Ferguson et al. (Eds.), *Out there: Marginalization and contemporary cultures* (pp. 241–243). Cambridge, MA: MIT.

Jaffe, S. (1996). *Scars make your body more interesting and other stories.* Boston, MA: Black Sparrow Press.

Jameson, F. (1981). *The political unconscious: Narrative as a socially symbolic act.* Ithaca, NY: Cornell University Press.

Kelley, R. D. G. (1997). *Yo' Mama's disfunktional! Fighting the culture wars in urban America.* Boston, MA: Beacon Press.

Lomawaima, K. T., & McCarty, T. L. (2006). *To remain an Indian: Lessons in democracy from a century of Native American education.* New York, NY: Teachers College Press.

Maldonado-Torres, N. (2007). On the coloniality of being. *Cultural Studies, 21*(2), 240–270.

Maldonado-Torres, N. (2009). Rousseau and Fanon on inequality and the human sciences. *The CLR James Journal: A Review of Caribbean Ideas, 15*(1), 1–29. Retrieved from http://trinity.duke.edu/.../wp.../reflections_Maldonado-Torres_respondent.pdf

Morris, R. (Ed.). (2010). *Can the subaltern speak? Reflections on the history of an idea.* New York, NY: Columbia University Press.

Morrison, T. (1987). *Beloved: A novel.* New York, NY: Knopf.

Moten, F., & Harney, S. (2010, March). Debt and study. *E-flux journal, 14.* Retrieved from http://www.e-flux.com/journal/view/119

Ndlvou-Gatsheni, S. (2011). *The logic of violence in Africa* (Ferguson Centre for African and Asian Studies, Working Paper No. 02). Retrieved from http:// www.open.ac.uk/ Arts/ferguson-centre/working-papers/working-paper-2.doc

Richardson, T. (2011). Navigating the problem of inclusion as enclosure in Native culture-based education: Theorizing shadow curriculum. *Curriculum Inquiry, 41(*3), 332–349.

Said, E. W. (1978). *Orientalism.* New York, NY: Pantheon Books.

Sedgwick, E. K. (1990). *Epistemology of the closet.* Berkeley: University of California Press.

Selden, S. (1999). *Inheriting shame: The story of eugenics and racism in America.* New York, NY: Teachers College Press.

Simpson, A. (2007). On ethnographic refusal: Indigeneity, "voice," and colonial citizenship. *Junctures, 9,* 67–80.

Skloot, R. (2010). *The immortal life of Henrietta Lacks.* New York, NY: Broadway Press.

Spivak, G. (2010). Can the subaltern speak? In. R. Morris (Ed.), *Can the subaltern speak? Reflections on the history of an idea* (pp. 21–80). New York, NY: Columbia University Press.

Tuck, E., & Guishard, M. (forthcoming). Uncollapsing ethics: Racialized sciencism, settler coloniality, and an ethical framework of decolonial participatory action research. In T. M. Kress, C. Malott, & B. Porfilio (Eds.), *Challenging status quo retrenchment: New directions in critical qualitative research.*

Tuck, E. (2009). Suspending damage: A letter to communities. *Harvard Educational Review, 79*(3), 409–427.

Tuck, E. (2010). Breaking up with Deleuze: Desire and valuing the irreconcilable. *The International Journal of Qualitative Studies in Education*, 23(5), 635–650.

Tuhiwai Smith, L. (1999). *Decolonizing methodologies: Research and Indigenous peoples.* Dunedin, NZ: Zed Books.

Veracini, L. (2011). Introducing settler colonial studies. *Settler Colonial Studies, 1,* 1–12. Retrieved July 10, 2011, from http://ojs.lib.swin.edu.au/index.php/settlercolonialstudies/ article/viewFile/239/223

Vizenor, G. R. (1993). The ruins of representation: Shadow survivance and the literature of dominance. *American Indian Quarterly, 17*(1), 7–30.

Vizenor, G. R. (Ed.). (2008). *Survivance: Narratives of Native presence.* Lincoln, NE: University of Nebraska Press.

Wolfe, P. (1999). *Settler colonialism and the transformation of anthropology: The politics and poetics of an ethnographic event.* New York, NY: Cassell.

Youngblood Jackson, A., & Mazzei, L. A. (2009). *Voice in qualitative inquiry: Challenging conventional, interpretive, and critical conceptions in qualitative research.* New York, NY: Routledge.

EPILOGUE

Reflecting Forward on Humanizing Approaches

Maisha T. Winn

After attending a production of *The Bluest Eye* with student and teaching artists from Girl Time, a playwriting and performance program for formerly incarcerated girls in which I was a participant observer for five years, I drove one student artist—Nia—home at her mother's request. Nia and I had an opportunity to use our "down time" (as one teaching artist called the rides home, as well as the pick-ups from and drop-offs to the train) to discuss how we experienced the production and our work with Girl Time. Down time became a critical component of my relationship with the girls as a teacher and a scholar asking questions about the role of playwriting and performance in creating and recreating literate identities for girls who found themselves "betwixt and between" incarcerated and liberated lives.

Nia navigated our way to her home through a series of neighborhoods that were unfamiliar to me. Uniform brick houses sat far from the streets among pine trees that seemed impossible to exist in a neighborhood within city limits. I had to be extremely cautious of the pedestrians who walked in the street because there were no sidewalks or streetlights. I certainly thought to myself that it was going to be difficult to find my way home. When we pulled up to Nia's house, a woman, who turned out to be Nia's mother, Ms. Johnson, and a man were standing outside in the dark. When Ms. Johnson approached the car, I recognized her familiar face, and we exchanged our gratitude for each other. She began to explain that she thought it was too late for Nia to ride the train, and I assured her that giving Nia a ride was the least I could do. Ms. Johnson insisted that I come inside to see how she had "redecorated" Nia's room. I must have looked a bit surprised, as it was now after 11:00 p.m. and I had no idea where I was. And who, I wondered to myself, was that man standing outside the house? I was ashamed of my reaction yet feeling justified. Nia's neighborhood was not that much different from the neighborhood where I was raised the first half of my life; however, I knew the cast of characters on my block. Was I embodying the same fear that I cautioned against in my scholarly work? I am sure my pause caused alarm with Nia, who told her mother firmly, "Mama, that woman is tired! Let her be on her way home. She don't have time for all that." As I listened to and looked at Nia, I realized that she thought of herself as protecting me—and herself—so that I would not have to say no and so she would not have to witness hearing me say no. I turned off the car and jumped out before I could think too much more about it.

It was evident that Ms. Johnson really wanted to invite me into her home, and in many ways to show me how much she loved her daughter. After all, hadn't enough people judged Ms. Johnson once they learned her daughter had become entangled in the school-to-prison pipeline, thus leading to her serving time in a youth detention center? And hadn't she seen the grimace behind people's affirming nods when she tried to explain how she was unable to get her out of a jail for children? Nia, Ms. Johnson, and I stood in the doorway of Nia's room, and it took me back to my teenage room with the proper posters of the music artists she loved. I reminisced about my New Edition, Michael Jackson, and Prince posters, and we laughed at the changing same of it all. Ms. Johnson pointed out the new matching curtains and comforter set she had surprised her daughter with, while Nia smiled shyly. We quietly took it all in and were deep in our own thoughts before Nia, again trying to look out for me, told her mother, "Let this lady get back to her house, Mama! It's late!"

As I close this volume of scholarship focused on decolonizing research methods, I am reminded of this scene with Nia and Ms. Johnson. As scholars working with youth and communities, all of us in this volume have been granted access to the lives of people in various contexts. Like Green, in this volume, I found myself in a "double dutch" game of sorts, trying to figure out when and where I was supposed to enter as well as exit. What I learned was that it was not always, if ever, up to me to walk away from a "participant," a "site," or a "study," because they were so much more than these scientific labels. These were so much more than "participants"; like Blackburn and Jocson in their critical ethnographic work, I had the privilege of working with young people who *schooled me* through our collaborative process. These were more than "sites"; rather, they were communities that I was invited into and where I was made to feel like one of the family. For many in this volume, like Romero-Little, Sims, and Romero, this idea of the research "site" is a label used for communities that are and have always been homelands. For many others in this volume, we navigate the borders of our own communities and those of others seeking the ground of common purpose toward equity. My projects with Nia and her peers were also much more than "studies" and "research projects"; I asked questions and, as in the participatory traditions described by Irizarry and Brown, and McCarty, Wyman, and Nicholas, I often co-constructed questions and solutions with the young people and their teachers. When I drove Nia home and her mother invited me inside, it was imperative that I accept her invitation and redirect my initial hesitation. In this context, Nia and her family taught me that I was not the one who solely got to say when and where I entered, and certainly not when and where—to recall Mangual Figueroa's experience with La Carta de Responsabilidad—I made my exit. Nia trusted me with their stories, and she needed to know that I was a worthy witness to her lived experi-ences. In a sense, she needed to know, as Kirkland's Guys did, who I was in this work. Ms. Johnson trusted me with her daughter, and she needed to know that this same person could walk into her house and witness that she, like so many other parents, was doing the best she could by her child in the face of a world that did not often value her daughter or her daughter's family. As Strong, Duarte, Gomez, and Meiners remind researchers in this volume, we can never be "too close to the work" if we are asking critical questions that can transform policies that are oppressive and colonizing. Through listening and "storying," as offered by Kinloch and San Pedro, and through "Critical Narrative Analysis," as put forward by Souto-Manning, scholars are able to resist the desire to control every aspect of their work in a way that allows them to develop new questions. The storying throughout this volume is an attempt to "refuse"—to paraphrase Tuck and Yang— the kind of research that does not take as a starting point the humanity and dignity of all people.

CONTRIBUTORS

Mollie Blackburn is Associate Professor of Teaching and Learning at The Ohio State University, where she co-coordinates the Sexuality Studies program. She is the author of *Interrupting Hate: Homophobia in Schools and What Literacy Can Do About It*, the co-editor of *Acting Out! Combating Homophobia Through Teacher Activism*, and *Literacy Research for Political Action*. Her scholarship has received the American Educational Research Association's Queer Studies special interest group's Body of Work Award and she has also received the Alan C. Purves Award for articles in *Research in the Teaching of English* that have been deemed rich with classroom implications, among other awards.

Tara M. Brown is Assistant Professor of Education at Brandeis University. She holds an EdD from Harvard University and is the recipient of a Spencer Research Fellowship and a Jacobs Foundation Dissertation Fellowship. Tara is a former secondary classroom teacher, having worked in alternative education. Her research addresses issues of educational justice, particularly as they pertain to urban schooling. Tara's research focuses on disciplinary exclusion and dropout, using participatory action research methodologies with youth. Tara's most recent study focuses on the educational and socioeconomic implications of school dropout among young adults living in rustbelt cities in the Northeast.

Daysi Diaz-Strong has been a community college administrator in Illinois for eight years. In her various roles she has worked closely with underrepresented students and developed programs to improve the success of low-income and underrepresented students. Additionally, Ms. Diaz-Strong teaches a first-year experience course. She obtained an M.A. in Educational Leadership from Northeastern Illinois University. Ms. Diaz-Strong's research interests include education, immigration, and identity. Currently she is conducting research on the experiences of undocumented students in higher education, and she has co-authored various articles on research findings.

Christina Gómez is Professor of Sociology and coordinator of the Latino and Latin American Studies Program at Northeastern Illinois University. Her research focuses on race relations, discrimination, and immigration. Her book *Mi Vida, Mi Voz: Latino College Students Tell Their Stories* is an edited anthology of 15 essays written by students growing up Latino in the United States. She has published numerous articles on Latino identity, skin color, and discrimination and Latino education.

Keisha L. Green earned her PhD in Educational Studies from Emory University, specializing in language, literacy, and culture. Currently, she is a postdoctoral fellow at Rutgers University in Learning and Teaching at the Graduate School of Education. Her most recent study explored the intersection of youth radio, literacy, and civic engagement. Keisha is a former National Council of Teachers of English Cultivating New Voices fellow. Her recent publications focus on arts and social justice education and the school-to-prison pipeline and include *The United States Social Forum: Perspectives of a Movement*; *Race, Ethnicity, and Education*; and *Reading African American Experiences in the Obama Era: Theory, Advocacy, Activism*.

Jason G. Irizarry is Associate Professor of Multicultural Education in the Department of Curriculum and Instruction in the Neag School of Education and Faculty Associate in the Institute for Puerto Rican and Latino Studies at the University of Connecticut. His research focuses on urban teacher recruitment, preparation, and retention with an emphasis on increasing the number of teachers of color, culturally responsive pedagogy, youth participatory action research, and Latino students in U.S. schools. A central focus of his work involves promoting the academic achievement of youth in urban schools by addressing issues associated with teacher education. Dr. Irizarry is the author of *The Latinization of U.S. Schools: Successful Teaching and Learning in Shifting Cultural Contexts* (2011).

Korina Jocson is Assistant Professor of Education in Arts and Sciences at Washington University at Saint Louis. Her research and teaching interests include literacy, youth, and cultural studies in education. Central to her work are sociocultural approaches in examining the changing nature of literacies and media technologies across educational contexts. Her current research projects include "mapping literacies" to investigate broader ecological dimensions that shape literate activities of children and youth. In the past decade, Jocson has collaborated with university programs, schools, and community-based organizations to promote literacy learning and development among nondominant populations. She has published in several scholarly journals and is the author of *Youth Poets: Empowering Literacies In and Out of Schools*. Presently, she is the convener of "Cultural Transformations: Youth in the Age of New Media," a multiyear faculty seminar series sponsored by the Center for the Humanities in Arts & Sciences.

Valerie Kinloch is Associate Professor in Literacy Studies at The Ohio State University. Her research examines the lives, literacy learning, and collaborative engagements of youth and adults in and outside of school spaces. Valerie's award-winning book is titled *Harlem On Our Minds: Place, Race, and the Literacies of Urban Youth* (2010), and her most recent books include *Urban Literacies: Critical Perspectives on Language, Learning, and Community* (2011) and *Crossing Boundaries: Teaching and Learning With Urban Youth* (2012). Valerie is the recipient of the 2010 AERA Scholars of Color Early Career Award, and the 2012 AERA Outstanding Book Award.

David E. Kirkland is a transdisciplinary scholar of language, literacy, and urban education, who explores the intersections among urban youth culture, gender, and language and literacy practices. He has received many awards for his work, including the NAEd/Spencer Foundation Postdoctoral Fellowship Award, the Ford Foundation Postdoctoral Fellowship Award, the NCTE Cultivating New Voices Fellowship Award, and the 2006 AERA Division G Dissertation Award. His most recent articles appear in the *Journal of Adolescent and Adult Literacy*, *Language Arts*, *Teachers College Record*, *English Education*, and *Reading Research Quarterly*. He recently completed his fourth book, *A Search Past Silence: A Counter Narrative of Black Males and Literacy*. Dr. Kirkland believes that, in their language and literacies, youth take on new meanings, beginning with a voice and verb, where words when spoken or written have the power to transform the world inside-out.

María E. Luna-Duarte is Interim Director at Northeastern Illinois University–El Centro Campus. She has ample experience coordinating programs that serve the Latino community. As the Interim Director of NEIU–El Centro Campus, Ms. Luna-Duarte has been a key stakeholder in the development and implementation of NEIU–El Centro Campus programs and services. She has worked as the Community Liaison for the Chicago ENLACE (Engaging Latino Communities for Education) partnership program at NEIU, where she assisted with projects concerning the retention of Latinos in higher education. Ms. Luna-Duarte is bilingual (Spanish/English) and possesses an in-depth understanding of and experience with the educational, economic, and cultural needs of Latino students. Ms. Luna-Duarte received a B.A. in Sociology and an M.A. in Higher Education and Leadership from Northeastern Illinois University. She is currently pursuing a doctorate in Policy Studies in Urban Education at the University of Illinois at Chicago.

Ariana Mangual Figueroa is Assistant Professor of Language Education in the Graduate School of Education at Rutgers, the State University of New Jersey. Her research examines the language socialization experiences of multilingual Latino communities living in the United States. Her most recent ethnographic study of mixed-status families tracks how parents and children talk about citizenship in their everyday lives, exploring how learning and language use are shaped by immigration and educational policies. Her work has been published in *Anthropology & Education Quarterly* and is forthcoming in the *Journal of Language, Identity, and Education.*

Teresa L. McCarty is the Alice Wiley Snell Professor of Education Policy Studies and Applied Linguistics and co-director of the Center for Indian Education at Arizona State University. An educational anthropologist, she has worked with Indigenous education programs throughout North America and is the former codirector of the American Indian Language Development Institute at the University of Arizona. Her recent books include *Language, Literacy, and Power in Schooling* (2005); *A Place To Be Navajo—Rough Rock and the Struggle* *for Self-Determination in Indigenous Schooling* (2002); *"To Remain an Indian":* *Lessons in Democracy From a Century of Native American Education* (with K. T. Lomawaima, 2006), and *Ethnography and Language Policy* (2011).

Erica R. Meiners is Professor of Education, Women's Studies, and Latino and Latin American Studies at Northeastern Illinois University. She has written about her ongoing labor and learning in antimilitarization campaigns, educational justice struggles, prison abolition and reform movements, and queer and immigrant rights organizing in *Flaunt It! Queers Organizing for Public Education and Justice* (2009); *Right to Be Hostile: Schools, Prisons and the Making of Public Enemies* (2007); and numerous journals, including *Radical Teacher*, *Meridians*, and *Women's Studies Quarterly*. She is the 2011–2012 Visiting Scholar in Residence at the Institute for Research on Race and Public Policy at the University of Illinois at Chicago.

Sheilah E. Nicholas is a member of the Hopi Tribe and Assistant Professor in the Department of Teaching, Learning, and Sociocultural Studies at the University of Arizona. She is coordinator of the UA Bureau of Applied Research and Anthropology Hopi Children's Word Book Project, and a member of the Hopi Education Endowment Fund Executive Committee. She has served as a consultant to the Hopi Tribe in planning and implementing Hopi language teacher training at the Hopilavayi Summer Institute. Her research has been published in numerous edited volumes, in *American Indian Culture and Research Quarterly,* and in the *Journal of Language, Identity, and Education.*

A-dae Romero (Cochiti/Kiowa), independent scholar, was born, raised, and enrolled in Cochiti Pueblo, New Mexico. A graduate of Princeton University's Woodrow Wilson School of Public and International Affairs, Romero received her juris doctorate degree from the Sandra Day O'Connor College of Law at Arizona State University. She currently serves as a pro tem judge and program consultant for Native Nations and organizations in New Mexico, California, and Alaska.

Eunice Romero-Little is Associate Professor in the School of Social Transformation and American Indian Studies at Arizona State University. Dr. Romero-Little's past and current research and scholarship reflect an unwavering desire to improve education for Native children by expanding the theoretical and everyday boundaries of our understanding of their in- and out-of-school learning experiences. Her research and scholarship grows out of a solid grounding as an education practitioner and as an Indigenous language activist who assisted in establishing a language revitalization program in her home community of Cochiti Pueblo, New Mexico.

Timothy San Pedro is a PhD Candidate in English Education at Arizona State University, where he has conducted three years of ethnographic research in a Native American Literature classroom in a state that has banned ethnic studies programs in public schools. He taught Alaska Native high school students for the

Cook Inlet Tribal Council and grew up on the Flathead Indian Reservation in western Montana. He is also a scholar, regional director, and mentor for the Gates Millennium Scholarship Program; a Ford Foundation Dissertation fellow; and a Cultivating New Voices Among Scholars of Color fellow. San Pedro's research interests include Native American urban education and socioculturally responsive pedagogies.

Christine Sims is Assistant Professor in the Department of Language, Literacy, and Sociocultural Studies in the College of Education at the University of New Mexico. Dr. Sims specializes in Indigenous language revitalization and maintenance issues, providing technical assistance to tribes in Native language program planning, and training language teachers through the UNM College of Education's American Indian Language Policy Research and Teacher Training Center. Dr. Sims was selected by the National Association for Bilingual Education as the 2002 recipient of the Ramon L. Santiago President's Award for research and advocacy on language rights issues for Native American communities and the 2002 New Mexico Association for Bilingual Education award for contributions to Native American bilingual education in New Mexico. She is a tribal member of Acoma Pueblo and resides with her family on the Acoma Pueblo Indian reservation in northwestern New Mexico.

Mariana Souto-Manning is Associate Professor in the Department of Curriculum and Teaching at Teachers College, Columbia University. From a critical perspective, her research examines the sociocultural and historical foundations of early schooling, language development, and literacy practices in pluralistic settings. She studies how children, families, and teachers from diverse backgrounds shape and are shaped by discursive practices. She has authored *Freire, Teaching, and Learning: Culture Circles Across Contexts*; *Teachers Act Up! Creating Multicultural Learning Communities Through Theatre*; and articles in journals such as *Journal of Early Childhood Literacy*, *Research in the Teaching of English*, *English Education*, and *Teachers College Record*.

Eve Tuck is Assistant Professor of Educational Foundations at the State University of New York at New Paltz. She has conducted participatory action research with New York City youth on the uses and abuses of the GED option, the impacts of mayoral control, and school noncompletion. Her publications are concerned with research methodology and ethics, Indigenous social thought, and settler colonialism. Tuck is the author of *Urban Youth and School Pushout: Gateways, Get-Aways, and the GED* (2012). She is an enrolled member of the Tribal Government of St. Paul Island, in Alaska.

Leisy T. Wyman is Associate Professor in the Language, Reading and Culture program, and affiliate faculty in American Indian Studies and Second Language Acquisition and Teaching at the University of Arizona. As a teacher-researcher and linguistic anthropologist of education, she has collaborated with Yup'ik adults and youth on books of Yup'ik elders' narratives (Fredson et al., 1998).

Additional works include the book *Youth Culture, Language Endangerment and Linguistic Survivance* (2012); a theme issue on Indigenous youth language for the *Journal of Language, Identity and Education* (McCarty & Wyman, 2009); and a book in progress on Indigenous youth language in North America (Wyman, McCarty, & Nicholas, Eds., forthcoming).

K. Wayne Yang is Assistant Professor in the Department of Ethnic Studies and affiliated with the Urban Studies & Planning Program and Department of Education Studies at the University of California San Diego. He was the co-founder of the Avenues Project, a nonprofit youth development organization, and also the co-founder of East Oakland Community High School. His research focuses on the role of youth popular culture and pedagogy in the emergence of social movements. Sometimes he writes as La Paperson, an avatar that irregularly calls, as in the article "The Postcolonial Ghetto: Seeing Her Shape and His Hand" in the *Berkeley Review of Education*.

AUTHOR INDEX

SUBJECT INDEX

Note: In page references, f indicates figures and t indicates tables.

⑤SAGE research**methods**

The essential online tool for researchers from the world's leading methods publisher

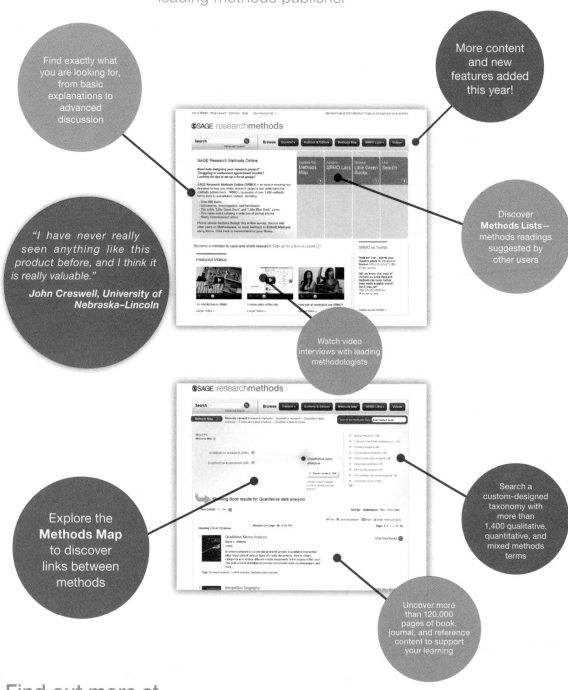

Find exactly what you are looking for, from basic explanations to advanced discussion

More content and new features added this year!

"I have never really seen anything like this product before, and I think it is really valuable."

John Creswell, University of Nebraska–Lincoln

Discover **Methods Lists**— methods readings suggested by other users

Watch video interviews with leading methodologists

Explore the **Methods Map** to discover links between methods

Search a custom-designed taxonomy with more than 1,400 qualitative, quantitative, and mixed methods terms

Uncover more than 120,000 pages of book, journal, and reference content to support your learning

Find out more at
www.sageresearchmethods.com